A Book

D0355462

A Book of India

B.N. Pandey

Rupa . Co.

This reprint in Rupa Paperback 2002
Second impression 2004

Published by
Rupa & Co
7/16, Ansari Road, Daryaganj,
New Delhi 110 002

Sales Centres:

Allahabad Bangalore Chandigarh
Chennai Hyderabad Jaipur Kathmandu
Kolkata Ludhiana Mumbai Pune

ISBN 81-7167-616-2

Printed in India by
Gopsons Papers Ltd., A-14 Sector 60, Noida 201 301

Contents

People Great and Small

Humour and Sentiment

Manners and Customs

Amusements and Festivals

Poems, Songs and Tales

Religions and Beliefs

The Evolution of Hinduism

Jainism

Buddhism

Acknowledgements

The publishers gratefully acknowledge the co-operation of the authors, owners of copyright and publishers who have given permission for poems and prose extracts to appear in these pages.

Every care has been taken to trace the holders of copyright for the pieces used in this anthology. Should any have been overlooked, the publishers hope that the information will be communicated to them so that appropriate acknowledgement may be made in future editions.

GEORGE ALLEN & UNWIN LTD. for the poems "Let no one be a Girl", "Twin Hills", "The End of Youth", "Ecstasy", "Waxing Moon", and "Ocean of Nectar", from *Love Songs of Vidyapati* translated by D. Bhattacharya.

EDWARD ARNOLD LTD. and Harcourt, Brace & World Inc. for the extract from *The Hills of Devi* by E.M. Forster.

SRI AUROBINDO ASHRAM for the poem "Hail to thee, Mother" by Bankim Chandra Chatterjee, translated by A. Ghose in *Collected Poems and Plays*.

ASIA PUBLISHING HOUSE for the poem "Raksha Bandhan" from *The Feather of the Dawn* by Sarojini Naidu and the extracts from *Tales from the Indian Classics* by V. S. Naravane.

MRS BAMBRIDGE AND HODDER & STOUGHTON LTD. for the poems "The Beasts are Very Wise" and "Pigs and Buffaloes" from the definitive edition of *Rudyard Kipling Verse*.

BASIL BLACKWELL & MOTT LTD. for the poem "The Indian Palm Squirrel" from *The Gold and the Grey* by Hilton Brown.

CAMBRIDGE UNIVERSITY PRESS for the poems "What are thine idols but lumps of stone", "Thou art the Heavens, and Thou the Earth" and "Slay first the thieves — desire, lust and pride" by Lalla, translated by Sir R.C. Temple in *The World of Lalla*.

THE JOHN DAY COMPANY INC., Asia Publishing House and Mrs. Indira Nehru Gandhi for the extracts from *The Discovery of India* by J.L. Nehru.

CHATTO AND WINDUS LTD., and HARPER & ROW INC. for the extracts from *Jesting Pilate* by Aldous Huxley.

THE CLARENDON PRESS for the extracts from *Jaina Sutras* translated by H. Jacobi; the extracts from *Hindu Manners, Customs and Ceremonies* by J.A. Dubois, translated by H. Beauchamp and the translations from *The Sikh Religion* by M.A. Macauliffe.

COLUMBIA UNIVERSITY PRESS for the extracts from *Sources* of *Indian Tradition* edited by D. Barry.

CONSTABLE AND COMPANY LIMITED for the extract from *Cities of India* by Sir G. Forrest.

THE CORNHILL MAGAZINE AND LAURENCE POLLINGER LIMITED for the extract from an article entitled *The Cave-Temples of Ajanta* by Alan Moorehead.

J.M. DENT & SONS LTD. and E.P. DUTTON & CO. INC. for the extracts from *Shakuntala* by Kalidasa, translated by A.W. Ryder, in "Everyman's Library".

HARVARD UNIVERSITY PRESS for the extracts from *The Little Clay Cart* translated by A.W. Ryder in the "Harvard Oriental Series".

LONGMANS, GREEN & CO. Limited for the extracts from *Studies from an Eastern Home* by Sister Nivedita.

MACMILLAN & CO. LTD. and THE TRUSTEES OF THE RABINDRANATH TAGORE ESTATE for the poems "None Lives for Ever",

"Anxious Love", "God is Not in Thy Temple", "The Bondage of Finery" and "Let My Country Awake" from *Collected Poems and Plays of Rabindranath Tagore*.

METHUEN & CO. LTD. and THE MICHIGAN STATE UNIVERSITY PRESS for the extract from *The Bachelor of Arts* by R. K. Narayan.

JOHN MURRAY for the poems "India (Bharat)" and "Taj-Mahal" from *A Flight of Swans* by Rabindranath Tagore, the poem "The Young Bride" from *The Herald of Spring* by Rabindranath Tagore, the poems "O Poet, Take your Last Ablution", "The Dog", "I have Never Put my Trust in Deeds" and "At Morn, as Soon as I Open my Eyes" from *Wings of Death* by Rabindranath Tagore, and the extract from *Siksha-Samuccaya* by Santideva.

NAVAJIVAN TRUST for the extracts from the following works by Mahatma Gandhi: *Non-violence in Peace and War; Communal Unity; My Experiments with Truth*.

OXFORD UNIVERSITY PRESS for the poems "Soul, the Finest Essence" and "He is God" *The 13 Principal Upanishads* by R.E. Hume; the extract from *Islam in India* by Jafar Shariff, translated by G.A. Herklots and the extract from *Sanyutha-Nikaya* translated by F.L. Woodward.

PRINCETON UNIVERSITY PRESS for the extract from *A Source Book in Indian Philosophy* by S. Radhakrishnan and Moore.

ARTHUR PROBSTHAIN for the extracts from *Mohenjo Daro and the Indus Civilisation* (copyright Government of India) by Sir John Marshall.

ATMA RAM & SONS and J.N. KAUL for the poems from *Poems of Ghalib*.

ROUTLEDGE & KEGAN PAUL LTD. for the poems "Jaipur" and "The Rock Temples, Ellora", from *Indian Landscape* by R.N. Curry; the extracts from *Hiuen Tsiang's Travels in India*, translated by S. Beal; the poems "Travel not with a Fool", "Easy and Hard Life", "By Self Alone", "Mind

Shapes the Character", "Conquest of Fear" and "Victory Breedeth Anger" from *Dhammapada,* translated by A.J. Edmunds and the extract from *The Travels of Fa-Hsien,* translated by H.A. Giles.

SEELEY, SERVICE & CO. Ltd. for the extract from *In Himalayan Tibet* by A.R. Heber and K. M. Heber.

SH. MUHAMMAD ASHRAF for the extract from *Speeches and Writings of Mr. Jinnah.*

THE UNIVERSITY OF CHICAGO PRESS for the extracts from *The Ten Princes* by Dandin, translated by A.W. Ryder.

THE UNIVERSITY OF MICHIGAN PRESS for the extract from *India* by Percival Spear.

YALE UNIVERSITY PRESS for the extract from *The Grateful Elephant and Other Stories* by E. W. Burlingame.

Y.M.C.A. PUBLISHING HOUSE, New Delhi for the poems "Seeking", "God Dwells in All", "The Restless Heart", "Keep me from Vanity", "Love finds out God" and "God's Counterfeit" from *Psalms of the Maratha Saints* by Nicol Macnicol and the poem "Lord Siva" from *Hymns of the Tamil Saivite Saints,* translated by E. Kingsbury and G.E. Phillips

Introduction

In compiling an anthology in English about a non-English speaking country, the editor is faced with the problem of finding an English translation of every piece of literature which he wishes to include in his collection. The task becomes particularly difficult in the case of India. Indians speak 845 languages and dialects, of which at least fifteen are major languages. Some of them rank with the oldest living languages of the world, possessing a highly developed grammar and a very rich literature. These Indian languages can be broadly classified into two groups — Aryan and Dravidian. That branch of the Aryan people who invaded India in the second millennium B.C. spoke a number of dialects, one of which achieved a literary form and came to be known as Sanskrit. Sanskrit, therefore, is derived from the same common ancestor as Persian, Greek, Latin, Avestic and the later Germanic Slavic languages. Sanskrit gave rise to various dialects, of which Pali was the principal one, spoken in North India in the 6th century B.C. Pali became the sacred language of the Buddhists, as Sanskrit was of the Hindus. About A.D. 1,000 some of the modern Indian languages began to develop from Sanskrit and Pali. Of these the most important are Hindi, Rajasthani, Gujarati, Punjabi, Sindhi, Kashmiri, Marathi and Bengali. Broadly speaking the Aryan group of languages is spoken in northern and central India. To the Dravidian group of languages belong Tamil, Telugu, Kannada and Malayalam. These languages were spoken by people who inhabited India long before the Aryans came and who had developed a civilisation which was in many ways superior to that of the early Aryan invaders of India. These Dravidian languages are today spoken principally by the people who inhabit the southern part of India. Only a fraction of the literature contained in these languages has so far been translated into English, and of these translations only a few have any literary merit whatsoever. This may partly explain why I have been unable to include the works of certain Indian writers.

There are, however, some compensations. During the British occupation of India many English and quite a few Indians wrote about India in English and some of them wrote very well. In fact the ancient civilisation and literature of India were discovered for the western world by the British scholar-administrators who learnt the classical languages of India, translated some of her greatest literature into English and thereby revealed to the world her glorious past. *Shakuntala,* the masterpiece of India's greatest Sanskrit poet — Kalidasa (c. 400-500 A.D.) — was translated into English in 1789 by one of the most brilliant scholars of the 18th century, Sir William Jones (1746-94) who went to Calcutta in 1783 as a judge of the Supreme Court. Many translations of Sanskrit poetry were made by Sir Edwin Arnold (1832-1904) and these, though their style now seems rather old fashioned, still have charm, and convey something of the originals. In the 19th century many Indologists worked on the literary remains of ancient India, perhaps the most outstanding being the great German Sanskritist F. Max Mueller (1832-1900), most of whose working life was spent at the University of Oxford. It was only at the turn of the last century that scientific archaeological excavation began in India and it was only as recently as 1922 that Sir John Marshall and Dr. R. D. Banerji discovered at Mohenjo Daro in Sind the remains of a great pre-Aryan civilisation which flourished in the third millennium B.C.

Another source of information about India is the accounts of travellers. The earliest significant to have survived is that of Megasthenes, the Seleucid Ambassador who visited India about 300 B.C. The Chinese travellers visited ancient India to collect information and materials about Buddha's life and teachings. West European and Russian travellers visited India in medieval and modern times. These travellers have left description of the people and their life as they saw them in India and most of their works have been translated into English.

In this collection of prose and verse, therefore, I have drawn freely on the English writings of Indians, Americans and Englishmen and on the English translations of original materials in Greek, Sanskrit, Pali, Arabic, Persian, Chinese, French, Hindi, Urdu, Bengali, Punjabi, Marathi, Kashmiri, Tamil and Telugu.

India's physical, religious and racial variety is as immense as its linguistic diversity. It is a huge country — twenty times bigger than England and Wales — and has every variety of climate from the scorching heat of the plains to the Arctic cold of the Himalayan region. The rainfall varies from 3 inches a year in Saurashtra, western India, to 460 inches in Cherrapunji, Assam. There is, on the one hand, the very fertile Gangetic plain in which anything will grow, and there are, on the other, the sandy deserts of Rajputana and Cutch. In the north, India is bounded by the mighty Himalayan mountains and in the south it is encircled by the ocean. The people vary in their physical features and pigmentation. An Indian can be fair or dark. People of all races and religions inhabit India, though the large majority of Indians are Hindus of Aryan or Dravidian stock. The Dravidians with their dark skin, small stature and long heads, inhabited the whole of India in prehistoric times. They now remain predominant in the south, which extends from the Vindhya mountains through the Deccan plateau to Cape Comorin. The people of the Punjab, Rajasthan, Kashmir and a part of Uttar Pradesh (usually abbreviated as U.P.) have mostly the characteristic Aryan features — tall, long-headed and a narrow and prominent nose. The people of central India, Bihar and other parts of U.P. are of mixed Aryo-Dravidian type; they are of medium or tall stature, their colour is light to dark brown; they are long-headed with a medium-sized nose. The people of Bengal, Orissa and Assam are a mixture of Mongolian and Dravidian stock. They are of small to medium height, dark, with broad faces and noses.

India has been the birth place of four religions — Hinduism, Buddhism, Jainism and Sikhism — of which the first two are among the major religions of the world. From outside there came to India Muslims as invaders, Zoroastrians (Parsees) and Jews as traders and adventurers, and Christians as traders and missionaries.

But underneath this Indian diversity lies the continuity of Indian civilisation and social structure from the very earliest times until the present day. A book of this size cannot claim to give a full picture of the variety of Indian life. All I have tried to do is to present a few landmarks in Indian history and some main trends and facets of Indian civilisation and culture.

This book follows the general arrangement of preceding volumes on Australia, Scotland and England, except that I have added a new chapter on Amusements and Festivals. Perhaps more religious festivals are celebrated in India than in any other country of the world. A visitor to India may notice almost every fortnight a religious procession or festivity. Instead of ballads I have added to the chapter on Poems and Songs a few tales from the *Jatakas* and the *Panchatantra*, the world famous treasuries of moral stories. The chapters on History and on Religions and Beliefs are longer than the other chapters. India has a recorded history of nearly five thousand years and its present social structure is deeply rooted in the remote past. In the chapter on the religions of India is included Islam which, though not an indigenous religion, did influence and was in turn influenced by the Hindu religion and beliefs.

The advent of Christian missionaries during the first century of British rule in India led to the Hindu revivalist and reformist movements of the 19th century. Hindu religious leaders like Raja Ram Mohan Roy, Ramakrishna Paramahamsa, Vivekananda and Dayanand attempted to free Hinduism from the accretions of superstition and revive its true essence. Christianity has not been given a separate treatment in this book, but the indirect results of its impact are shown in the preachings and writings of Hindu reformers.

I have not tried to show either the influence of Indian civilisation and culture on South East Asia and the Far East, or India's contribution to world civilisation. We are now living in an age where sharp cultural differences are beginning to disappear. An Indian today feels as comfortable in a suit as an Englishman in a pair of pyjamas. The fact that the Indians took the suit from the British and the British borrowed the pyjama from India now does not matter. The isolation, which persisted for thousands of years on account of differences in religion, nationality and language and of difficulties of transport, has suddenly begun to disappear. We are now living in a small world where ideas are no sooner born than they shed their national colours. It is only for historical interest that contributors and their contributions need be recorded. The whole of South East Asia received most of its culture from India and Indian cultural influences in the from of Buddhism spread through central Asia to China.

Apart from her influence on western philosophy and literature, India has given to the world rice, cotton, the sugar cane, spices, the domestic fowl, the game of chess, "and, most important of all, the decimal system of numeral notation, the invention of an unknown Indian mathematician early in the Christian era." (A.L. Basham *The Wonder that was India*. p. 485.) Certain Indian ideas and systems are called Arabic in the western world because they were brought thither by the Arabs who traded with India.

India suffered an immense loss this year in the death of Jawaharlal Nehru. The most beloved sons of India in this century have been Mahatma Gandhi and Nehru. But whereas Gandhi was loved and revered as a saint, Nehru was loved and respected as a man. He was indeed a great man, a great statesman and, last but not least, a prolific writer. His great book *The Discovery of India,* is one of the best interpretations of the uniqueness of India and of its national spirit. I have drawn freely on this book in this collection to reveal some glimpses of Nehru's personality and character through his writings.

I am deeply indebted to Professor A.L. Basham, Professor of the History of South Asia in the University of London, for his most valuable suggestions on the source-materials for ancient Indian history, civilisation and literature. He has himself translated two Sanskrit poems into English especially for this book. He has also permitted me to include in this collection two of his poems (*The Victoria Memorial* and *Kalighat*) which he wrote for his personal pleasure while in India and never intended to publish. I have also benefited immensely from the expert technical advice of J.B. Foreman and his colleagues in the firm of Collins, particularly in the matter of selecting illustrations.

London
15 June 1964

B.N. Pandey
Lecturer in Modern　Indian History
School of Oriental and African Studies
University of London

Prologue
India (Bharat)

On the shores of Bharat,
Where men of all races have come together,
Awake, O my Mind!
Standing here with outstretched arms,
I send my salutations to the God of Humanity,
And in solemn chant sing His praises.
At whose call no one knows,
Came floating streams of men
And merged into the sea of Bharat.
The Aryan, the Non-Aryan, the Dravidian,
The Huns, the Pathans and the Moghuls —
They all have merged here into one body.
Today the West has opened its doors,
And from thence come gifts.
Giving and taking,
All will be welcome on the shores of Bharat,
Where men of all races have come together.
Come, O Aryan and Non-Aryan,
Hindu and Muslim,
Come, O English and you Christian,
Come, O Brahmin,
Purify your mind and clasp the hands of all;
Come, O downtrodden,

And let vanish all burdens of your humiliation.
Tarry not, but come you all
To anoint the Mother,
On the shores of Bharat,
Where men of all races have come together.

RABINDRANATH TAGORE (1861-1941)
A Flight of Swans
translated by AUROBINDO BOSE

History

The Indus Civilisation

c. 2500-1550 B.C.

Hitherto it has commonly been supposed that the pre-Aryan peoples of India were on an altogether lower plane of civilisation than their Aryan conquerors; that to the latter they were much what the Helots were to the Spartans, or the Slavs to their Byzantine overlords — a race so servile and degraded, that they were commonly known as Dasas or slaves. The picture of them gleaned from the Hymns of the Rigveda was that of black skinned, flat-nosed barbarians, as different from the fair Aryans in physical aspect as they were in speech and religion, though at the same time it was evident that they must have been rich in cattle, good fighters, and possessed of many forts in which they defended themselves against the invaders. These "forts", however, were explained by Vedic scholars as being no more than occasional places of refuge — simple earthworks, that is to say, surrounded, may be, by palisades or rough stone walls; for, seeing that the Aryans themselves were still in the village state and that their society was in other respects correspondingly primitive, it was deemed impossible that the older races of India — the contemptible, outcast Dasas — could already have been living in well-built cities or fortresses, or in other respects have attained to a higher state of culture. Mentally, physically, socially, and religiously, their inferiority to their conquerors

3

was taken for granted, and little or no credit was given them
for the achievements of Indian civilisation. Never for a moment
was it imagined that five thousand years ago, before ever the
Aryans were heard of, the Panjab and Sind, if not other parts
of India as well, were enjoying an advanced and singularly
uniform civilisation of their own, closely akin but in some
respects even superior to that of contemporary Mesopotamia
and Egypt. Yet this is what the discoveries at Harappa and
Mohenjo-daro have now placed beyond question. They exhibit
the Indus peoples of the fourth and third millennia B.C., in
possession of a highly developed culture in which no vestige
of Indo-Aryan influence is to be found. Like the rest of
Western Asia, the Indus country is still in the Chalcolithic Age
— that age in which arms and utensils of stone continue to
be used side by side with those of copper or bronze. Their
society is organised in cities; their wealth derived mainly from
agriculture and trade, which appears to have extended far and
wide in all directions. They cultivate wheat and barley as well
as the date palm. They have domesticated the humped zebu,
buffalo, and short horned bull, besides the sheep, pig, dog,
elephant, and camel; but the cat and probably the horse are
unknown to them. For transport they have wheeled vehicles,
to which oxen doubtless were yoked. They are skilful metal
workers, with a plentiful supply of gold, silver, and copper.
Lead, too, and tin are in use, but the latter only as an alloy
in the making of bronze. With spinning and weaving they are
thoroughly conversant. Their weapons of war and of the
chase are the bow and arrow, spear, axe, dagger, and mace.
The sword they have not yet evolved; nor is there any evidence
of defensive body armour. Among their other implements,
hatchets, sickles, saws, chisels, and razors are made of both
copper and bronze; knives and celts sometimes of these metals,
sometimes of chert or other hard stones. For the crushing of
grain they have the muller and saddle-quern but not the

circular grindstone. Their domestic vessels are commonly of earthenware turned on the wheel and not infrequently painted with encaustic designs; more rarely they are of copper, bronze, or silver. The ornaments of the rich are made of the precious metals or of copper, sometimes overlaid with gold, of faience, ivory, carnelian, and other stones; for the poor, they are usually of shell or terracotta. Figurines and toys, for which there is a wide vogue, are of terracotta, and shell and faience are freely used, as they are in Sumer and the West generally, not only for personal ornaments but for inlay work and other purposes. With the invention of writing the Indus peoples are also familiar, and employ for this purpose a form of script which, though peculiar to India, is evidently analogous to other contemporary scripts of Western Asia and the Nearer East.

To the extent thus briefly summarised the Indus culture corresponded in its general features with the Chalcolithic cultures of Western Asia and Egypt. In other respects, however, it was peculiar to Sind and the Panjab and as distinctive of those regions as the Sumerian culture was of Mesopotamia or the Egyptian of the Valley of the Nile. Thus, to mention only a few salient points, the use of cotton for textiles was exclusively restricted at this period to India and was not extended to the Western world until two or three thousand years later. Again, there is nothing that we know of in prehistoric Egypt or Mesopotamia or anywhere else in Western Asia to compare with the well-built baths and commodious houses of the citizens of Mohenjo-daro. In those countries, much money and thought were lavished on the building of magnificent temples for the gods and on the palaces and tombs of kings, but the rest of the people seemingly had to content themselves with insignificant dwellings of mud. In the Indus Valley, the picture is reversed and the finest structures are those erected for the convenience of the citizens. Temples, palaces, and tombs there may of course have been, but if so, they are either still undiscovered or so like other edifices as not to be readily distinguishable from them. At Ur, it is true, Mr. Woolley has unearthed a group of moderate-sized houses of burnt brick which constitute a notable exception to the general rule; but these disclose such a striking similarity to the latest levels at Mohenjo-daro, that there can be little doubt as to the influence under which they were erected. Be this, however, as it may, we are justified in seeing in the Great Bath of Mohenjo-daro and in its roomy and serviceable houses, with their ubiquitous wells and bathrooms and elaborate systems of drainage, evidence that the ordinary townspeople enjoyed here a degree of comfort and luxury unexampled in other parts of the then civilised world.

SIR JOHN MARSHALL
Mohenjo-daro and the Indus Civilisation

The Aryan Prayer for Victory

The Aryans entered India in the 2nd millennium B.C. They had perfected a very advanced poetic technique for the composition of hymns to be sung in praise of their gods. These hymns, which were handed down by word of mouth, were collected and arranged in the 1st millennium B.C. in the Vedas, of which *Rigveda* is the oldest and the most sacred text of the Hindus.

> Let me win glory, Agni, in our Battles: enkindling thee,
> may we support our bodies.
> May the four regions bend and bow before me: with thee
> for guardian may we win in combat.
> May all the gods be on my side in battle, the Maruts led
> by Indra, Vishnu, Agni.

Mine be the middle air's extended region, and may the wind blow favouring these my wishes.

May the gods grant me riches, may the blessing and invocation of the gods assist me.

Foremost in fight be the divine invokers: may we, unwounded, have brave heroes round us.

For me let them present all mine oblations, and let my mind's intention be accomplished.

May I be guiltless of the least transgression: and, all ye gods, do ye combine to bless us.

Ye six divine Expanses, grant us freedom: here, all ye gods, acquit yourselves like heroes.

Let us not lose our children or our bodies: let us not benefit the foe, king Soma!

Baffling the wrath of our opponents, Agni, guard us as our infallible protector.

Let these thy foes turn back and seek their houses, and let their thought who watch at home be ruined.

Lord of the world, creator of creators: the saviour god who overcomes the foeman.

May gods, Brihaspati, both Asvins shelter from ill this sacrifice and sacrificer.

Foodful, and much-invoked, at this our calling may the great Bull vouchsafe us wide protection.

Lord of bay coursers, Indra, bless our children: harm us not, give us not as prey to others.

Let those who are our foemen stay afar from us: with Indra and with Agni we will drive them off.

Vasus, Adityas, Rudras have exalted me, made me far-reaching, mighty, thinker, sovran lord.

The Rigveda (1200-900 B.C.) X. Hymn 128
translated by R.T.H. GRIFFITH

The Qualities of a King

The king, the minister, the country, the fort, the treasury, the army and the friend are the elements of sovereignty. Of these, the best qualities of the king are:

Born of a high family, godly, possessed of valour, seeing through the medium of aged person, virtuous, truthful, not of a contradictory nature, grateful, having large aims, highly enthusiastic, not addicted to procrastination, powerful to control his neighbouring kings, of resolute mind, having an assembly of ministers of no mean quality, and possessed of a taste for discipline — these are the qualities of an inviting nature.

Inquiry, hearing, perception, retention in memory, reflection, deliberation, inference and steadfast adherence to conclusions are the qualities of the intellect.

Valour, determination of purpose, quickness, and probity are the aspects of enthusiasm.

Possessed of a sharp intellect, strong memory, and keen mind, energetic, powerful, trained in all kinds of arts, free from vice, capable of paying in the same coin by way of awarding punishments or rewards, possessed of dignity, capable of taking remedial measures against dangers, possessed of foresight, ready to avail himself of opportunities when afforded in respect of place, time, and manly efforts, clever enough to discern the causes necessitating the cessation of treaty or war with an enemy, or to lie in wait keeping treaties, obligations and pledges, or to avail himself of his enemy's weak points, making jokes with no loss of dignity or secrecy, never brow-beating and casting haughty and stern looks, free from passion, anger, greed, obstinacy, fickleness, haste and back-biting habits, talking to other with a smiling

face, and observing customs as taught by aged persons —
such is the nature of self-possession.

KAUTILYA
Arthasâstra (321-300 B.C.)
translated by R. SHAMASASTRY

The Welfare of the People

Asoka's inscriptions are the oldest surviving Indian
written documents of historical importance. They consist
of a series of edicts engraved on rocks and pillars at widely
scattered points all over India.

Thus saith King Priyadarsi [Asoka], Beloved of the Gods.
Formerly, in the ages gone by, there was no transaction of
state business and no reporting of incidents at all hours. So
I have made the following arrangement, viz. that the reporters
may appear before me for reporting the affairs of the people
at any time and place, whether I am engaged in eating or
in the harem or in the bed-chamber or on a promenade or
in the carriage or on the march. And I am now attending
to people's affairs at all places. And, when I issue an order
orally in connection with any donation or proclamation or
when an emergent work presses itself upon the Mahamatras
and in case there is in that connection a controversy among
the Ministers of the Council or an argumentation in the
Council in favour of a particular view, the fact must be
reported to me immediately at any place and at any time.
Thus have I ordered.

I am never complacent in regard to my exertions or the
dispatch of people's business by me. I consider it my only duty
to promote the welfare of all men. But exertion and prompt

dispatch of business lie at the root of that. There is verily no duty which is more important to me than promoting the welfare of all men. And whatever effort I make is made in order that I may discharge the debt which I owe to all living beings, that I may make them happy in this world, and that they may attain heaven in the next world.

Therefore this record relating to Dharma has been caused to be written by me on stone for the following purpose, viz. that it may last for a long time and that my sons, grandsons and great-grandsons may conform to it for the welfare of all men. This, however, is difficult to accomplish without the utmost exertion.

Inscriptions of Asoka (269-232 B.C.)
Rock Edict 6
translated by D.C. SIRCAR

The Father King

He does not seek — until a father's care
Is shown his subjects — rest in solitude;
As a great elephant recks not of the sun
Until his herd is sheltered in the wood.

KALIDASA (c. A.D. 400-500)
Shakuntala
translated by A.W. RYDER

King's Bodyguard

Alexander's general Seleucus Nicator was defeated by Emperor Chandragupta Maurya in 305 B.C. and a peace was concluded by a matrimonial alliance. Seleucus sent an ambassador, Megasthenes, to reside at the Mauryan court at Pataliputra (modern Patna) and the ambassador wrote a detailed account of India.

The care of the king's person is entrusted to women, who also are brought from their parents. The guards and the rest of the soldiery attend outside the gates. A woman who kills the king when drunk becomes the wife of his successor. The sons succeed the father. The king may not sleep during the daytime, and by night he is obliged to change his couch from time to time, with a view to defeat plots against his life.

The king leaves his palace not only in time of war, but also for the purpose of judging causes. He then remains in court for the whole day, without allowing the business to be interrupted, even though the hour arrives when he must needs attend to his person — that is, when he is to be rubbed with cylinders of wood. He continues hearing cases while the friction, which is performed by four attendants, is still proceeding. Another purpose for which he leaves his palace is to offer sacrifice; a third is to go to the chase, for which he departs in Bacchanalian fashion. Crowds of women surround him, and outside of this circle spearmen are ranged. The road is marked off with ropes, and it is death, for man and woman alike, to pass within the ropes. Men with drums and gongs lead the procession. The king hunts in the enclosures and shoots arrows from a platform. At his side stand two or three armed women. If he hunts in the open grounds he shoots from the back of an elephant. Of the women, some are in chariots, some on horses, and some even on elephants, and they are

equipped with weapons of every kind, as if they were going
on a campaign.

Megasthenes (302 B.C.)
translated by J.W. MCCRINDLE

Slaves and their Protection

I

There are slaves of seven kinds, viz. he who is made
a captive under a standard, he who serves for his daily
food, he who is born in the house, he who is bought and he
who is given, he who is inherited from ancestors, and he who
is enslaved by way of punishment.

A wife, a son, a slave, these three are declared to have
no property; the wealth which they earn is acquired for him
to whom they belong.

The Laws of Manu (A.D. 100-200)
VIII. 415-16
translated by G. BUEHLER

II

Deceiving a slave of his money or depriving him of the
privileges he can exercise as an Arya shall be punished with
half the fine levied for enslaving the life of an Arya.

A man who takes in mortgage a person who runs away,
or who dies or who is incapacitated by disease, shall be
entitled to receive back from the mortgager the value he paid
for the slave.

Employing a slave to carry the dead or to sweep ordure,
urine, or the leavings of food; or a female slave to attend on

her master while he is bathing naked; or hurting or abusing him or her, or violating the chastity of a female slave shall cause the forfeiture of the value paid for him or her. Violation of the chastity of nurses, female cooks, or female servants of the class of joint cultivators or of any other description shall at once earn their liberty for them. Violence towards an attendant of high birth shall entitle him to run away. When a master has connection with a nurse or pledged female slave against her will, he shall be punished with the first amercement; a stranger doing the same shall be punished with the middlemost amercement. When a man commits or helps another to commit rape with a girl or a female slave pledged to him, he shall not only forfeit the purchase-value, but also pay a certain amount of money to her and a fine of twice the amount to the government.

KAUTILYA
Arthasâstra (321-300 B.C.)
translated by R. SHAMASASTRY

Justice and its Administration

I

Justice, being violated, destroys; justice, being preserved, preserves: therefore justice must not be violated, lest violated justice destroy us.

For divine justice is said to be a bull; that man who violates it the gods consider to be a man despicable like a Sudra; let him, therefore, beware of violating justice.

The only friend who follows men even after death is justice; for everything else is lost at the same time when the body perishes.

One quarter of the guilt of an unjust decision falls on him who committed the crime, one quarter on the false witness; one quarter on all the judges, one quarter on the king.

But where he who is worthy of condemnation is condemned, the king is free from guilt, and the judges are saved from sin; the guilt falls on the perpetrator of the crime alone.

*

Let him never slay a Brahmana, though he may have committed all possible crimes; let him banish such an offender, leaving all his property to him and his body unhurt.

No greater crime is known on earth than slaying a Brahmana; a king, therefore, must not even conceive in his mind the thought of killing a Brahmana.

The Laws of Manu (A.D. 100-200)
VIII. 15-19, 380-81
translated by G. BUEHLER

II

The Mahamatras of Tosali; who are the judicial officers of the city, have to be addressed in the following words of the Beloved of the Gods [Asoka].

As regards whatever good I notice, I desire that I may carry it out by deeds and accomplish it by proper means. And I consider the following to be the principal means to this end, viz. to impart instructions of you. For you are placed by me over many thousands of beings with the object that I may gain the affection of all men.

All men are my children. Just as, in regard to my own children, I desire that they may be provided with all kinds of welfare and happiness in this world and in the next, the same I desire also in regard to all men. But you do not understand how far my intention goes in this respect. A few amongst you per chance understand it; but even such of you understand it partly and not fully. Howsoever well-placed you may be, you have to pay attention to this matter.

In the administration of justice, it sometimes happens that some persons suffer imprisonment or harsh treatment. In such cases, a person may accidentally obtain an order cancelling his imprisonment, while many other persons in the same condition continue to suffer for a long time. In such a circumstance, you should so desire as to deal with all of them impartially.

But an officer fails to act impartially owing to the following dispositions, viz. jealousy, anger, cruelty, hastiness, want of perseverance, laziness and fatigue. Therefore, you should desire that these dispositions may not be yours. And the root of the complete success of an officer lies in the absence of anger and avoidance of hastiness. In the matter of administration of justice, an officer does not get up for work if he is fatigued; but he has to move, to walk and to advance. Whoever amongst you pays attention to this should tell other officers: "Pay attention to nothing except the duties assigned to you by the king. Such and such are the instructions of the Beloved of the Gods." The observance of this duty will produce great results for you; but its non-observance will produce great harm.

For, if you fail to observe this, there will be for you neither the attainment of heaven nor the attainment of the king's favour. Because indifferent observance of this duty on your part cannot make me excessively energetic in favouring you. If, however, you observe this duty, you will attain heaven and also discharge the debt you owe to me, your master.

This record has been written here for the following purpose, viz. that the judicial officers of the city may strive to do their duty at all times and that the people within their

charges suffer neither from unnecessary imprisonment nor
from unnecessary harassment....

Inscriptions of Asoka (269-232 B.C.)
Rock Edict 15
translated by D.C. SIRCAR

The Protection of the Animals

This record relating to Dharma has been caused to be
written by king Priyadarsi, [Asoka], Beloved of the Gods.
Here no living being should be slaughtered for sacrifice
and no festive gathering should be held. For King Priyadarsi,
Beloved of the Gods, sees manifold evil in festive gatherings.
There is, however, one kind of festive gathering which is
considered good by king Priyadarsi, Beloved of the Gods.

Many hundred thousands of living beings were formerly
slaughtered every day in the kitchen of Priyadarsi, Beloved
of the Gods, for the sake of curry. But now, when this record
relating to Dharma is written, only three living creatures are
killed daily for the sake of curry, viz. two birds and one
animal. Even this animal is also not slaughtered regularly.
These three living beings too shall not be killed in future.

*

Everywhere in the dominions of king Priyadarsi, Beloved of
the Gods, and likewise in the bordering territories such as
those of the Chodas and Pandyas as well as of the Satiyaputra
and the Keralaputra as far south as Tamraparni, and in the
territories of the Yavana king Antiyoka and also the kings who
are the neighbours of the said Antiyoka — everywhere king
Priyadarsi, Beloved of the Gods, has arranged for two kinds

of medical treatment, medical treatment for men and medical treatment for animals. And, wherever there were no medicinal herbs beneficial to men and animals, everywhere they have been caused to be imported and planted. Wherever there were no roots and fruits, everywhere they have been caused to be imported and planted. On the roads, wells have been caused to be dug and trees have been caused to be planted for the enjoyment of animals and men.

Inscriptions of Asoka (269-232 B.C.)
Rock Edict 2
translated by D.C. SIRCAR

Conquest by Love

The country of the Kalingas was conquered by king Priyadarsi [Asoka], Beloved of the Gods, eight years after his coronation. In this war in Kalinga, men and animals numbering one hundred and fifty thousands were carried away captive from that country, as many as one hundred thousands were killed there in action, and many times that number perished. After that, now that the country of the Kalingas has been conquered, the Beloved of the Gods is devoted to an intense practice of the duties relating to Dharma, to a longing for Dharma and to the inculcation of Dharma among the people. This is due to the repentance of the Beloved of the Gods on having conquered the country of the Kalingas.

Verily, the slaughter, death and deportation of men, which take place in the course of the conquest of an unconquered country, are now considered extremely painful and deplorable by the Beloved of the Gods ....

Now, really there is no person who is not sincerely devoted to a particular religious sect. Therefore the slaughter, death or deportation of even a hundredth or thousandth part of all those people who were slain or died or were carried away captive at that time in Kalinga, is now considered very deplorable by the Beloved of the Gods.

So, what is conquest through Dharma is now considered to be the best conquest by the Beloved of the Gods. And such a conquest has been achieved by the Beloved of the Gods not only here in his own dominions but also in the territories bordering on his dominions.

So, whatever conquest is achieved in this way, verily that conquest creates an atmosphere of satisfaction everywhere both among the victors and the vanquished. In the conquest through Dharma, satisfaction is derived by both the parties. But that satisfaction is indeed of little consequence. Only happiness of the people in the next world is what is regarded by the Beloved of the Gods as a great thing resulting from such a conquest.

And this record relating to Dharma has been written on stone for the following purpose, viz. that my sons and great-grandsons should not think of a fresh conquest by arms as worth achieving, that they should adopt the policy of forbearance and light punishment towards the vanquished even if they conquer people by arms, and that they should regard the conquest through Dharma as the true conquest. Such a conquest brings happiness to all concerned both in this world and in the next. And let all their intense joys be what is pleasure associated with Dharma. For this brings happiness in this world as well as in the next.

Inscriptions of Asoka (269-232 B.C.)
Rock Edict 13
translated by D.C. SIRCAR

Warfare

I proceed now to describe the mode in which the Indians equip themselves for war, premising that it is not to be regarded as the only one in vogue. The foot-soldiers carry a bow made of equal length with the man who bears it. This they rest upon the ground, and pressing against it with their left foot thus discharge the arrow, having drawn the string far backwards: for the shaft they use is little short of being three yards long, and there is nothing which can resist an Indian archer's shot — neither shield nor breast-plate, nor any stronger defence if such there be. In their left hand they carry bucklers made of undressed ox-hide, which are not so broad as those who carry them, but are about as long. Some are equipped with javelins instead of bows, but all wear a sword, which is broad in the blade, but not longer than three cubits; and this, when they engage in close fight (which they do with reluctance), they wield with both hands, to fetch down a lustier blow. The horsemen are equipped with two lances like the lances called *saunia*, and with a shorter buckler than that carried by the foot-soldiers. But they do not put saddles on their horses, nor do they curb them with bits like the bits in use among the Greeks or the Kelts, but they fit on round the extremity of the horse's mouth a circular piece of stitched raw ox-hide studded with pricks of iron or brass pointing inwards, but not very sharp: if a man is rich he uses pricks made of ivory. Within the horse's mouth is put an iron prong like a skewer, to which the reins are attached. When the rider, then, pulls the reins, the prong controls the horse, and the pricks which are attached to this prong goad the mouth, so that it cannot but obey the reins.

The Indians are in person slender and tall, and of much lighter weight than other men. The animals used by the common sort for riding on are camels and horses and asses, while the wealthy use elephants — for it is the elephant which in India carries royalty. The conveyance which ranks next in honour is the chariot and four; the camel ranks third; while to be drawn by a single horse is considered no distinction at all. But the Indian women, if possessed of uncommon discretion, would not stray from virtue for any reward short of an elephant, but on receiving this a lady lets the giver enjoy her person. Nor do the Indians consider it any disgrace to a woman to grant her favours for an elephant, but it is rather regarded as a high compliment to the sex that their charms should be deemed worth an elephant. They marry without either giving or taking dowries, but the women, as soon as they are marriageable, are brought forward by their fathers and exposed in public, to be selected by the victor in wrestling or boxing or running, or by someone who excels in any other manly exercise. The people of India live upon grain, and are tillers of the soil; but we must except the hillmen, who eat the flesh of beasts of chase.

Arian (2nd cent. A.D.)
translated by J.W. McCRINDLE

The Dress of the People

I

The character of the people is here, as elsewhere, formed by the position of their country and its climate. They cover their persons down to the feet with fine muslin, are shod with sandals, and coil round their heads cloths of linen (cotton). They hang precious stones as pendants from their

ears, and persons of high social rank, or of great wealth, deck
their wrist and upper arm with bracelets of gold. They
frequently comb, but seldom cut, the hair of their head. The
beard of the chin they never cut at all, but they shave off the
hair from the rest of the face, so that it looks polished. The
luxury of their kings, or as they call it, their magnificence,
is carried to a vicious excess without a parallel in the world.

When the king condescends to show himself in public his
attendants carry in their hands silver censers, and perfume
with incense all the road by which it is his pleasure to be
conveyed. He lolls in a golden palanquin, garnished with
pearls, which dangle all round it, and he is robed in fine
muslin embroidered with purple and gold. Behind his palanquin
follow men-at-arms and his bodyguards, of whom some carry
boughs of trees, on which birds are perched trained to interrupt
business with their cries. The palace is adorned with gilded
pillars clasped all round by a vine embossed in gold, while
silver images of those birds which most charm the eye diversify
the workmanship. The palace is open to all comers even when
the king is having his hair combed and dressed. It is then that
he gives audience to ambassadors, and administers justice to
his subjects. His slippers being after this taken off, his feet
are rubbed with scented ointments. His principal exercise is
hunting; amid the vows and songs of his courtesans he shoots
the game enclosed within the royal park. The arrows, which
are two cubits long, are discharged with more effort than
effect, for though the force of these missiles depends on their
lightness they are loaded with an obnoxious weight. He rides
on horseback when making short journeys, but when bound
on a distant expedition he rides in a chariot (howdah) mounted
on elephants, and, huge as these animals are, their bodies are
covered completely over with trappings of gold. That no form
of shameless profligacy may be wanting, he is accompanied
by a long train of courtesans carried in golden palanquins,

and this troop holds a separate place in the procession from
the queens' retinue, and is as sumptuously appointed. His
food is prepared by women, who also serve him with wine,
which is much used by all the Indians. When the king falls into
a drunken sleep his courtesans carry him away to his bedchamber
invoking the gods of the night in their native hymns.

Q. Curtius Rufus
translated by J.W. McCRINDLE

II

The dress worn by the Indians is made of cotton, as Nearchos
tells us — cotton produced from those trees of which mention
has already been made. But this cotton is either of a brighter
white colour than any cotton found elsewhere, or the darkness
of the Indian complexion makes their apparel look so much
the whiter. They wear an under-garment of cotton which
reaches below the knee half-way down to the ankles, and also .
an upper garment which they throw partly over their shoulders,
and partly twist in folds round their head. The Indians wear
also ear-rings of ivory, but only such of them do this as are
very wealthy, for all Indians do not wear them. Their beards,
Nearchos tells us, they dye of one hue and another, according
to taste. Some dye their white beards to make them look as
white as possible, but others dye them blue; while some again
prefer a red tint, some a purple, and others a rank green. Such
Indians, he also says, as are thought anything of, use parasols
as a screen from the heat. They wear shoes made of white
leather, and these are elaborately trimmed, while the soles are
variegated, and made of great thickness, to make the wearer
seem so much the taller.

Arian (2nd cent. A.D.)
translated by J.W. McCRINDLE

Some Glimpses of the Golden Period A.D. 320-455

To the south of this, the country is called the Middle Kingdom (of the Brahmans). It has a temperate climate, without frost or snow; and the people are prosperous and happy, without registration or official restrictions. Only those who till the king's land have to pay so much on the profit they make. Those who want to go away, may go; those who want to stop, may stop. The king in his administration uses no corporal punishments; criminals are merely fined according to the gravity of their offences. Even for a second attempt at rebellion the punishment is only the loss of the right hand. The men of the king's bodyguard have all fixed salaries. Throughout the country no one kills any living thing, nor drinks wine, not eats onions or garlic; but chandalas are segregated. Chandala is their name for foul men (lepers). These live away from other people; and when they approach a city or market they beat a piece of wood, in order to distinguish themselves. Then people know who they are and avoid coming into contact with them.

In this country they do not keep pigs or fowls, there are no dealings in cattle, no butcher's shops or distilleries in their market-places. As a medium of exchange they use cowries. Only the chandalas go hunting and deal in flesh.

*

The elders and gentry of these countries have instituted in their capitals free hospitals, and hither come all poor or helpless patients, orphans, widowers, and cripples. They are well taken care of, a doctor attends to them, food and medicine being supplied according to their needs. They are all made quite comfortable, and when they are cured they go away.

The Travels of Fa-hsien (A.D. 399-414)
translated by H.A. GILES

Food and Drink

In cultivating the land, those whose duty it is sow and reap, plough and harrow (*weed*), and plant according to the season; and after their labour they rest a while. Among the products of the ground, rice and corn are most plentiful. With respect to edible herbs and plants, we may name ginger and mustard, melons and pumpkins, the *Heun-to (Kandu?)* plant, and others. Onions and garlic are little grown; and few persons eat them; if anyone uses them for food, they are expelled beyond the walls of the town. The most usual food is milk, butter, cream, soft sugar, sugar-candy, the oil of the mustard seed, and all sorts of cakes made of corn are used as food. Fish, mutton, gazelle, and deer they eat generally fresh, sometimes salted; they are forbidden to eat the flesh of the ox, the ass, the elephant, the horse, the pig, the dog, the fox, the wolf, the lion, the monkey, and all the hairy kind. Those who eat them are despised and scorned, and are universally reprobated; they live outside the walls, and are seldom seen among men.

With respect to the different kinds of wine and liquors, there are various sorts. The juice of the grape and sugar-cane, these are used by the Kshattriyas as drink; the Vaisyas use strong fermented drinks; the Sramans and Brahmans drink a sort of syrup made from the grape or sugar-cane, but not of the nature of fermented wine.

The mixed classes and base-born differ in no way *(as to food or drink)* from the rest, except in respect of the vessels they use, which are very different both as to value and material. There is no lack of suitable things for household use. Although they have saucepans and stewpans, yet they do not know the steamer used for cooking rice. They have many vessels made of dried clay; they seldom use red copper vessels: they eat from one vessel, mixing all sorts of condiments together, which they take up with their fingers. They have no spoons or cups, and in short no sort of chopsticks. When sick, however, they use copper drinking cups.

Hiuen Tsiang's Travels in India (A.D. 629-45)
translated by S. BEAL

Administration

As the administration of the government is founded on benign principles, the executive is simple. The families are not entered on registers, and the people are not subject to forced labour (conscription). The private demesnes of the crown are divided into four principal parts; the first is for carrying out the affairs of state and providing sacrificial offerings; the second is for providing subsidies for the ministers and chief officers of state; the third is for rewarding men of distinguished ability; and the fourth is for charity to religious bodies, whereby the field of merit is cultivated (planted). In this way the taxes on the people are light, and the personal service required of them is moderate. Each one keeps his own worldly goods in peace, and all till the ground for their subsistence. Those who cultivate the royal estates pay a sixth part of the produce as tribute. The merchants who engage in commerce come and go in carrying out their transactions. The payment is in strict proportion to the work done.

*

With respect to the ordinary people, although they are naturally light-minded, yet they are upright and honourable. In money matters they are without craft, and in administering justice they are considerate. They dread the retribution of another state of existence, and make light of the things of the present world. They are not deceitful or treacherous in their conduct, and are faithful to their oaths and promises. In their rules of government there is remarkable rectitude, whilst in their behaviour there is much gentleness and sweetness. With respect to criminals or rebels, these are few in number, and only occasionally troublesome. When the laws are broken or the power of the ruler violated, then the matter is clearly sifted and the offenders imprisoned. There is no infliction of corporal punishment; they are simply left to live or die, and are not counted among men.

Hiuen Tsiang's Travels in India (A.D. 629-45)
translated by S. BEAL

Towns and Buildings

The towns and villages have inner gates; the walls are wide and high; the streets and lanes are tortuous, and the roads winding. The thoroughfares are dirty and the stalls arranged on both sides of the road with appropriate signs. Butchers, fishers, dancers, executioners, and scavengers, and so on, have their abodes without the city. In coming and going these persons are bound to keep on the left side of the road till they arrive at their homes. Their houses are surrounded by low walls, and form the suburbs. The earth being soft and muddy, the walls of the towns are mostly built of brick or tiles. The towers on the walls are constructed of wood or bamboo; the houses have balconies and belvederes, which are made of wood, with a coating of lime or mortar, and covered with tiles. The different buildings have the same form as those in China: rushes, or dry branches, or tiles, or boards are used for covering them. The walls are covered with lime and mud, mixed with cow's dung for purity. At different seasons they scatter flowers about. Such are some of their different customs.

Hiuen Tsiang's Travels in India (A.D. 629-45)
translated by S. BEAL

The Beginnings of the Caste System

The coming of the Aryans into India raised new problems — racial and political. The conquered race, the Dravidians, had a long background of civilisation behind them, but there is little doubt that the Aryans considered themselves vastly superior and a wide gulf separated the two races. Then there were also the backward aboriginal tribes, nomads or forest-dwellers. Out of this conflict and interaction of races gradually arose the caste system, which, in the course of succeeding centuries, was to affect Indian life so profoundly. Probably caste was neither Aryan nor Dravidian. It was an attempt at the social organisation of different races, a rationalisation of the facts as they existed at the time. It brought degradation in its train afterwards, and it is still a burden and a curse; but we can hardly judge it from subsequent standards or later developments. It was in keeping with the spirit of the times and some such grading took place in most of the ancient civilisations, though apparently China was free from it. There was a four-fold division in that other branch of the Aryans, the Iranians, during the Sassanian period, but it did not petrify into caste. Many of these old civilisations, including that of Greece, were entirely dependent on mass slavery. There was no such mass or large-scale labour slavery in India, although there were relatively small numbers of domestic slaves. Plato in his *Republic* refers to a division similar to that of the four principal castes. Mediaeval catholicism knew this division also.

Caste began with a hard and fast division between Aryans and non-Aryans, the latter again being divided into the Dravidian races and the aboriginal tribes. The Aryans, to begin with, formed one class and there was hardly any specialisation. The word Arya comes from a root word meaning to till, and the Aryans as a whole were agriculturists and agriculture was considered a noble occupation. The tiller of the soil functioned also as priest, soldier, or trader, and there was no privileged order of priests. The caste divisions, originally intended to separate the Aryans from the non-Aryans, reacted on the Aryans themselves, and as division of functions and specialisation increased, the new classes took the form of castes.

Thus at a time when it was customary for the conquerors to exterminate or enslave the conquered races, caste enabled a more peaceful solution which fitted in with the growing specialisation of functions. Life was graded and out of the mass of agriculturists evolved the Vaishyas, the agriculturists, artisans, and merchants; the Kshatriyas, or rulers and warriors; and the Brahmins, priests and thinkers who were supposed to guide policy and preserve and maintain the ideals of the nation. Below these three there were the Shudras or labourers and unskilled workers, other than the agriculturists. Among the indigenous tribes many were gradually assimilated and given a place at the bottom of the social scale, that is among the Shudras. This process of assimilation was a continuous one. These castes must have been in a fluid condition; rigidity came in much later. Probably the ruling class had always great latitude, and any person who by conquest or otherwise assumed power, could, if he so willed, join the hierarchy as a Kshatriya, and get the priests to manufacture an appropriate genealogy connecting him with some ancient Aryan hero.

The word Arya ceased to have any racial significance and came to mean "noble", just as anarya meant ignoble and was usually applied to nomadic tribes, forest-dwellers, etc.

The Indian mind was extraordinarily analytical and had a passion for putting ideas and concepts, and even life's activities, into compartments. The Aryans not only divided society into four main groups but also divided the individual's life into four parts: the first part consisted of growth and adolescence, the student period of life, acquiring knowledge, developing self-discipline and self-control, continence; the second was that of the householder and man of the world; the third was that of the elder statesman, who had attained a certain poise and objectivity, and could devote himself to public work without the selfish desire to profit by it; and the last stage was that of the recluse, who lived a life largely cut off from the world's activities. In this way also they adjusted the two opposing tendencies which often exist side by side in man — the acceptance of life in its fullness and the rejection of it.

J.L. NEHRU (1889-1964)
The Discovery of India

The Advantages of Castes

Many persons study so imperfectly the spirit and character of the different nations that inhabit the earth, and the influence of climate on their manners, customs, predilections, and usages, that they are astonished to find how widely such nations differ from each other. Trammelled by the prejudices of their own surroundings, such persons think nothing well regulated that is not included in the polity and government of their own country. They would like to see all nations of the earth placed on precisely the same footing as themselves. Everything which differs from their own customs they consider either uncivilised or ridiculous. Now, although man's nature is pretty much the same all the world over; it is subject to so many differentiations caused by soil, climate, food, religion, education, and other circumstances peculiar to different countries, that the system of civilisation adopted by one people would plunge another into a state of barbarism and cause its complete downfall.

I have heard some persons, sensible enough in other respects, but imbued with all the prejudices that they have brought with them from Europe, pronounce what appears to me an altogether erroneous judgement in the matter of caste divisions amongst the Hindus. In their opinion, caste is not only useless to the body politic, it is also ridiculous, and even calculated to bring trouble and disorder on the people. For my part, having lived many years on friendly terms with the Hindus, I have been able to study their national life and character closely, and I have arrived at a quite opposite decision on this subject of caste. I believe caste division to be in many respects the *chef-d'oeuvre*, the happiest effort, of Hindu legislation. I am persuaded that it is simply and solely due to the distribution of the people into castes that India did not lapse into a state of barbarism, and that she preserved and perfected the arts and sciences of civilisation whilst most other nations of the earth remained in a state of barbarism. I do not consider caste to be free from many great drawbacks; but I believe that the resulting advantages, in the case of a nation constituted like the Hindus, more than outweigh the resulting evils.

To establish the justice of this contention we have only to glance at the condition of the various races of men who live in the same latitude as the Hindus, and to consider the past and present status of those among them whose natural disposition and character have not been influenced for good by the purifying doctrines of Revealed Religion. We can judge what the Hindus would have been like, had they not been held within the pale of social duty by caste regulations, if we glance at neighbouring nations west of the Peninsula and east of it beyond the Ganges as far as China. In China itself a temperate climate and a form of government peculiarly adapted to a people unlike any other in the world have produced the same effect as the distinction of caste among the Hindus.

After much careful thought I can discover no other reason except caste which accounts for the Hindus not having fallen into the same state of barbarism as their neighbours and as almost all nations inhabiting the torrid zone. Caste assigns to each individual his own profession or calling; and the handing down of this system from father to son, from generation to generation, makes it impossible for any person or his descendants to change the condition of life which the law assigns to him for any other. Such an institution was probably the only means that the most clear-sighted prudence could devise for maintaining a state of

civilisation amongst a people endowed with the peculiar
characteristics of the Hindus.

ABBE J.A. DUBOIS
Hindu Manners, Customs and Ceremonies (1816)
translated by H. BEAUCHAMP

India Conquered by the Muslims

The Muslims first invaded India in 711 A.D. By the
middle of the 13th century they had conquered a major
part of Northern India and made Delhi their capital.

Happy Hindustan, the splendour of Religion, where the
Law finds perfect honour and security. In learning Delhi can
now compete with Bokhárá, for Islám has been made manifest
by its kings. The whole country, by means of the sword of
our holy warriors, has become like a forest denuded of its
thorns by fire. The land has been saturated with the water
of the sword, and the vapours of infidelity have been
dispersed. The strong men of Hind have been trodden under
foot, and all are ready to pay tribute. Islám is triumphant,
idolatry is subdued. Had not the law granted exemption
from death by the payment of poll-tax, the very name of
Hind, root and branch, would have been extinguished. From
Ghazni to the shore of the ocean you see all under the
dominion of Islám. Cawing crows see no arrows pointed at
them; nor is the Tarsá (Christian) there, who does not fear
(taras) to render the servant equal with God; nor the Jew
who dares to exalt the Pentateuch to a level with the Kurán;
nor the Magh who is delighted with the worship of fire, but
of whom the fire complains with its hundred tongues. The

four sects of Musulmáns are at amity, and the very fish are
Sunnis.

AMIR KHUSRU (1253-1325)
Ashika
translated by ELLIOT AND DOWSON

Persecution of the Hindus

The Hindus and idol-worshippers had agreed to pay the
money for toleration *(zar-i zimmiya)*, and had consented
to the poll tax *(jizya)*, in return for which they and their
families enjoyed security. These people now erected new idol-
temples in the city and the environs in opposition to the Law
of the Prophet which declares that such temples are not to
be tolerated. Under Divine guidance I destroyed these edifices,
and I killed those leaders of infidelity who seduced others into
error, and the lower orders I subjected to stripes and
chastisement, until this abuse was entirely abolished. The
following is an instance:— In the village of Maluh there is
a tank which they call *kund*. Here they had built idol-temples,
and on certain days the Hindus were accustomed to proceed
thither on horseback, and wearing arms. Their women and
children also went out in palankins and carts. There they
assembled in thousands and performed idol worship. This
abuse had been so overlooked that the bazar people took out
there all sorts of provisions, and set up stalls and sold their
goods. Some graceless Musulmans, thinking only of their own
gratification, took part in these meetings. When intelligence
of this came to my ears my religious feelings prompted me
at once to put a stop to this scandal and offence to the religion
of Islám. On the day of the assembling I went there in person,

and I ordered that the leaders of these people and the promoters of this abomination should be put to death. I forbade the infliction of any severe punishments on the Hindus in general, but I destroyed their idol-temples, and instead thereof raised mosques. I founded two flourishing towns *(kasba)*, one called Tughlikpur, the other Salarpur. Where infidels and idolators worshipped idols, Musulmans now, by God's mercy, perform their devotions to the true God. Praises of God and the summons to prayer are now heard there, and that place which was formerly the home of infidels has become the habitation of the faithful, who here repeat their creed and offer up their praises to God.

SULTAN FIROZ SHAH (1351-1388)
Futuhat-i Firoz Shahi
translated by ELLIOT and DOWSON

The Mughal Conquest of India
1526

The first Mughal Emperor of India, Babar (1483-1530), a direct descendant of Timur and of Chingiz Khan, succeeded to the principality of Faraghana (now in Soviet Turkestan) when twelve, occupied Kabul in 1504, invaded India for the fifth time in 1526, defeated the Muslim Emperor Ibrahim Lodi on the famous battlefield of Panipat near Delhi in 1526 and established a line of Mughal rule in India which lasted until 1858, when Queen Victoria assumed the Sovereignty of India.

Ambition admits not of inaction;
The world is his who exerts himself,

In wisdom's eye, every condition
May find repose, but royalty alone.

On Thursday, the 28th of Rajeb, [10 May], about the hour
of afternoon prayers, I entered Agra, and took up my residence
at Sultan Ibrahim's palace. From the time when I conquered
the country of Kabul, which was in the year 910 [1504], till
the present time, I had always been bent on subduing
Hindustan. Sometimes, however, from the misconduct of my
Amirs and their dislike of the plan, sometimes from the cabals
and opposition of my brothers, I was prevented from
prosecuting any expedition into that country, and its provinces
escaped being overrun. At length these obstacles were removed.
There was now no one left, great or small, noble or private
man, who could dare to utter a word in opposition to the
enterprise. In the year 925 [1519], I collected an army, and
having taken the fort of Bajour by storm in two or three
gharis, put all the garrison to the sword. I next advanced into
Behreh, where I prevented all marauding and plunder, imposed
a contribution on the inhabitants, and having levied it to the
amount of four hundred thousand *shahrokhis* in money and
goods, divided the proceeds among the troops who were in
my service, and returned to Kabul. From that time till the year
932 [1526], I attached myself in a peculiar degree to the
affairs of Hindustan, and in the space of these seven or eight
years entered it five times at the head of an army. The fifth
time, the Most High God, of his grace and mercy, cast down
and defeated an enemy so mighty as Sultan Ibrahim, and made
me the master and conqueror of the powerful empire of
Hindustan. From the time of the blessed Prophet (on whom
and on his family be peace and salvation!) down to the present
time, three foreign kings had subdued the country, and acquired
the sovereignty of Hindustan. One of these was Sultan Mahmud
Ghazni [A.D. 977-1030], whose family long continued to fill

the throne of that country. The second was Sultan Shahabeddin Ghuri [A.D. 1157-1203], and for many years his slaves and dependants swayed the sceptre of these realms. I am the third. But my achievement is not to be put on the same level with theirs; for Sultan Mahmud, at the time when he conquered Hindustan, occupied the throne of Khorasan, and had absolute power and dominion over the Sultans of Khwariam and the surrounding chiefs. The King of Samarkand, too, was subject to him. If his army did not amount to two hundred thousand, yet grant that it was only one hundred thousand, and it is plain that the comparison between the two conquests must cease. Moreover, his enemies were Rajas. All Hindustan was not at that period subject to a single Emperor: every Raja set up for a monarch on his own account, in his own petty territories. Again, though Sultan Shahabeddin Ghuri did not himself enjoy the sovereignty of Khorasan, yet his elder brother, Sultan Ghiaseddin Ghuri, held it. In the *Tabakat-e-Nasiri* it is said, that on one occasion he marched into Hindustan with one hundred and twenty thousand cataphract horse. His enemies, too, were Rais and Rajas; a single monarch did not govern the whole of Hindustan. When I marched into Behreh, we might amount to one thousand five hundred, or two thousand men at the utmost. When I invaded the country for the fifth time, overthrew Sultan Ibrahim, and subdued the empire of Hindustan, I had a larger army than I had ever before brought into it. My servants, the merchants and their servants and the followers of all descriptions that were in the camp along with me, were numbered, and amounted to twelve thousand men. The kingdoms that depended on me were Badakhshan, Kunduz, Kabul, and Kandahar; but these countries did not furnish me with assistance equal to their resources; and, indeed, some of them, from their vicinity to the enemy, were so circumstanced, that, far from affording me assistance, I was obliged to send them extensive supplies from my other territories. Besides this, all Maweralnaher was occupied by the Khans and Sultans of the Uzbeks, whose armies were calculated to amount to about a hundred thousand men, and who were my ancient foes. Finally, the whole empire of Hindustan, from Behreh to Behar, was in the hands of the Afghans. Their prince, Sultan Ibrahim, from the resources of his kingdom, could bring into the field an army of five hundred thousand men. At that time some of the Amirs to the east were in a state of rebellion. His army on foot was computed to be a hundred thousand strong; his own elephants, with those of his Amirs, were reckoned at nearly a thousand. Yet, under such circumstances, and in spite of this power, placing my trust in God, and leaving behind me my old and inveterate enemy the Uzbeks, who had an army of a hundred thousand men, I advanced to meet so powerful a prince as Sultan Ibrahim, the lord of numerous armies, and emperor of extensive territories. In consideration of my confidence in Divine aid, the Most High God did not suffer the distress and hardships that I had undergone to be thrown away, but defeated my formidable enemy, and made me the conqueror of the noble country of Hindustan. This success I do not ascribe to my own strength, nor did this good fortune flow from my own efforts, but from the fountain of the favour and mercy of God.

*

Return a hundred thanks, O Babur! for the bounty of the
      merciful God
Has given you Sind, Hind, and numerous kingdoms;
If unable to stand the heat, you long for cold,
You have only to recollect the frost and cold of Ghazni.

BABAR (1483-1530)
Memoirs
translated by W. ERSKINE

The Artists

Want of genius, therefore, is not the reason why works of superior art are not exhibited in the capital. If the artists and manufacturers were encouraged, the useful and fine arts would flourish; but these unhappy men are condemned, treated with harshness, and inadequately remunerated for their labour. The rich will have every article at a cheap rate. When an *Omrah* or *Mansebdar* requires the services of an artisan, he sends to the bazaar for him, employing force, if necessary, to make the poor man work; and after the task is finished, the unfeeling lord pays, not according to the value of the labour, but agreeably to his own standard of fair remuneration; the artisan having reason to congratulate himself if the korrah has not been given in part payment. How then can it be expected that any spirit of emulation should animate the artist or manufacturer? Instead of contending for a superiority of reputation, his only anxiety is to finish his work, and to earn the pittance that shall supply him with a piece of bread. The artists, therefore, who arrived at any eminence in their art are those only who are in the service of the King or of some powerful Omrah, and who work exclusively for their patron.

FRANCIS BERNIER (1620-88)
Travels in the Moghul Empire (1656-68)
translated by A. CONSTABLE

The Mughal Classification of the People

When the auspicious throne of royalty was filled by this dignified and brave monarch [Humayun], all the officers of the State and inhabitants of the kingdom were divided into three classes. The brothers and relations of the King, the nobles and ministers, as well as the military men, were called *Ahl-i Daulat* (officers of the State), because it is evident that — according to the words, "There can be no dominion without men" — no degree of wealth and prosperity can be attained without the assistance of this class of brave and courageous people; and no one can obtain the throne and power without the aid of warriors and heroes.

Kings, with the assistance of their army,
Place their feet upon the throne of empires.
He alone can obtain wealth and rank
Who is assisted by his army.

The holy persons, the great *mushaikhs* (religious men), the respectable *saiyids*, the literati, the law officers, the scientific persons, poets, besides other great and respectable men, formed the second class, and were denominated *Ahl-i Sa'ádat* (good men), because to observe, honour, and regard these people, and to associate with such men, secures eternal prosperity, and enables men to rise to high dignities and ranks.

Virtue is the gift of God:
It is not in the power of the mighty man to obtain it.
If you wish to obtain fortune,
You must associate with virtuous men.

Those who possessed beauty and elegance, those who

were young and most lovely, also clever musicians and sweet singers, composed the third class, and the appellation of *Ahl-i Murád* (people of pleasure) was conferred on them, because most people take great delight in the company of such young-looking men, of rosy cheeks and sweet voices, and are pleased by hearing their songs, and the pleasing sound of the musical instruments, such as the harp, the sackbut, and the lute.

> The hope of the heart of lovers
> Is never realised but when they meet persons whose cheeks
>   are rosy.
> He who is fond of hearing songs and music
> Has the gates of happiness opened for himself.

KHONDAMIR (1475-1533)
Humayun-Nama
translated by ELLIOT and DOWSON

Letter from King James to Emperor Jahangir
1614-15

James, by the Grace of Almightie God, the Creator of Heauen and Earth, King of Great Britaine, France and Ireland, Defender of the Christian Faith, etc.

To the high and mightie Monarch the Great Mogor, King of the Orientall Indies, of Chandahar, of Chismer and Corazon, etc. Greeting.

We hauing notice of your great favour towards Vs and Our Subjects, by Your Great Firma to all Your Captaines of Riuers and Offices of Your Customes, for the entertaynment of Our louing Subjects the English Nation with all kind respect, at what time soeuer they shall arrive at any of the Ports within Your Dominions, and that they may have quiet Trade and Commerce without any kind of hinderance or molestation, etc., As by the Articles concluded by Suc Suff, Gouernour of the Guzerats, in Your Name, with Our louing Subiect Captaine Thomas Best appeareth: Have thought it meete to send vnto You Our Ambassadour, which may more fully and at large handle and treate of such matters as are fit to be considered of, concerning that good and friendly correspondence, which is so lately begunne betweene Vs, and which will without doubt redound to the honour and vtilitie of both Nations. In which consideration, and for the furthering of such laudable Commerce, Wee have made choice of Sir Thomas Roe, Knight, one of the principall Gentlemen of Our Court, to whom Wee have giuen Commission vnder Our Great Seale of England, together with directions and instructions further to treate of such matters as may be for the continuance and increase of the vtilitie and profit of each others Subjects: to whom We pray You to giue favour and credit in whatsoeuer Hee shall mooue or propound toward the establishing and enlarging of the same. And for confirmation of our good inclination and well-wishing toward You, We pray You to accept in good part the Present, which our said Ambassadour will deliuer vnto You. And so doe commit You to the mercifull protection of Almightie God.

The Embassy of Sir Thomas Roe to India
1615-19

Bengal in the 17th Century

Egypt has been represented in every age as the finest and most fruitful country in the world, and even our modern writers deny that there is any other land so peculiarly favoured by nature: but the knowledge I have acquired of *Bengale*, during two visits paid to that kingdom, inclines me to believe that the pre-eminence ascribed to Egypt is rather due to *Bengale*. The latter country produces rice in such abundance that it supplies not only the neighbouring but remote states. It is carried up the Ganges as far as Patna, and exported by sea to Maslipatam and many other ports on the coast of Koromandel. It is also sent to foreign kingdoms, principally to the island of *Ceylon* and the *Maldives*. *Bengale* abounds likewise in sugar, with which it supplies the kingdoms of *Golkonda* and the *Karnatic*, where very little is grown, *Arabia* and *Mesopotamia*, through the towns of Moka and Bassora, and even Persia, by way of Bender-Abbasi. *Bengale* likewise is celebrated for its sweetmeats, especially in places inhabited by Portuguese, who are skilful in the art of preparing them, and with whom they are an article of considerable trade. Among other fruits, they preserve large citrons, such as we have in Europe, a certain delicate root about the length of sarsaparilla, that common fruit of the Indies called amba, another called ananas, small mirobolans, which are excellent, limes and ginger.

Bengale, it is true, yields not so much wheat as Egypt; but if this be a defect, it is attributable to the inhabitants, who live a great deal more upon rice than the Egyptians, and seldom taste bread. Nevertheless, wheat is cultivated in sufficient quantity for the consumption of the country, and for the making of excellent and cheap sea-biscuits, with which the crews of European ships, English, Dutch and

Portuguese, are supplied. The three or four sorts of vegetables which, together with rice and butter, form the chief food of the common people, are purchased for the merest trifle, and for a single roupie twenty or more good fowls may be bought. Geese and ducks are proportionably cheap. There are also goats and sheep in abundance; and pigs are obtained at so low a price that the Portuguese, settled in the country, live almost entirely upon pork. This meat is salted at a cheap rate by the Dutch and English, for the supply of their vessels. Fish of every species, whether fresh or salt, is in the same profusion. In a word, *Bengale*, abounds with every necessary of life; and it is this abundance that has induced so many Portuguese, Half-castes, and other Christians, driven from their different settlements by the Dutch, to seek an asylum in this fertile kingdom. The Jesuits and Augustins, who have large churches and are permitted the free and unmolested exercise of their religion, assured me that Ogouli [Hoogli] alone contains from eight to nine thousand Christians, and that in other parts of the kingdom their number exceeded five-and-twenty thousand. The rich exuberance of the country, together with the beauty and amiable disposition of the native women, has given rise to a proverb in common use among the Portuguese, English, and Dutch, that the Kingdom of *Bengale* has a hundred gates open for entrance, but not one for departure.

FRANCIS BERNIER (1620-88)
Travels in the Moghul Empire (1656-68)
translated by A. CONSTABLE

The Decay of India

The search for the sources of India's strength and for her deterioration and decay is long and intricate. Yet the recent causes of that decay are obvious enough. She fell behind in the march of technique, and Europe, which had long been backward in many matters, took the lead in technical progress. Behind this technical progress was the spirit of science and a bubbling life and spirit which displayed itself in many activities and in adventurous voyages of discovery. New techniques gave military strength to the countries of western Europe and it was easy for them to spread out and dominate the East. That is the story not only of India, but of almost the whole of Asia.

Why this should have happened so is more difficult to unravel, for India was not lacking in mental alertness and technical skill in earlier times. One senses a progressive deterioration during centuries. The urge to life and endeavour becomes less, the creative spirit fades away and gives place to the imitative. Where triumphant and rebellious thought had tried to pierce the mysteries of nature and the universe, the wordy commentator comes with his glosses and long explanations. Magnificent art and sculpture give way to meticulous carving of intricate detail without nobility of conception or design. The vigour and richness of language, powerful yet simple, are followed by highly ornate and complex literary forms. The urge to adventure and the overflowing life which led to vast schemes of distant colonisation and the transplantation of Indian culture in far lands: all these fade away and a narrow orthodoxy taboos even the crossing of the high seas. A rational spirit of inquiry, so evident in earlier times, which might well have led to the further growth of science, is replaced by irrationalism and a blind idolatory of the past. Indian life becomes a sluggish stream, living in the past, moving slowly through the accumulations of dead centuries. The heavy burden of the past crushes it and a kind of coma seizes it. It is not surprising that in this condition of mental stupor and physical weariness India should have deteriorated and remained rigid and immobile, while other parts of the world marched ahead.

J.L. NEHRU (1889-1964)
The Discovery of India

The English Army

I now considered myself an experienced soldier, as I had suffered defeats, and had helped to win victories; I had served with Sahebs, and white soldiers; and, in my opinion, the reason that the English are invincible is, they do not care for defeat: four times have I seen a European regiment driven back with terrible slaughter, yet their fifth attack was as fierce as the first. A wonderful thing is, they do not get in confusion when their leader is killed — another officer takes his place, and the men obey him just the same. Now, in a Native army, if the Sirdar or leader is killed, the whole army falls into confusion, and generally takes to flight — the men will not follow the next leader. And the chief reason for this great difference is, the Rajahs or Nawabs generally fight for their own benefit, and they collect all the plunder in their own *tosahkanas* (coffers), to spend upon themselves and their favourites alone, not for the good of their subjects; so of course the people do not care about the war, any further than by it there is the chance of getting plunder, or of rising to power. Another reason is, few Princes of Hindoostan ever regularly pay their troops, and when an army is allowed to pay itself by plunder, there can be no real discipline, although every individual may be brave. Princes seldom grant pensions to the families of those killed in their service, and care but little about the soldier when once he is disabled and of no further use to them. The Sirkar's officers fight, but their whole object is not plunder alone — the strict rules of the army prevent this to any great extent; they receive their pay regularly, and they feel sure they will get it; also if their *kismut* (fate) is, that they are to be wounded, they will still be cared for, and oftentimes rewarded.

Autobiography of Subadar Sita Ram (1861)
translated by NORGATE

The Western Impact

The impact of western culture on India was the impact of a dynamic society, of a "modern" consciousness, on a static society wedded to medieval habits of thought which, however, sophisticated and advanced in its own way could not progress because of its inherent limitations. And yet, curiously enough the agents of this historic process were not only wholly unconscious of their mission in India but, as a class, actually represented no such process. In England their class fought this historic process but the forces opposed to them were too strong and could not be held back. In India they had a free field and were successful in applying the brakes to that very change and progress which, in the larger context, they represented. They encouraged and consolidated the position of the socially reactionary groups in India, and opposed all those who worked for political and social change.

If change came it was in spite of them or as an incidental and unexpected consequence of their activities. The introduction of the steam engine and the railway was a big step towards a change of the medieval structure, but it was intended to consolidate their rule and facilitate the exploitation for their own benefit of the interior of the country. This contradiction between the deliberate policy of the British authorities in India and some of its unintended consequences produces a certain confusion and masks that policy itself. Change came to India because of this impact of the west, but it came almost in spite of the British in India. They succeeded in slowing down the pace of that change to such an extent that even today the transition is very far from complete.

*

Individual Englishmen, educationists, orientalists, journalists, missionaries, and others played an important part in bringing western culture to India, and in their attempts to do so often came into conflict with their own Government. That Government feared the effects of the spread of modern education and put many obstacles in its way, and yet it was due to the pioneering efforts of able and earnest Englishmen, who gathered enthusiastic groups of Indian students around them, that English thought and literature and political tradition were introduced to India. (When I say Englishmen I include, of course, people from the whole of Great Britain and Ireland, though I know this is improper and incorrect. But I dislike the word Britisher, and even that probably does not include the Irish. My apologies to the Irish, the Scots, and the Welsh. In India they have all functioned alike and have been looked upon as one indistinguishable group.) Even the British Government, in spite of its dislike of education, was compelled by circumstances to arrange for the training and production of clerks for its growing establishment. It could not afford to bring out from England large numbers of people to serve in this subordinate capacity. So education grew slowly and, though it was a limited and perverted education, it opened the doors and windows of the mind to new ideas and dynamic thoughts. The printing press and indeed all machinery were also considered dangerous and explosive for the Indian mind, not to be encouraged in any way lest they led to the spread of sedition and industrial growth. There is a story that the Nizam of Hyderabad once expressed a desire to see European machinery and thereupon the British Resident procured for him an air-pump and a printing press. The Nizam's momentary curiosity having been satisfied, these were stored away with other gifts and curiosities. But when the Government in Calcutta heard of this they expressed their displeasure to their Resident and rebuked him especially for introducing a printing press in an Indian state. The Resident offered to get it broken up secretly if the Government so desired.

J.L. Nehru (1889-1964)
The Discovery of India

To India — My Native Land

Why hang'st thou lonely on yon withered bough?
Unstrung, forever, must thou there remain?
Thy music once was sweet — who hears it now?
Why doth the breeze sigh over thee in vain? —
Silence hath bound thee with her fatal chain;
Neglected, mute and desolate art thou
Like ruined monument on desert plain —
O! many a hand more worthy far than mine
Once they harmonious chords to sweetness gave,

And many a wreath for them did Fame entwine
Of flowers still blooming on the minstrel's grave;
Those hands are cold — but if thy notes divine
May be by mortal wakened once again,
Harp of my country, let me strike the strain!
My country! in thy day of glory past
A beauteous halo circled round thy brow,
And worshipped as a deity thou wast.
Where is that glory, where that reverence now?
The eagle pinion is chained down at last,
And grovelling in the lowly dust art thou:
Thy minstrel hath no wreath to weave for thee
Save the sad story of thy misery!
Well — let me dive into the depths of time,
And bring from out the ages that have rolled
A few small fragments of those wrecks sublime,
Which human eye may never more behold;
And let the guerdon of my labour be,
My fallen country! one kind wish from thee!

HENRY LOUIS VIVIAN DEROZIO (1809-31)
Poems of Henry Derozio

The Introduction of
English Education
1835

In the 1830s the British in India were divided between Orientalists and Anglicists on the question of education. The Orientalists were in favour of giving government support for the study of Persian, Arabic and Sanskrit and they owed much to Sir William Jones (1746-1794) who had praised Sanskrit for its "wonderful structure more perfect than the Greek, more copious than the Latin and more exquisitely refined than either." The Anglicists, on the other hand, believed in the supremacy of English language and literature and the practical advantages that would follow its introduction into India. The Government supported the Anglicists' viewpoint in 1835.

To sum up what I have said, I think it clear that we are not fettered by the Act of Parliament of 1813; that we are not fettered by any pledge expressed or implied; that we are free to employ our funds as we choose; that we ought to employ them in teaching what is best worth knowing; that English is better worth knowing than Sanscrit or Arabic; that the natives are desirous to be taught English, and are not desirous to be taught Sanscrit or Arabic; that neither as the languages of law, nor as the languages of religion, have the Sanscrit and Arabic any peculiar claim to our engagement; that it is possible to make natives of this country thoroughly good English scholars; and that to this end our efforts ought to be directed.

In one point I fully agree with the gentlemen to whose general views I am opposed. I feel with them, that it is impossible for us, with out limited means, to attempt to educate the body of the people. *We must at present do our best to form a class who may be interpreters between us* and the millions whom we govern; a class of persons, Indian in blood and colour, but English in taste, in opinions, in morals, and in intellect. To that class we may leave it to refine the vernacular dialects of the country, to enrich those dialects with terms of science borrowed from the Western nomenclature, and to render them by degrees fit vehicles for conveying knowledge of the great mass of the population.

T.B. MACAULAY (1800-59)
Minute on Education

Advantages and Disadvantages of British Rule in India

1871

Dadabhai Naoroji was thrice elected the President of Indian National Congress and was the first Indian to be elected member of British Parliament. The following is an extract from a paper on India which he presented to a learned society in London.

Credit — *In the Cause of Humanity:* Abolition of suttee and infanticide.

Destruction of Dacoits, Thugs, Pindarees* and other such pests of Indian Society.

Remarriage of Hindoo widows, and charitable aid in time of famine.

Glorious work all this, of which any nation may well be proud, and such as has not fallen to the lot of any people in the history of mankind.

In the Cause of Civilisation: Education, both male and female. Though yet only partial, an inestimable blessing as far as it has gone, and leading gradually to the destruction of superstition, and many moral and social evils. Resuscitation of India's own noble literature, modified and refined by the enlightenment of the West.

The only pity is that as much has not been done as might have been in this noble work; but still India must be, and is, deeply grateful.

Politically: Peace and order. Freedom of speech and liberty of the Press. Higher political knowledge and aspirations. Improvement of government in the native States.

---

* Armed thieves, highway murderers, robber bands

Security of life and property. Freedom from oppression caused by the caprice or avarice of despotic rulers, and from devastation by war. Equal justice between man and man (sometimes vitiated by partiality to Europeans). Services of highly educated administrators, who have achieved the above-mentioned good results.

Materially: Loans for railways and irrigation. (I have been particularly charged with ignoring this, but I consider it one of the greatest benefits you have conferred upon India, inasmuch as it has enabled us to produce more than we could before, though there is not yet enough for all of India's ordinary wants, and I have said this in my paper.) I cannot ascertain the exact amount of investments in irrigation works, but I take them to be about £10,000,000 making the total £110,000,000. The development of a few valuable products, such as indigo, tea, coffee, silk, etc. Increase of exports. Telegraphs.

Generally: A slowly growing desire of late to treat India equitably, and as a country held in trust. Good intentions.

No nation on the face of the earth has ever had the opportunity of achieving such a glorious work as this, I hope in this credit side of the account I have done no injustice, and if I have omitted any item which anyone may think of importance, I shall have the greatest pleasure in inserting it. I appreciate, and so do my countrymen, what England has done for India, and I know that it is only in British hands that her regeneration can be accomplished. Now for the debit side.

Debit — *In the Cause of Humanity:* Nothing. Everything, therefore, is in your favour under this head.

In the Cause of Civilisation: As I have said already, there has been a failure to do as much as might have been done, but I put nothing to the debit. Much has been done, or I should not be standing here this evening.

Politically: Repeated breach of pledges to give the natives a fair and reasonable share in the higher administration of their own country, which has much shaken confidence in the good faith of the British word. Political aspirations and the legitimate claim to have a reasonable voice in the legislation and the imposition and disbursement of taxes, met to a very slight degree, thus treating the natives of India not as British subjects, to whom representation is a birthright.

(I stop here a moment to say a word as to a mistake into which my friend, Mr. Hyde Clark, fell, in supposing that I desired the government of India to be at once transfered to the natives. In my belief a greater calamity could not befall India than for England to go away and leave her to herself.)

Consequent on the above, an utter disregard of the feelings and views of the natives. The great moral evil of the drain of the wisdom and practical administration and statesmanship, leaving none to guide the rising generation. (Here, again, have I been misunderstood. I complain not of Englishmen returning to their own country, but of the whole administration being kept entirely in English hands, so that none of the natives are brought up to and taught the responsibilities and duties of office, so that we have none amongst ourselves to guide us as our elders and teach us our duties as citizens and as moral beings. A foster mother or nurse will never supply the place of the real mother, and the natives will therefore naturally follow their own leaders, unless you prove more kind, humane and considerate. Draw these leaders on your side.) The indifference to India, even of a large portion of those who have had an Indian career, and who are living on Indian pensions. The culpable indifference of a large portion of the people, the public Press, and Parliament of this country to the interests of India; therefore, periodical committees of inquiry are absolutely necessary, for the knowledge that such will take place would be a check on careless administration. With regard to the native states, though their system is improving, it is most unjust that their cases should be decided in secret.

The frequent change of officials is a constant source of disturbance in policy, and though it may be unavoidable, it is none the less hard upon India.

Financially: All attention is engrossed in devising new modes of taxation, without any adequate effort to increase the means of the people to pay; and the consequent vexation and oppressiveness of the taxes imposed, imperial and local. Inequitable financial relations between England and India, i.e. the political debt of £100,000,000 clapped on India's shoulders, and all home charges also, though the British exchequer contributes nearly £3,000,000 to the expenses of the colonies. The crushing and economically rude and unintelligent policy of making the present generation pay the whole cost of public works for the benefit of the future instead of making the political like all other machinery, and distributing the weight so as to make a small power lift a large weight by the aid of time. The results of trying to produce something out of nothing, of the want of intelligent adaptation of financial machinery, and of much reckless expenditure; in financial embarrassments, and deep discontent of the people.

Materially: The political drain, up to this time, from India to England, of above £500,000,000, at the lowest computation, in principal alone, which with interest would be some thousands of millions. The further continuation of this drain at the rate, at present, of above £12,000,000, with a tendency to increase. (I do not mean this as a complaint; you must have a return for the services rendered to India, but let us have the means of paying. If I have a manager to whom I pay £1,000 a year, and he only makes the business produce £400, so that £600 a year must be paid him out of capital, any man of business can see what will be the result. Peace and order will soon be completely established by the closing of the concern.)

The consequent continuous impoverishment and exhaustion of the country, except so far as it has been very partially relieved and replenished by the railway and irrigation loans, and the windfall of the consequences of the American war, since 1850. Even with this relief, the material condition of India is such that the great mass of the poor people have hardly 2d a day and a few rags, or a scanty subsistence.

The famines that were in their power to prevent, if they had done their duty, as a good and intelligent government. The policy adopted during the last fifteen years of building railways, irrigation works, etc. is hopeful, has already resulted in much good to your credit, and if persevered in, gratitude and contentment will follow.

An increase of exports (without adequate compensation); (a) loss of manufacturing industry and skill. Here I end the debit side....

To sum up the whole, the British rule has been — morally, a great blessing; politically peace and order on one hand, blunders on the other, materially, impoverishment (relieved as far as the railway and other loans go). The natives call the British system *Sakar ki Churi*, the knife of sugar. That is to say there is no oppression, it is all smooth and sweet, but it is the knife, notwithstanding. I mention this that you should know these feelings. Our great misfortune is that you do not know our wants. When you will know our real wishes, I have not the least doubt that you would do justice. The genius and spirit of the British people is fair play and justice. The great problems before the English statesman are two: (1) To make the foreign rule self-supporting, either by returning to India, in some shape or other, the wealth that has been, and is being drawn from it, or by stopping that drain in some way till India is so far improved in its material condition as to be able to produce enough for its own ordinary wants and the extraordinary ones of a costly distant rule. If you cannot feel yourself actuated by the high and noble ambition of the amelioration of 200,000,000 of human beings, let your self-interest suggest to you to take care of the bird that gives the golden egg of £12,000,000 a year to your nation, and provisions to thousands of your people of all classes. In the name of humanity, I implore our rulers to make up their minds not to prevent the restoration of the equilibrium, after the continuous exhaustion by drain and by horrible famines. I do not in the least grudge any legitimate benefit England may derive for its rule in India. On the contrary, I am thankful for its invaluable moral benefits; but it is the further duty of England to give us such a government, and all the benefit of its power and credit, as to enable us to pay, without starving or dying by famine, the tribute or price for the rule; (2) How to satisfy reasonably the growing political aspirations and just rights of a people called British subjects to have a fair share in the administration and legislation of their own country. If the Select Committee solve these two problems, before which all other difficulties, financial or others, are as nothing, they will deserve the blessings of 200,000,000 of the human race.

DADABHAI NAOROJI (1825-1917)
Essays, Speeches, Addresses and Writings

The Principles of British Government in India

1883

One great practical inference is that government in India must proceed upon principles different from and in some respects opposed to those which prevail in England, and which, since the outbreak of the French Revolution, have acquired in many parts of Europe something like the consistency and energy of a new religion. In England, and in countries which derive their political institutions from our own, the government has come directly to represent the great body of the people; all modern legislation has been directed to a great extent towards the object of making that representation more and more complete, and the action of the constituents upon the representatives more and more direct and peremptory. In India the opposite is the case. The government which now exists has not been chosen by the people. It is not, and if it is to exist at all, it cannot look upon itself as being, the representative of the general wishes and average way of thinking of the bulk of the population which it governs. It is the representative of a totally different order of ideas from those prevalent among the natives of India.

Another practical inference from the fact that the British power is founded on conquest is that it must be absolute. The British Government of India differs from the various native governments which it has successively conquered, and on the conquest of which it is founded, not in its origin, but by its objects. The rule of the Queen, and that of the Moghuls whom she displaced, differ, not in the foundation on which they rest, nor in the extent of the power which they possess, but in the spirit in which they rule and the principles by which they govern themselves. The great peculiarity of the British Government in India is that it is essentially both Eastern and European. It rests on the foundation common to all Eastern governments. It is animated by a spirit and principles essentially European. My proposition is that it is absolutely essential to its existence, and to its utility both to England and to India, that the foundation on which it rests should be as distinctly acknowledged and borne in mind in practice as the principles by which it is animated; and I further say that much of the language recently used by persons high in authority, both in India and in England, either conceals this fact or shows that the writer or speaker is afraid or ashamed of it.

In the first place, then, it should be observed that the strong association which exists in the minds of most English people between good government and representative government is likely to mislead them in dealing with the Government of India. I cannot even glance in this place at the reasons which have created this association of ideas, or at the limitations which even in this country ought to be imposed upon it.

I think however, that it may be safely asserted that the absolute government has its own merits and conveniences; that it is, so to speak, as legitimate a form of government as any other; and that if it exists, if it is well and successfully administered, and if it is suited to the circumstances and tastes of those amongst whom it exists, there is no reason why those who administer it should seek to substitute for it a representative system, or should feel in any respect ashamed of their position as absolute rulers, or desirous to lay it down. Much of the language used about the British Government in India implies, if it does not exactly state, a doctrine which might perhaps be called the doctrine of the Divine Right of Representative Institutions, or of the Sovereignty of the People; it seems to assume that the exercise of absolute power can never be justified except as a temporary expedient used for the purpose of superseding itself, and as a means of educating those whom it affects into a fitness for parliamentary institutions. The point at which I differ from many of those who write and speak upon the Government of India is that I do not in any degree share in this view, whether it is regarded as a doctrine or a sentiment. I do not think that the permanent existence of such a Government as ours in India must be in itself a bad thing; that we ought not to desire its permanence even if we can secure it; and that the establishment of some kind of parliamentary system instead of it is an object which ought to be distinctly contemplated, and, as soon as it is practicable, carried out.

SIR JAMES FITZJAMES STEPHEN
The Foundation of the Government of India
from *Nineteenth Century*, October 1883
(Sir James was legal member of the
Supreme Council of India, 1869-72,
and judge of the High Court, 1879-91)

Hail to the Mother

Bankim Chandra Chatterjee's poem 'Bande Mataram' (Hail to the Mother) first appeared in his novel Anandamath (The Abbey of Bliss) 1882, and soon became the Marseillaise of the nationalist movement throughout India.

Mother, I bow to thee!
Rich with thy hurrying streams,
Bright with thy orchard gleams,
Cool with thy winds of delight,
Dark fields waving, Mother of might,
Mother free.
Glory of moonlight dreams
Over thy branches and lordly streams,
Clad in thy blossoming tress,
Mother, giver of ease,
Laughing low and sweet!
Mother, I kiss thy feet,
Speaker sweet and low!
Mother, to thee I bow.
Who hath said thou art weak in thy land,
When the swords flash out in twice seventy million hands

And seventy million voices roar*
Thy dreadful name from shore to shore?
With many strengths who are mighty and stored,
To thee I call, Mother and Lord!
Thou who savest, arise and save!
To her I cry who ever her foemen drave
Back from plain and sea
And shook herself free.
Thou art wisdom, thou art law,
Thou our heart, our soul, our breath,
Thou the love divine, the awe
In our hearts that conquers death.
Thine the strength that nerves the arm,
Thine the beauty, thine the charm.
Every image made divine
In our temples is but thine.
Thou art Durga,** Lady and Queen,
With her hands that strike and her swords of sheen,
Thou art Lakshmi*** lotus-throned,
And the Muse a hundred-toned.
Pure and Perfect without peer,
Mother, lend thine ear.
Rich with thy hurrying streams,
Bright with thy orchard gleams,
Dark of hue, O candid-fair
In thy soul, with jewelled hair
And thy glorious smile divine
Loveliest of all earthly lands,
Showering wealth from well-stored hands!

---

*   When used as a national anthem, this figure was changed to 300
      million.
**   The Goddess Mother, much-worshipped in Bengal.
***   The Goddess of Wealth.

Mother, mother mine!
Mother sweet, I bow to thee
Mother great and free!

> BANKIM CHANDRA CHATTERJEE (1838-94)
> translated by A. GHOSE

The Goal of the Indian National Congress
1905

The goal of the Congress is that India should be governed in the interests of the Indians themselves, and that in course of time a form of Government should be attained in this country similar to what exists in the self-governing Colonies of the British Empire. For better, for worse, our destinies are now linked with those of England and the Congress freely recognises that whatever advance we seek must be within the Empire itself. That advance, moreover, can only be gradual, as at each stage of the progress it may be necessary for us to pass through a brief course of apprenticeship before we are enabled to go to the next one; for it is a reasonable proposition that the sense of responsibility, required for the proper exercise of the political institutions of the West, can be acquired by an Eastern people through practical training and experiment only. To admit this is not to express any agreement with those who usually oppose all attempts at reform on the plea that the people are not ready for it. While, therefore, we are prepared to allow that an advance towards our goal may be only by reasonably cautious steps, what we emphatically insist on is that the resources of the country should be primarily devoted to the work of qualifying the people by means of education and in other ways, for such advance. Even the most bigoted champion of the existing system of administration will not pretend that this is in any degree the case at present. Our net revenue is about 44 million sterling. Of this very nearly one-half is now eaten up by the Army. The Home Charges, exclusive of their military portion absorb nearly one-third. These two, between them, account for about 34 millions out of 44. Then over three millions are paid to European officials in civil employment. This leaves only about 7 millions at the disposal of the Government to be applied to other purposes. Can anyone, who realises what this means, wonder that the Government spends only a miserable three-quarters of a million out of State funds on the education of the people — primary, secondary and higher, all put together? Japan came under the influence of Western ideas only forty years ago, and yet she is in a line with the most advanced nations of the West in matters of mass education, the State finding funds for the education of every child of school-going age. We have now been a hundred years under England's rule, and yet today four villages out of every five are without a school-house and seven children out of eight are allowed to grow up in ignorance and in darkness! Militarism, Service interests and the interest of the English capitalists — all take precedence today of the true interest of the Indian people in the administration of the country. Things cannot be otherwise, for it is the Government of the people of one country by the people of another, and this, as Mill points out, is bound to produce great evils. Now the Congress wants that all this should change and that India should be governed, first and foremost, in the interests of the Indians themselves. This result will be achieved only in proportion as we obtain more and more voice in the government of our country.

On the moral side, the present situation is steadily destroying our capacity for initiative and dwarfing us as men of action. On the material side, it has resulted in a fearful impoverishment of the people. For a hundred years and more now India has been for members of the dominant race, a country where fortunes were to be made to be taken out and spent elsewhere. As in Ireland, the evil of absentee landlordism has in the past aggravated the racial domination of the English over the Irish, so in India what may be called absentee capitalism has been added to the racial ascendancy of Englishmen. A great and ruinous drain of wealth from the country has gone on for many years, the next excess of exports over imports (including treasure) during the last forty years amounting to no less than a thousand millions sterling. The steady rise in the death-rate of the country — from 24 per thousand, the average for 1882-84, to 30 per thousand, the average for 1892-94, and 34 per thousand, the present average — is a terrible and conclusive proof of this continuous impoverishment of the mass of our people. India's best interests — material and moral — no less than the honour of England, demand that the policy of equality for the two races promised by the Sovereign and by Parliament should be faithfully and courageously carried out.

G.K. GOKHALE (1866-1915)
Report of the 21st Indian National Congress 1905

This Government does not Suit Us
1907

In 1906 the Indian National Congress split up into two parties — the Moderates and the Extremists — led respectively by G.K. Gokhale and B.G. Tilak.

Two new words have recently come into existence with regard to our politics, and they are *Moderates* and *Extremists*. These words have a specific relation to time, and they, therefore, will change with time. The Extremists of today will be Moderates tomorrow, just as the Moderates of today were Extremists yesterday. When the National Congress was first started and Mr. Dadabhai's views, which now go for Moderates, were given to the public, he was styled an Extremist, so that you will see that the term Extremist is an expression of progress. We are extremists today and our sons will call themselves Extremists and us Moderates.

One thing is granted, viz. that this Government does not suit us. As has been said by an eminent statesman — the Government of one country by another can never be a successful, and therefore, a permanent Government. There is no difference of opinion about this fundamental proposition between the Old and New schools. One fact is that this alien Government has ruined the country. We believed in the benevolent intentions of the Government, but in politics there is no benevolence. Benevolence is used to sugar-coat the declarations of self-interest, and we were in those days deceived by the apparent benevolent intentions under which rampant self-interest was concealed.

It is said there is a revival of Liberalism, but how long will it last? Next year it might be, they are out of power, and are we to wait till there is another revival of Liberalism, and then again if that goes down and a third revival of Liberalism takes place; and after all what can a liberal Government do? I will quote the observation of the father of the Congress, Mr. A.O. Hume. This was made in 1893. Let the Government be Liberal or Conservative, rest sure that they will not yield to you willingly anything. I laughed when I read the proceedings of the meeting in Calcutta, congratulating people on the appointment of Mr. Morley to the Secretaryship of State for India. Passages were read from Mr. Morley's books. There are the interested Anglo-Indians and the Secretary of State is the head of the Anglo-Indian bureaucracy whose mouth-piece he is. Do you mean to say that when the whole bureaucracy, the whole body of Anglo-Indians, is against you, the Secretary of State will set aside the whole bureaucracy and give you rights? Has he the power? If he does, will he not be asked to walk away? So then it comes to this that the whole British electorate must be converted. So you are going to convert all persons who have a right to vote in England, so as to get the majority on your side, and when this is done and when by that majority the Liberal party is returned to Parliament bent upon doing good to India and it appoints a Secretary of State as good as Mr. Morley, then you hope to get something of the old methods. The new Party has realised this position. The whole electorate of Great Britain must be converted by lectures. You cannot touch their pocket or interest, and that man must be a fool indeed who would sacrifice his own interest on hearing a philosophical lecture. To convert the whole electorate of England to your opinion and then to get indirect pressure to bear upon the Members of Parliament, they in their turn to return a Cabinet favourable to India and the whole Parliament, the Liberal party and the Cabinet to bring pressure on the bureaucracy to yield — we say this is hopeless. You can now understand the difference between the Old and the New Parties. Appeals to the bureaucracy are hopeless. On this point both the New and Old Parties are agreed. The Old Party believes in appealing to the British nation and we do not. That being our position, it logically follows we must have some other method. There is another alternative. We are not going to sit down quiet. We shall have some other method by which to achieve what we want. We are not disappointed, we are not pessimists. It is the hope of achieving the goal by our own efforts that has brought into existence this new New Party.

We have come forward with a scheme which if you accept, shall better enable you to remedy this state of things than the scheme of the Old school. Your industries are ruined utterly, ruined by foreign rule; your wealth is going out of the country and you are reduced to the lowest level which no human being can occupy. In this state of things, is there any other remedy by which you can help yourself? The remedy is not petitioning but boycott. We say prepare your forces, organise your power, and then go to work so that they cannot refuse you what you demand. We are not armed, and there is no necessity for arms either. We have a stronger weapon, a political weapon, in boycott. We have perceived one fact, that the whole of this administration, which is carried on by a handful of Englishmen, is carried on with our assistance. We are all in subordinate service. The whole Government is carried on with our assistance and they try to keep us in ignorance of our power of co-operation between ourselves but that which is in our own hands at present can be claimed by us and administered by us. The point is to have the entire control in our hands. I want to have the key of my house, and not merely one stranger turned out of it. Self-Government is our goal; we want a control over our administrative machinery. What the New Party wants you to do is to realise the fact that your future rests entirely in your own hands. If you mean to be free, you can be free; if you do not mean to be free, you will fall and be for ever fallen.

B.G. TILAK (1856-1920)
Speeches and Writings

And then Gandhi Came

What could we do? How could we pull India out of this quagmire of poverty and defeatism which sucked her in? Not for a few years of excitement and agony and suspense, but for long generations our people had offered their "blood and toil, tears and sweat". And this process had eaten its way deep into the body and soul of India, poisoning every aspect of our corporate life, like that fell disease which consumes the tissues of the lungs and kills slowly but inevitably. Sometimes we thought that some swifter and more obvious process resembling cholera or the bubonic plague, would have been better; but that was a passing thought, for adventurism leads nowhere, and the quack treatment of deep-seated diseases does not yield results.

And then Gandhi came. He was like a powerful current of fresh air that made us stretch ourselves and take deep breaths; like a beam of light that pierced the darkness and removed the scales from our eyes; like a whirlwind that upset many things, but most of all the working of people's minds. He did not descend from the top; he seemed to emerge from the millions of India, speaking their language and incessantly drawing attention to them and their appalling condition. Get off the backs of these peasants and workers, he told us, all you who live by their exploitation; get rid of the system that produces this poverty and misery. Political freedom took new shape then and acquired a new content. Much that he said we only partially accepted or sometimes did not accept at all. But all this was secondary. The essence of his teaching was fearlessness and truth, and action allied to these, always keeping the welfare of the masses in view. The greatest gift for an individual or a nation, so we had been told in our ancient books, was *abhaya* (fearlessness), not merely bodily courage but the absence of fear from the mind. Janaka and Yajnavalka had said, at the dawn of our history, that it was the function of the leaders of a people to make them fearless. But the dominant impulse in India under British rule was that of fear — pervasive, oppressing, strangling fear; fear of the army, the police, the widespread secret service; fear of the official class; fear of laws meant to suppress and of prison; fear of the landlord's agent; fear of the money-lender; fear of unemployment and starvation, which were always on the threshold. It was against this all-pervading fear that Gandhi's quiet and determined voice was raised: Be not afraid. Was it so simple as all that? Not quite. And yet fear builds its phantoms which are more fearsome than reality itself, and reality, when calmly analysed and its consequences willingly accepted, loses much of its terror.

So, suddenly, as it were, that black pall of fear was lifted from the people's shoulders, not wholly of course, but to an amazing degree. As fear is close companion to falsehood, so truth follows fearlessness. The Indian people did not become much more truthful than they were, nor did they change their essential nature overnight; nevertheless a sea-change was visible as the need for falsehood and furtive behaviour lessened. It was a psychological change, almost as if some expert in psycho-analytical methods had probed deep into the patient's past, found out the origins of his complexes, exposed them to his view, and thus rid him of that burden.

There was that psychological reaction also, a feeling of

shame at our long submission to an alien rule that had degraded
and humiliated us, and a desire to submit no longer whatever
the consequences might be.

*

Gandhi for the first time entered the Congress organisation
and immediately brought about a complete change in its
constitution. He made it democratic and a mass organisation.
Democratic it had been previously also but it had so far been
limited in franchise and restricted to the upper classes. Now
the peasants rolled in and, in its new garb, it began to assume
the look of a vast agrarian organisation with a strong sprinkling
of the middle classes. This agrarian character was to grow.
Industrial workers also came in but as individuals and not in
their separate organised capacity.

Action was to be the basis and objective of this organisation,
action based on peaceful methods. Thus far the alternatives
had been just talking and passing resolutions, or terroristic
activity. Both of these were set aside and terrorism was
especially condemned as opposed to the basic policy of the
Congress. A new technique of action was evolved which,
though perfectly peaceful, yet implied non-submission to what
was considered wrong and, as a consequence, a willing
acceptance of the pain and suffering involved in this. Gandhi
was an odd kind of pacifist, for he was an activist full of
dynamic energy. There was no submission in him to fate or
anything that he considered evil; he was full of resistance,
though this was peaceful and courteous.

The call of action was two-fold. There was, of course, the
action involved in challenging and resisting foreign rule; there
was also the action which led us to fight our own social evils.
Apart from the fundamental objective of the Congress — the
freedom of India — and the method of peaceful action, the
principal plans of the Congress were national unity, which

involved the solution of the minority problems, and the raising of the depressed classes and the ending of the curse of untouchability.

Realising that the main props of British rule were fear, prestige, the co-operation, willing or unwilling, of the people, and certain classes whose vested interests were centred in British rule, Gandhi attacked these foundations. Titles were to be given up and though the title-holders responded to this only in small measure, the popular respect for these British-given titles disappeared and they became symbols of degradation. New standards and values were set up and the pomp and splendour of the viceregal court and the princes, which used to impress so much, suddenly appeared supremely ridiculous and vulgar and rather shameful, surrounded as they were by the poverty and misery of the people. Rich men were not so anxious to flaunt their riches; outwardly at least many of them adopted simpler ways, and in their dress, became almost indistinguishable from humbler folk.

The older leaders of the Congress, bred in a different and more quiescent tradition, did not take easily to these new ways and were disturbed by the upsurge of the masses. Yet so powerful was the wave of feeling and sentiment that swept through the country, that some of this intoxication filled them also. A very few fell away and among them was Mr. M.A. Jinnah. He left the Congress not because of any difference of opinion on the Hindu-Moslem question but because he could not adapt himself to the new and more advanced ideology, and even more so because he disliked the crowds of ill-dressed people, talking in Hindustani, who filled the Congress. His idea of politics was of a superior variety, more suited to the legislative chamber or to a committee-room. For some years he felt completely out of the picture and even decided to leave India for good. He settled down in England and spent several years there.

It is said, and I think with truth, that the Indian habit of mind is essentially one of quietism. Perhaps old races develop that attitude to life; a long tradition of philosophy also leads to it and yet Gandhi, a typical product of India, represents the very antithesis of quietism. He has been a demon of energy and action, a hustler, and a man who not only drives himself but drives others. He has done more than anyone I know to fight and change the quietism of the Indian people.

He sent us to the villages, and the countryside hummed with the activity of innumerable messengers of the new gospel of action. The peasent was shaken up and he began to emerge from his quiescent shell. The effect on us was different but equally far-reaching, for we saw, for the first time as it were, the villager in the intimacy of his mud-hut, and with the stark shadow of hunger always pursuing him we learnt our Indian economics more from these visits than from books and learned discourses. The emotional experience we had already undergone was emphasised and confirmed and henceforward there could be no going back for us to our old life or our old standards, howsoever much our views might change subsequently....

What was his idea of India which he was setting out to mould according to his own wishes and ideals? "I shall work for an India in which the poorest shall feel that it is their country, in whose making they have an effective voice, an India in which there shall be no high class and low class of people, an India in which all communities shall live in perfect harmony ... There can be no room in such an India for the curse of untouchability or the curse of intoxicating drinks and drugs ... Women will enjoy the same rights as men ... This is the India of my dreams." Proud of his Hindu inheritance as he was, he tried to give to Hinduism a kind of universal attire and included all religions within the fold of truth. He refused to narrow his cultural inheritance. "Indian culture," he wrote, "is neither Hindu, Islamic, nor any other, wholly. It is a fusion of all." Again he said: "I want the culture of all lands to be blown about my house as freely as possible. But I refuse to be blown off my feet by any. I refuse to live in other peoples' houses as an interloper, a begger, or a slave." Influenced by modern thought currents, he never let go of his roots and clung to them tenaciously.

And so he set about to restore the spiritual unity of the people and to break the barrier between the small westernised group at the top and the masses, to discover the living elements in the old roots and to build upon them, to waken these masses out of their stupor and static condition and make them dynamic. In his single-track and yet many-sided nature the dominating impression that one gathered was his identification with the masses, a community of spirit with them, an amazing sense of unity with the dispossessed and poverty-stricken not only of India but of the world. Even religion, as everything else, took second place to his passion to raise these submerged people. "A semi-starved nation can have neither religion, nor art nor organisation. Whatever can be useful to starving millions is beautiful to my mind. Let us give today first the vital things of life, and all the graces and ornaments of life will follow ... I want art and literature that can speak to millions." These unhappy dispossessed millions haunted him and everything seemed to revolve round them. "For millions it is an eternal vigil or an eternal trance." His ambition, he said, was "to wipe every tear from every eye."

It is not surprising that this astonishingly vital man, full of self-confidence and an unusual kind of power, standing for equality and freedom for each individual, but measuring all this in terms of the poorest, fascinated the masses of India and attracted them like a magnet. He seemed to them to link up the past with the future and to make the dismal present appear just as a stepping-stone to the future of life and hope.

And not the masses only but intellectuals and others also, though their minds were often troubled and confused and the change-over for them from the habits of a lifetime was more difficult. Thus he effected a vast psychological revolution not only among those who followed his lead but also among his opponents and those many neutrals who could not make up their minds what to think and what to do.

J.L. NEHRU (1889-1964)
The Discovery of India

Means and End

They say "means are after all means." I would say "means are after all everything." As the means so the end. There is no wall of separation between means and end. Indeed the Creator has given us control (and that too very limited) over means, none over the end. Realisation of the goal is in exact proportion to that of the means. This is a proposition that admits of no exception.

*

Means and end are convertible terms in my philosophy of life.

MAHATMA GANDHI (1869-1948)
Young India

Non-Violence

I do justify entire non-violence, and consider it possible in relation between man and man and nation; but it is not "a resignation from all real fighting against wickedness." On the contrary, the non-violence of my conception is a more active and more real fighting against wickedness than retaliation whose very nature is to increase wickedness. I contemplate a mental, and therefore a moral, opposition to immoralities. I seek entirely to blunt the edge of the tyrant's sword, not by putting up against it a sharper-edged weapon, but by disappointing his expectation that I should be offering physical resistance. The resistance of the soul that I should offer instead would elude him. It would at first dazzle him, and at last compel recognition from him, which recognition would not humiliate him but would uplift him. It may be urged that this again is an ideal state. And so it is. The propositions from which I have drawn my arguments are as true as Euclid's definitions, which are none the less true, because in practice we are unable even to draw Euclid's line on a blackboard. But even a geometrician finds it impossible to get on without bearing in kind Euclid's definitions. Nor may we, the German friend, his colleagues and myself, dispense with the fundamental propositions on which the doctrine of satyagraha is based.

I have often noticed that weak people have taken shelter under the Congress creed or under my advice, when they have simply by reason of their cowardice, been unable to defend their own honour or that of those who were entrusted to their care. I recall the incident that happened near Bettiah when non-co-operation was at its height. Some villagers were looted. They had fled, leaving their wives, children and belongings to the mercy of the looters. When I rebuked them for their cowardice in thus neglecting their charge, they shamelessly pleaded non-violence. I publicly denounced their conduct and said that my non-violence fully accommodated violence offered by those who did not feel non-violence and who had in their keeping the honour of their women-folk and little children. Non-violence is not a cover for cowardice, but it is the supreme virtue of the brave. Exercise of non-violence requires far greater bravery than that of swordsmanship. Cowardice is wholly inconsistent with non-violence. Translation from swordsmanship to non-violence is possible and, at times, even an easy stage. Non-violence, therefore, presupposes ability to strike. It is a conscious deliberate restraint put upon one's desire for vengeance. But vengeance is any day superior to passive, effeminate and helpless submission. Forgiveness is higher still. Vengeance too is weakness. The desire for vengeance comes out of fear of harm, imaginary or real. A dog barks and bites when he fears. A man who fears no one on earth would consider it too troublesome even to summon up anger against one who is vainly trying to injure him. The sun does not wreak vengeance upon little children who throw dust at him. They only harm themselves in the act.

*

I do believe that, where there is only a choice between cowardice and violence, I would advise violence. Thus when my eldest son asked me what he should have done, had he been present when I was almost fatally assaulted in 1908, whether he should have used his physical force which he could and wanted to use, and defended me, I told him that it was his duty to defend me even by using violence. Hence it was that I took part in the Boer War, the so-called Zulu Rebellion and the late war. Hence also do I advocate training in arms for those who believe in the method of violence. I would rather have India resort to arms in order to defend her honour than that she should, in a cowardly manner, become or remain a helpless witness to her own dishonour.

But I believe that non-violence is infinitely superior to violence, forgiveness is more manly than punishment. Forgiveness adorns a soldier. But abstinence is forgiveness only when there is the power to punish; it is meaningless when it pretends to proceed from a helpless creature. A mouse hardly forgives a cat when it allows itself to be torn to pieces by her. I therefore appreciate the sentiment of those who cry out for the condign punishment of General Dyer and his ilk. They would tear him to pieces, if they could. But I do not believe India to be helpless. I do not believe myself to be a helpless creature. Only I want to use India's and my strength for a better purpose....

I am not a visionary. I claim to be a practical idealist. The religion of non-violence is not meant merely for the *rishis* and saints. It is meant for the common people as well. Non-violence is the law of our species as violence is the law of the brute. The spirit lies dormant in the brute, and he knows no law but that of physical might. The dignity of man requires obedience to a higher law — to the strength of the spirit.

I have therefore ventured to place before India the ancient law of self-sacrifice. For *satyagraha* and its offshoots, non-co-operation and civil resistance are nothing but new names for the law of suffering. The rishis, who discovered the law of non-violence in the midst of violence, were greater geniuses than Newton. They were themselves greater warriors than Wellington. Having themselves known the use of arms, they realised their uselessness, and taught a weary world that its salvation lay not through violence but through non-violence.

Non-violence in its dynamic condition means conscious suffering. It does not mean meek submission to the will of the evil-doer, but it means the pitting of one's whole soul against the will of the tyrant. Working under this law of our being, it is possible for a single individual to defy the whole might of an unjust empire to save his honour, his religion, his soul, and lay the foundation for that empire's fall or its regeneration.

*

Ahimsa is not the way of the timid or the cowardly. It is the way of the brave ready to face death. He who perishes of sword in hand is no doubt brave, but he who faces death without raising his little finger and without flinching is braver. But he who surrenders his rice bags for fear of being beaten is a coward and no votary of *ahimsa*. He is innocent of ahimsa. He who, for fear of being beaten, suffers the women of his household to be insulted, is not manly but just the reverse. He is fit to be neither a husband nor a father nor a brother. Such people have no right to complain.

These cases have nothing to do with inveterate enmity between the Hindus and Mussulmans. Where there are fools there are bound to be knaves, where there are cowards there are bound to be bullies, whether they are Hindus or Mussulmans. Such cases used to happen even before the outbreak of these communal hostilities. The question here, therefore, is not how to teach one of the two communities a lesson or how to humanise it, but how to teach a coward to be brave.

MAHATMA GANDHI (1869-1948)
Non-violence in Peace and War

Satyagraha

For the past thirty years, I have been preaching and practising *satyagraha*. The principles of *satyagraha*, as I know it today, constitute a gradual evolution.

Satyagraha differs from Passive Resistance as the North Pole from the South. The latter has been conceived as a weapon of the weak and does not exclude the use of physical force or violence for the purpose of gaining one's end, whereas the former has been conceived as a weapon of the strongest and excludes the use of violence in any shape or form.

The term *satyagraha* was coined by me in South Africa to express the force that the Indians there used for full eight years, and it was coined in order to distinguish it from the movement then going on in the United Kingdom and South Africa under the name of Passive Resistance.

On the political field, the struggle on behalf of the people mostly consists in opposing error in the shape of unjust laws. When you have failed to bring the error home to the law-giver by way of petitions and the like, the only remedy open to you, if you do not wish to submit to error, is to compel him by physical force to yield to you or by suffering in your own person by inviting the penalty for the breach of the law. Hence *satyagraha* largely appears to the public as Civil Disobedience or Civil Resistance. It is civil in the sense that it is not criminal.

The law-breaker breaks the law surreptitiously and tries to avoid the penalty; not so the civil resister. He ever obeys the laws of the state to which he belongs, not out of fear of the sanctions, but because he considers them to be good for the welfare of society. But there come occasions, generally rare, when he considers certain laws to be so unjust as to render obedience to them a dishonour. He then openly and civilly breaks them and quietly suffers the penalty for their breach. And in order to register his protest against the action of the law-givers, it is open to him to withdraw his co-operation from the state by disobeying such other laws whose breach does not involve moral turpitude.

In my opinion, the beauty and efficacy of *satyagraha* are so great and the doctrine so simple that it can be preached even to children. It was preached by me to thousands of men, women and children commonly called indentured Indians with excellent results.

*

I do not want Britain to be defeated, nor do I want her to be victorious in a trial of brute strength, whether expressed through the muscle or the brain. Your muscular bravery is an established fact. Need you demonstrate that your brain is also as unrivalled in destructive power as your muscle? I hope you do not wish to enter into such an undignified competition with the Nazis. I venture to present you with a nobler and a braver way, worthy of the bravest soldier. I want you to fight Nazism without arms, or if I am to retain the military terminology, with non-violent arms. I would like you to lay down the arms you have as being useless for saving you or humanity. You will invite Herr Hitler and Signor Mussolini to take what they want of your beautiful island, with your many beautiful buildings. You will give all these but neither your souls, nor your minds. If these gentlemen choose to occupy your homes, you will vacate them. If they do not give you free passage out, you will allow yourselves man, woman and child, to be slaughtered, but you will refuse to owe allegiance to them.

This process or method, which I have called non-violent non-cooperation is not without considerable success in its use in India. Your representatives in India may deny my claim.

If they do, I shall feel sorry for them. They may tell you that our non-cooperation was not wholly non-violent, that it was born of hatred. If they give that testimony, I will not deny it. Had it been wholly non-violent, if all the non-cooperators had been with goodwill towards you, I make bold to say that you who are India's masters would have become her pupils and, with much greater skill than we have, perfected this matchless weapon and met the German and Italian friends' menace with it. Indeed the history of Europe during the past few months would then have been written differently. Europe would have been spared seas of innocent blood, the rape of so many small nations, and the orgy of hatred.

This is no appeal made by a man who does not know his business. I have been practising with scientific precision non-violence and its possibilities for an unbroken period of over fifty years. I have applied it in every walk of life, domestic, institutional, economic and political. I know of no single case in which it has failed. Where it has seemed sometimes to have failed, I have ascribed it to my imperfections. I claim no perfection for myself. But I do claim to be a passionate seeker after Truth, which is but another name for God. In the course of that search the discovery of non-violence came to me. Its spread is my life mission. I have no interest in living except for the prosecution of that mission.

I claim to have been a lifelong and wholly disinterested friend of the British people. At one time I used to be also a lover of your empire. I thought that it was doing good to India. When I saw that in the nature of things it could do no good, I used, and am still using, the non-violent method to fight imperialism. Whatever the ultimate fate of my country, my love for you remains, and will remain, undiminished. My non-violence demands universal love, and you are not a small part of it. It is that love which has prompted my appeal to you.

May God give power to every word of mine. In His name I began to write this, and in His name I close it. May your statesman have the wisdom and courage to respond to my appeal. I am telling His Excellency the Viceroy that my services are at the disposal of His Majesty's Government, should they consider them of any practical use in advancing the object of my appeal.

MAHATMA GANDHI (1869-1948)
Young India

The Proposal for the Creation of Pakistan

1930

Communalism, in its higher aspect, then, is indispensable to the formation of a harmonious whole in a country like India. The Muslim demand for the creation of a Muslim India is, therefore, perfectly justified. The resolution of the All-Parties Muslim Conference at Delhi is to my mind wholly inspired by this noble ideal of a harmonious whole which, instead of stifling the respective individualities of its component wholes, affords them chances of fully working out the possibilities that may be latent in them. And I have no doubt that this house will emphatically endorse the Muslim demand embodied in this resolution. Personally I would go further than the demands embodied in it. I would like to see the Punjab, North-West Frontier Province, Sind and Baluchistan amalgamated into a single state. Self-Government within the British Empire, or without the British Empire, the formation of a consolidated North-West Indian Muslim state appears to me to be the final destiny of the Muslims at least of North-West India. The proposal was put forward before the Nehru Committee. They rejected it on the ground that, if carried into effect, it would give a very unwieldy state. This is true in so far as the area is concerned; in point of population the state contemplated by the proposal would be much less than some of the present Indian provinces. The idea need not alarm the Hindus or non-Muslim minorities within the area. The idea need not alarm the Hindus or the British. India is the greatest Muslim country in the world. The life of Islam as a cultural force in this living country very largely depends on its centralisation in a specified territory. Thus, possessing full opportunity of development within the body-politic of India, the North West Indian Muslims will prove the best defenders of India against a foreign invasion, be that invasion the one of ideas or bayonets. The Punjab with fifty-six per cent Muslim population supplies fifty-four per cent of the total combatant troops in the Indian army and if the nineteen thousand Gurkhas recruited from the independent state of Nepal are excluded, the Punjab contingent amounts to sixty-two per cent of the whole Indian Army. This percentage does not take into account nearly six thousand combatants supplied to the Indian Army by the North-West Frontier Province and Baluchistan. From this you can easily calculate the possibilities of North-West Indian Muslims in regard to the defence of India against foreign aggression. The Right Hon'ble Mr. Srinivasa Sastri thinks that the Muslims' demand for the creation of autonomous Muslim states along the North-West border is actuated by a desire "to acquire means of exerting pressure in emergencies on the Government of India." I may frankly tell him that the Muslim demand is not actuated by the kind of motive he imputes to us; it is actuated by a genuine desire for free development which is practically impossible under the type of unitary government contemplated by the nationalist Hindu politicians with a view to secure permanent communal dominance in the whole of India.

MUHAMMAD IQBAL (1873-1938)
Indian Quarterly Register vol. 2 (1930)

Demand for Pakistan
1940

The problem in India is not of an inter-communal character but manifestly of an international one, and it must be treated as such. So long as this basic and fundamental truth is not realised, any constitution that may be built will result in disaster and will prove destructive and harmful not only to the Musalmans but to the British and Hindus also. If the British Government are really in earnest and sincere to secure peace and happiness of the people of the sub-continent, the only course open to us all is to allow the major nations separate homelands by dividing India into "autonomous national states." There is no reason why these states should be antagonistic to each other. On the other hand, the rivalry and the natural desire and efforts on the part of one to dominate the social order and establish political supremacy over the other in the government of the country will disappear. It will lead more towards natural goodwill by international pacts between them, and they can live in complete harmony with their neighbours. This will lead further to a friendly settlement all the more easily with regard to minorities by reciprocal arrangements and adjustments between Muslim India and Hindu India, which will far more adequately and effectively safeguard the rights and interests of Muslims and various other minorities.

It is extremely difficult to appreciate why our Hindu friends fail to understand the real nature of Islam and Hinduism. They are not religions in the strict sense of the word, but are, in fact, different and distinct social orders, and it is a dream that the Hindus and Muslims can ever evolve a common nationality, and this misconception of one Indian nation has gone far beyond the limits and is the cause of most of your troubles and will lead India to destruction if we fail to revise our notions in time. The Hindus and Muslims belong to two different religious philosophies, social customs, literatures. They neither intermarry nor interdine together and, indeed, they belong to two different civilisations which are based mainly on conflicting ideas and conceptions. Their outlooks on life and of life are different. It is quite clear that Hindus and Musalmans derive their inspiration from different sources of history. They have different epics, different heroes, and different episodes. Very often the hero of one is the foe of the other and, likewise, their victories and defeats overlap. To yoke together two such nations under a single state, one as a numerical minority and the other as a majority, must lead to growing discontent and final destruction of any fabric that may be so built up for the government of such a state.

The present artificial unity of India dates back only to the British conquest and is maintained by the British bayonet, but termination of the British regime, which is implicit in the recent declaration of his Majesty's Government, will be the herald of the entire break-up with worse disaster than has ever taken place during the last one thousand years under Muslims. Surely that is not the legacy which Britain would bequeath to India after 150 years of her rule, nor would Hindu and Muslim India risk such a sure catastrophe.

Muslim India cannot accept any constitution which must necessarily result in a Hindu majority government. Hindus and Muslims brought together under a democratic system forced upon the minorities can only mean Hindu Raj. Democracy of the kind with which the Congress High Command is enamoured would mean the complete destruction of what is most precious in Islam. We have had ample experience of the working of the provincial constitutions during the last two and a half years and any repetition of such a government must lead to civil war.

M.A. JINNAH (1876-1948)
Speeches and Writings of Mr. Jinnah

1942

What happened in India in August 1942, was no sudden development but a culmination of all that had gone before. Much has been written about it, in attack, criticism or defence, and many explanations given. And yet most of this writing misses the real meaning, for it applies purely political considerations to something that was deeper than politics. Behind it all lay an intense feeling that it was no longer possible to endure and live under foreign autocratic rule. All other questions became secondary — whether under that rule it was possible to make improvements or progress in some directions, or whether the consequences of a challenge might be more harmful still. Only the overwhelming desire to be rid of it and to pay any price for the riddance remained, only the feeling that whatever happened this could not be endured.

That feeling was no new sensation; it had been there for many years. But previously it had been restrained in many

ways and disinclined to keep pace with events. The war itself
was both a restraining and releasing factor. It opened out our
minds to vast developments and revolutionary changes, to the
possibility of the realisation of our hopes in the near future;
and it put a brake on much that we might otherwise have done
because of our desire to help, and certainly not to hinder in
any way, the struggle against the Axis powers.

*

In the early morning of August 9th, 1942, numerous arrests
were made all over India. What happened then? Only scraps
of news trickled through to us after many weeks, and even
now we can form only an incomplete picture of what took
place. All the prominent leaders had been suddenly removed
and no one seemed to know what should be done. Protest,
of course, there had to be, and there were spontaneous
demonstrations. These were broken up and fired upon, and
tear-gas bombs were used; all the usual channels of giving
expression to public feeling were stopped. And then all these
suppressed emotions broke out and crowds gathered in cities
and rural areas and came in conflict with the police and the
military. They attacked especially what seemed to them the
symbols of British authority and power, the police stations,
post offices, and railway stations; they cut the telegraph and
telephone wires. These unarmed and leaderless mobs faced
police and military firing, according to official statements, on
538 occasions, and they were also machine-gunned from low-
flying aircraft. For a month or two or more these disturbances
continued in various parts of the country and then they
dwindled away and gave place to sporadic occurrences. "The
disturbances" said Mr. Churchill in the House of Commons,
"were crushed with all the weight of the Government," and
he praised "The loyalty and steadfastness of the brave Indian
police as well as the Indian official class generally whose

behaviour has been deserving of the highest praise." He added that "larger reinforcements have reached India and the number of white troops in that country is larger than at any time in the British connection." These foreign troops and the Indian police had won many a battle against the unarmed peasantry of India and crushed their rebellion; and that other main prop of the British Raj in India, the Official class, had helped, actively or passively, in the process.

*

The sudden, unorganised demonstrations and outbreaks on the part of the people, culminating in violent conflicts and destruction, and continued against over-whelming and powerful armed forces, were a measure of the intensity of their feelings. Those feelings had been there even before the arrest of their leaders, but the arrests and the frequent firings that followed them, roused the people to anger and to the only course that an enraged mob can follow. For a time there seems to have been a sense of uncertainty as to what should be done. There was no direction, no programme. There was no well-known person to lead them or tell them what to do, and yet they were too excited and angry to remain quiescent. As often happens in these circumstances, local leaders sprang up and were followed for the moment. But even the guidance they gave was little; it was essentially a spontaneous mass upheaval. All over India, the younger generation, especially university students, played an important part in both the violent and peaceful activities of 1942. Many universities were closed. Some of the local leaders attempted even then to pursue peaceful methods of action and civil disobedience, but this was difficult in the prevailing atmosphere. The people forgot the lesson of non-violence which had been dinned into their ears for more than twenty years, and yet they were wholly unprepared, mentally or otherwise, for any effective violence. That very teaching of non-violent methods produced doubt and hesitation and came in the way of violent action. If the Congress, forgetful of its creed, had previously given even a hint of violent action, there is no doubt that the violence that actually took place would have increased a hundred-fold.

But no such hint had been given, and, indeed, the last message of the Congress had again emphasised the importance of non-violence in action. Yet perhaps one fact had some effect on the public mind. If, as we had said, armed defence was legitimate and desirable against an enemy aggressor, why should that not apply to other forms of existing aggression? The prohibition of violent methods of attacks and defence once removed had unintended results, and it was not easy for most people to draw fine distinctions. All over the world extreme forms of violence were prevailing and incessant propaganda encouraged them. It became then a question of expediency and of intensity of feeling. Then there were also people, outside or in the Congress, who never had any belief in non-violence and who were troubled with no scruples in regard to violent action.

But in the excitement of the moment few people think; they act in accordance with their long-suppressed urges which drive them forward. And so, for the first time since the great revolt of 1857, vast numbers of people again rose to challenge by force (but a force without arms!) the fabric of British rule in India. It was a foolish and inopportune challenge, for all the organised and armed force was on the other side, and in greater measure indeed than at any previous time in history. However great the numbers of the crowd, it cannot prevail in a contest of force against armed forces. It had to fail unless those armed forces themselves changed their allegiance. But those crowds had not prepared for the contest or chosen the time for it. It came upon them unawares and in their immediate reaction to it, however unthinking and misdirected it was,

they showed their love of India's freedom and their hatred
of foreign domination.

Though the policy of non-violence went under, for the time
being at least, the long training that the people had received
under it had one important and desirable result. In spite of the
passions aroused there was very little, if any, racial feeling, and,
on the whole, there was a deliberate attempt on the part of
the people to avoid causing bodily injury to their opponents.
There was a great deal of destruction of communications and
governmental property, but even in the midst of this destruction
care was taken to avoid loss of life. This was not always possible
or always attempted, especially in actual conflicts with the
police or other armed forces. According to official reports, so
far as I have been able to find them, about 100 persons were
killed by mobs in the course of the disturbances all over India.
This figure is very small considering the extent and area of the
disturbances and the conflicts with the police.

J.L. NEHRU (1889-1964)
The Discovery of India

India Divided

1947

I beg to move, "That the Bill be now read a Second time."
This Bill brings to an end one chapter in the long
connection between Britain and India, but it opens another.
British rule which has endured so long is now, at the instance
of this country, coming to an end.

There have been many instances in history when States
at the point of the sword have been forced to surrender

government over another people. It is very rare for a people that have long enjoyed power over another nation to surrender it voluntarily. My mind recalls as the nearest parallel the action of the Liberal Government of Sir Henry Campbell Bannerman, in 1906, when he gave back to the Dutch in South Africa the freedom to manage their own affairs which they had lost in the South African war. That was a great act of faith, an act of faith which bore fruit both in 1914 and 1939. I have often heard that great South African statesman, General Smuts, describing it as marking the end of imperialism.

We can recall how, 90 years ago, the Government of the East India Company came to an end when Parliament assumed responsibility for Indian affairs. During those long years there has been a change in the spirit of British administration. In the earlier days we were concerned mainly with trade providing opportunities for making fortunes. In the eighteenth century British citizens returning from India had often made fortunes and were known as nabobs. But, as time went on, there was an increasing appreciation of the responsibility for the lives of many millions who sought justice and a quiet life. The British administrator in India became more and more deeply concerned with the well-being of that great congeries of people divided by race, by caste, language and religion in this sub-continent.

To this change of spirit the House of Commons, in many famous debates from the time of Burke onwards, made a most notable contribution. Perhaps it is not always realised how early that change took place. It was long before the transfer of sovereignty to the Crown. In the early days of the nineteenth century, great men, such as Sir Thomas Munro in Madras, set the standards which have since been followed by so many who have served India. Looking back today over the years, we may well be proud of the work which our fellow citizens have done in India. There have, of course, been mistakes, there have been failures, but we can assert that our rule in

India will stand comparison with that of any other nation which has been charged with the ruling of a people so different from themselves.

There has been a great succession of Viceroys who have made their particular contributions and sought to serve India faithfully. I think not least among them would be accounted the present Viceroy. There is a roll of names of eminent Governors of Provinces, high among which is that of the right hon. Gentleman the Member for Scottish Universities (Sir J. Anderson). There has been a multitude of administrators, soldiers, missionaries and others who have served India with great devotion and have loved the Indian people. In every part of India are the graves of those who died in her service. Not least among those who have served India are the men who in the difficult and exacting times of the last four decades, under the stress of two great wars with all their repercussions on Indian life, have worked in the changing conditions that have resulted from the rise of Indian nationalism and the development of self-government. May I recall here a thing that is not always remembered, that just as India owes her unity and freedom from external aggression to the British, so the Indian National Congress itself was founded and inspired by men of our own race, and further, that any judgement passed on our rule in India by the Indians is passed on the basis, not of what obtained in the past in India, but on the principles which we have ourselves instilled into them. I am well aware that many of those who have been closely associated with India are anxious about the future of the millions for whom we are now relinquishing responsibility. I can understand their anxiety. They fear that the work to which they have devoted themselves for so many years may be brought to nought. They are anxious for those who would suffer most from a breakdown of administration — the poorest sections of the community.

We must all be anxious, but I think everybody realises that the service of Britain to India must now take another form. The constitutional change vital as it is, does not, of course, mean the disappearance of the civilian European community in India. Not a few of those of the British race who have been in the Services in India will, we confidently expect, be willing, at the invitation of the two new Governments, to continue in official service in India and Pakistan. The business community in India has still, I am confident, a role to play in maintaining, between the populations in India and this country, trade and commerce, to the great benefit of both. To those men and women, who, although domiciled in the United Kingdom, are intending to remain in India after Partition I would say, "You have a great task in front of you, namely, to cement the bonds of friendship between this country, India and Pakistan. You can accomplish at least as much in achieving this end as can the British Government."

Many years ago, when we began the association of Indians in the responsibility of Government and set ourselves to train them in the methods of democracy, it was obvious that the time would come, sooner or later, when Indians would seek to secure the entire management of their own affairs. This was clear many years ago to some of our wisest administrators, and I quote from a letter of Mountstuart Elphinstone as long ago as 1854:

The moral is that we must not dream of perpetual possession, but must apply ourselves to bring the natives into a state that will admit of their governing themselves in a manner that may be beneficial to our interests as well as their own, and that of the rest of the world; and to take the glory of the achievement and the sense of having done our duty for the chief reward of our exertions.

It has been the settled policy of all parties in this country for many years that Indians, in course of time, should manage their own affairs. The question has always been how and when? It would, I think, be unprofitable today to go back into the past and to question whether, if some particular action had been taken by a British Government earlier, or if a different line of conduct had been taken by the Indian political leaders on certain occasions, a more satisfactory solution might have been found than that which I am commending to the House today.

There are hon. Members of this House, such as the noble Lord the Member for Horsham (Earl Winterton) and the hon. Member for Aylesbury (Sir S. Reed), whose connection with the Indian problem goes back far beyond mine. Some 20 years ago, I was first brought into contact with it by being placed on the Simon Commission, and I think they would agree with me that the major difficulty that has faced all of us in considering the best way of achieving Indian self-government has been the absence of mutual trust and toleration between the communities. It has sometimes been said by our enemies that this was a difficulty created by ourselves in order to perpetuate our own rule. Nothing could be more untrue. This same difficulty, which faced Mr. Edwin Montagu and the Simon Commission, faced the President of the Board of Trade in his Mission and my three Cabinet colleagues in theirs, and it was still the outstanding difficulty of the present Viceroy when he took office. Everyone who has touched the Indian problem has been brought up against this stumbling-block. They have all wanted to maintain the unity of India, to give India complete self-government and to preserve the rights of minorities. Every one of them has hoped that a solution might be found without resorting to partition. I know that many Indians of all communities passionately desire this, but it has not been found to be practicable.

We and the Indian statesmen have had to accept the only alternative — partition. For myself, I earnestly hope that this severance may not endure, and that the two new Dominions which we now propose to set up may, in course of time, come together again to form one great member State of the British Commonwealth of Nations. But this is entirely a matter for the Indians themselves. The demand for self-government has been insistently pressed for many years by the leaders of political thought in India, and has been simulated by the external situation, and particularly by those great waves of nationalist feeling that accompanied both the great wars. This demand is not peculiar to India, but has spread throughout Asia. It is the natural result of contact by dwellers in other continents with European political thought. The chief question has been as to how this desire could be gratified. Delay in granting it has always led to more and more extreme demands.

There has been a tendency to consider that nothing short of complete and absolute severance would satisfy this urge. There is a desire by some to cut every tie which connects them with their former rulers. On the other hand, in the age in which we live, there are very strong reasons which militate against the complete isolation which some demand. Many countries that long enjoyed their freedom and independence have lost it either permanently or temporarily, and some form of association with others for security and greater prosperity is the desire of many peoples. The League of Nations and the United Nations Organisation express this desire, but the one great practical example of how complete freedom and independence can be combined with inclusion in a greater whole is the British Commonwealth of Nations.

The British Commonwealth of Nations is so unique that its nature is still not fully comprehended, and even many of our American friends do not understand that the Dominions are as free as Great Britain. They do not appreciate that membership of the British Commonwealth, in the words of the Prime Minister of New Zealand is, "independence with something added, not independence with something taken away". In this Bill, we set up two independent Dominions, free and equal, of no less status than the United Kingdom or the Dominion of Canada, completely free in all respects from any control by this country, but united by a common allegiance to the Sovereign and by a community of ideas, receiving from their membership of the Commonwealth great advantages, but in no way suffering any restriction. The Title of this Bill expresses this fact that the independence which has been the goal for so long of many Indians can be, and I believe will be realised within the British Commonwealth of Nations. It is my hope that these two new Dominions may continue in this great association, giving and receiving benefits.

I saw with great regret in one paper, and I think in one paper only, that the action which we are now taking was described as abdication. It is not the abdication, but the fulfilment of Britain's mission in India. It is the culminating point in a long course of events. The Morley-Minto proposals, the Montagu-Chelmsford proposals, the Simon Commission Report, the Round Table Conferences, the Act of 1935, the Declaration at the time of the Cripps Mission, the visit of my right hon. Friends to India last year, are all steps in the road that led up eventually to the proposals that I announced to the House on 3rd June last. This Bill is designed to implement those proposals, which met, I think, with general acceptance in this House and in the country.

C.R. ATTLEE
Speech on the Indian Independence Bill 10 July 1947

The Message of Asia

What I want you to understand is the message of Asia. It is not to be learnt through Western spectacles or by imitating the atom bomb. If you want to give a message to the West, it must be the message of love and the message of truth. I do not want merely to appeal to your head. I want to capture your heart.

In this age of democracy, in this age of awakening of the poorest of the poor, you can re-deliver this message with the greatest emphasis. You will complete the conquest of the West not through vengeance because you have been exploited, but with real understanding. I am sanguine if all of you put your hearts together — not merely heads — to understand the secret of the message these wise men of the East have left to us, and if we really become worthy of that great message, the conquest of the West will be completed. This conquest will be loved by the West itself.

The West is today pining for wisdom. It is despairing of a multiplication of atom bombs, because atom bombs mean utter destruction not merely of the West but of the whole world, as if the prophecy of the Bible is going to be fulfilled and there is to be a perfect deluge. It is up to you to tell the world of its wickedness and sin — that is the heritage your teachers and my teachers have taught Asia.

MAHATMA GANDHI (1869-1948)
Communal Unity

Places

The Himalayas

God of the distant north, the Snowy Range
O'er other mountains towers imperially;
Earth's measuring-rod, being great and free from change,
Sinks to the eastern and the western sea.

Whose countless wealth of natural gems is not
Too deeply blemished by the cruel snow;
One fault for many virtues is forgot,
The moon's one stain for beams that endless flow.

Where demigods enjoy the shade of clouds
Girding his lower crests, but often seek,
When startled by the sudden rain that shrouds
His waist, some loftier, ever sunlit peak.

Where bark of birch-trees makes, when torn in strips
And streaked with mountain minerals that blend
To written words 'neath dainty finger-tips,
Such dear love-letters as the fairies send.

Whose organ-pipes are stems of bamboo, which
Are filled from cavern-winds that know no rest,
As if the mountain strove to set the pitch
For songs that angels sing upon his crest.

Where magic herbs that glitter in the night
Are lamps that need no oil within them, when

They fill cave-dwellings with their shimmering light
And shine upon the loves of mountain men.

Who offers roof and refuge in his caves
To timid darkness shrinking from the day;
A lofty soul is generous; he saves
Such honest cowards as for protection pray.

Who brings to birth the plants of sacrifice;
Who steadies earth, so strong is he and broad.
The great Creator, for this service' price,
Made him the king of mountains, and a god.

KALIDASA (c. A.D. 400-500)
The Birth of the War-God
translated by A.W. RYDER

The Ganges

Vast as a sea the Ganges flows,
And fed by Himalaya's snows,
Or rushing rains, with giant force
Unwearied runs its fated course;
The banks that skirt its lengthened way
Boundless variety display;
The mural height, the level green,
The dangerous rock, the dark ravine,
The barren sand, the fertile mound
With maze of flowery thicket crowned.
The cheerful lawn, or frowning glade,
Embrowned by overhanging shade:
The spacious plain, that waving corn,
Orchards, or fragrant groves adorn;

Whilst towns and hamlets intervene
And gild with life the changing scene.

*

Close to the marge the cattle browse,
Or trail the rudely fashioned ploughs;
The buffalo, his sides to cool,
Stands buried in the marshy pool.
The wild duck nestles in the sedge;
The crane stands patient on the edge;
Watching to seize its finny prey;
Whilst high the skylark wings its way,
And in the shadow of a cloud
Warbles its song distinct and loud,
Though far removed from human eyes,
The songster sails the upper sky.
Scattered across the teeming plain
In groups the peasants glean the grain,
The sickle ply, or wield the hoe,
Or seeds for future harvests sow.
Some burthened with their homely ware
Journey to village *Hat* or fair,
And some suspend their toils to mark
Inquisitive the passing bark.
But most where to the river leads
The Ghat, or beaten path proceeds,
A never-ending train collects
Of every caste, and age, and sex.
Grave in the tide the Brahmin stands,
And folds his cord, or twirls his hands,
And tells his beads, and all unheard
Mutters a solemn mystic word.
With reverence the Sudra dips,
And fervently the current sips,

That to his humbler hopes conveys
A future life of happier days.
But chief do India's simple daughters
Assemble in these hallowed waters.
With vase of classic model laden,
Like Grecian girl or Tuscan maiden,
Collecting thus, their urns to fill
From gushing fount or trickling rill;
And still with pious fervour they
To Gunga veneration pay,
And with pretenceless rite prefer
The wishes of their hearts to her.
The maid or matron, as she throws
Champac or lotus, Bel or rose,
Or sends the quivering light afloat
In shallow cup or paper boat,
Prays for a parent's peace and wealth,
Prays for a child's success and health,
For a fond husband breathes a prayer,
For progeny their loves to share,
For what of good on earth is given
To lowly life, or hoped in Heaven.
Such are the scenes the Ganges shows,
As to the sea it rapid flows;
And all who love the works to scan
Of nature, or the thoughts of man,
May here unquestionably find
Pleasure and profit for the mind.

HORACE HAYMAN WILSON (1786-1866)

Elephanta

The dawn had hardly broken in the East when we went on board a small yacht to sail to Elephanta. After a couple of hours' sail the landing-place at Elephanta is reached. Here, in the days of old, there used to be a colossal stone elephant, from which the Portuguese named the place. After ascending a steep path, and a steeper flight of stairs, we find ourselves on a small plateau, and before us opens a wide cavern. We enter, and when the eye becomes accustomed to the darkness we see before us a gigantic *trimurti*, or three-formed god. The expression of the first face is one of far-off, deep contemplation, and is grand and noble in its calm serenity. It represents Shiv in the character of Brahma, the creator; in his left hand he holds a citron, an emblem of the womb. The right hand is broken. The breast is adorned with a necklace of pearls, and below it is a deep, richly-wrought, heart ornament. The head-dress consists of the hair raised and crowned by a royal tiara most beautifully carved. The face to the east, with its stern, commanding, Roman expression, is Shiv in the character of Buddha, the destroyer, and the brow has an oval swelling above the nose, representing a third eye. He is smiling at a cobra, which is twisted round his arms, and with stretched hood looks him in the face. Among his ornaments are some of the peculiar symbols of Shiv — a human skull over the temple, a leaf of the *Gloriosa superba*, a branch of the milk bush, twisted snakes instead of hair, and high up a cobra erect with outstretched hood. To the west there is a gentle, placid face, which is Shiv in the character of Vishnu the preserver, and he holds a lotus flower in his hand. The Trimurti is the main object of interest in the cavern, but many hours can be profitably spent in examining the different compartments, with their sculptures full of power and life, representing the gods and goddesses of the Hindu Pantheon, and the stories of their lives. Shiv, with his consort Parvati, is a favourite subject. In one compartment we have Shiv and Parvati seated on the holy hill of Kailas; and Parvati being in a pet, or *mana*, has her head slightly turned away. Legend says that the demon Ravan chanced to pass by at the time, and being angry at the hill stopping his progress, took it in his arms and shook it. Parvati, feeling the hill to move, ran for protection into Shiv's arms. One story states that Shiv in his rage stamped Ravan under foot; another (probably more true) that he blessed him for stopping Parvati's fit of ill temper. Behind Parvati is the figure of a nurse executed with great spirit, and she carries a child astraddle on her left hip, as carried in India at the present hour. These sculptures illustrate how unbroken in the East are the links between the past and the present; they are an epitome of the religious and social life that makes the continent of India so deeply interesting. The gross and passionate effigies of Hindu Mythology completely express the Oriental mind — "humorous, amorous, obscene, subtle, and refined."

G.W. FORREST
Cities of India (1903)

The Discovery of Ajanta Caves

The caves, we were told, lay in the side of a ravine in wild and desolate country some 350 miles to the north-west, at the extreme tip of Hyderabad State where it touches the Bombay province. Properly speaking they were not caves at all, but temples which had been excavated from the living rock by Buddhist monks. These monks had first come to the ravine somewhere in the second century before Christ, and they had begun by hacking out the rock by hand and hurling it down into the river below. Then, probably with large mirrors to reflect the sunshine from the ravine outside, they set about the decoration of the walls, the doorways and the ceilings. They continued for the next eight hundred years, always painting and sculpturing the Buddha, but setting him against an idyllic background of folk tales and the everyday life of their own time. In much the same way as in the Italian renaissance which over a thousand years later, the work was subsidised by the wealthy merchants and princes of the surrounding countryside.

No one knew why the monks had abandoned Ajanta: whether it was plague or persecution or for some other, more occult, reason. By A.D. 600 Buddhism itself was dying out in India (it has never succeeded in returning except in the Himalayas), and it may simply have been that the rich merchants refused to subscribe any more. At all events, somewhere in the seventh century A.D. the monks vanished, and the valley returned to its former desolation.

For the next twelve hundred years Ajanta appears to have been as effectively lost and forgotten to civilisation as Pompeii was after the eruption of Vesuvius in A.D. 79. Tigers and other wild game prowled through the fabulous halls and made their lairs among the paintings. Under the pressure of the monsoonal rains the doorways fell in, and shrubs and creepers overgrew the entrances. Perhaps from time to time hermits or wandering tribes may have made a home there, but as far as the outside world was concerned Ajanta ceased to exist. Then at last the caves were discovered again in 1819.

By this time I had a fairly good general knowledge of Ajanta and more particularly I had unearthed the strange, rather Rider Haggardish legend which has grown up around the caves since they were brought to light again in 1819. It seems that the actual discovery was made by a group of British officers attached to the Madras Army. They were taking a few days off from military manoeuvres in the Indhyadri hills, and had come up to the head of the gorge on a tiger-hunting expedition when they fell in with a half-wild boy who was minding a group of buffaloes. This boy said he knew of some tiger lairs and he led them down over rocky ground towards the bed of the river. Then, pointing through the trees he indicated a place in the cliff that was thickly overgrown with creepers and bushes. Hacking their way in through this undergrowth the officers suddenly found themselves confronted with a large doorway of carved stone. Beyond this a square cavern lined with pillars led back into the rock, and at the farther end a huge figure of the Buddha sat quietly smiling in the darkness. All the walls were covered with a series of brilliant paintings.

It is a pity that more is not known about these army officers or what they did at this first moment of discovery. One would like to think that, like Rider Haggard's heroes, they clutched up burning brands and plunged into the dark network of corridors; and it is not hard to imagine their echoing voices as perhaps they ran on excitedly from one new gallery to another. Other caves, of course, had been found in India and in just this accidental way, but none were so spectacular and none contained anything like this galaxy of painting. There would have been some dangers in such an exploration, for no one knew what snakes or wild animals were lurking in the darkness, or where some gaping hole had opened up in the uneven ground.

The feeling of movement is extraordinary. It is almost cinematographic. Wherever you look you see figures in a state of continuous motion, people gesticulating, dancing, stooping to kneel to the Buddha, half turning to one another as though some thought — something they eagerly *had* to say — had suddenly come into their minds. The immediate effect is to give you a sensation of warmth and gaiety. It is not at all like one's first impression of, say, the Michelangelo frescoes in the Sistine Chapel, where the figures are grander or nobler than life, or the Gozzoli murals in Florence in which the procession of the Medicis remains fixed in history. At Ajanta you, the observer, are part of the proceedings, and if you flash an electric light down the dark corridors the whole scene revolves around you like a ballet.

Wherever they could the artists painted groups of lovers. You see them everywhere, floating ecstatically in clouds across the ceilings, inclining towards one another in some palace garden, or standing two by two, carved in high relief in panels from the floor to the ceiling at nearly every doorway. Almost always it is the shy first moment of love where the man, in the sudden relief of unexpected happiness, has discovered that he is welcome. He supports the woman on his arm, or perhaps he is simply reaching out to touch her and he looks away in a daze. The woman leans back and glances upward half smiling into his face.

There is a curious grace about the Ajanta women, and quite clearly the artists adored painting them. Like elegant cats they seem to fall into natural attitudes of their own accord, even though their hour-glass figures appear to be wildly exaggerated to a western eye. Even Rubens in his most enthusiastic days could hardly have imagined such enormous high breasts and such tiny waists as these; and yet, after you have been looking at the frescoes for an hour or two it is difficult to think of the female figure in any other way.

In the Ajanta civilisation it was the rich, the privileged and the beautiful who went naked. Often you will see in the paintings a group of servant girls clothed drably from neck to knee, while the princess they are attending rises up like a flower out of the foliage with a towering head-dress, strings

of pearls falling down between her breasts and a strip of
transparent gauze around her loins. Apparently the underlying
idea was that if a woman was beautiful she should be seen,
and a kind of innocence was made of the human body. There
was no question of modesty or self-consciousness. Nakedness
was accepted as a natural thing, in the same way as children
accept it, and the jewels and the jungle flowers in the women's
hair were treated as delightful toys.

ALAN MOOREHEAD
The Cave-Temples of Ajanta
from *The Cornhill*, Spring 1955

Rock Temples, Ellora

What miracle formed these lovely matrices
Of stone-and-mortar buildings that had shape,
Colour and meaning under open skies?
What held men there through time and change of faith
Hollowing out a mountain — ecstasies
Of austere contemplation? — human hope
Of ruthless help from powerful deities? —
Or an artist's dream of half-outwitting death?

These vaults are far removed from warping sun,
Insinuating rain and normal danger
Of mankind's cruelty or the gods' anger;
How many masons, priests and gritty years
Carved out these saints, gods, demons, worshippers
Remote from love and light in the heart of stone?

After austere centuries monk-masons,
Carving their age's mind in disciplined rock,

Tapping and tapping while their chisels spoke
Of ever worldlier Buddhas, with musicians,
Dancers and patrons, animal decorations
About the dreaming heads, felt little shock
When under their chipping hammers the stone broke
Into a dancing riot of jungle visions.

Chisels carved through a stupa to a nandi,
A buddha to a lingam: then stopped short
To find an elephant's head, a wild boar's snout —
Or figuers locked in love along a frieze:
Ravanna, many-headed, shook Kailasa;
The temple broke its way through to the skies.

R.N. CURREY
Indian Landscape (1947)

Mathura

I shall never forget the feeling of joy with which I first gazed on the panorama of the buildings and ghats of Mathura, which rose as a vision before my eyes, across the spacious and limpid Jumna. I jumped from my seat in the railway carriage and rushed to the window and looked with delight on the far-famed classic town! The sacred Jumna flowed before me, temples and towers and graceful edifices rose beyond and were bathed in sunlight, and the memories of three thousand years sanctified the lovely scene. My thoughts flew back to the time when Mahmud of Ghazni, found it in all its loveliness and left it a ruin, — back to the time when Houen Tsang and Fa Hian found it ringing with joyous Buddhist celebrations and pompous gatherings, — back to those dim ages when Krishna and the Yadavas went as colonists from this spot and Hinduised the far shores of Gujarat! It is difficult to avoid sentimentalising when standing on this spot, for there are few spots which recall to the Hindu more vividly the memories of an ancient world and an ancient civilisation.

My feelings were not less keen when I entered Mathura, and when in the cool of the evening I strolled along its streets lined with ornate and beautiful old Hindu-style buildings, and paused on the river bank to witness religious celebrations. Sacred hymns were uttered and the sacred fire was lighted, and a crowd of pious and simple-hearted men and women rushed forward to receive the blessings and the benefit of the evening service. We took a boat the next morning and glided up and down the river, and we saw many a devout worshipper standing in water and hailing the rising sun with sacred hymns which were uttered by their ancestors in this same spot, three thousand years ago. The nation which has a past has a future also; and the faith and destiny of the great Hindu nation will survive the degradation of the present.

R.C. DUTT
Rambles in India

Benares

Thy Gods have wrapt thee round as with a shroud,
Saintly Benares, where from morn till night,
From mosque-crowned street and temple-haunted height,
Throb out the voiceful murmurs of the crowd,
Over thy hallowed Ganges echoing loud;
While in the deep nook of each flower-clasped shrine,
Ever the speechless Shape, in calm divine,

Broods o'er the suppliant heads before him bowed.
But the majestic River rolls beneath,
Serene, relentless, bearing toward the sea
The dust of those, who, happy in their death,
By her blest margin meet Eternity.
Last, the clear sunset throws a golden wreath,
And the sweet Night sinks down all silently.

C.A. KELLY (19th cent.)

The Temple of Jagannath

The home of the Jagannath on the coast of Coromandel
Is a temple town in the heart of the city of Puri.
The God with his brother and sister live deep in the
    Mandal;
Of Vishnu's shrines this is the holiest sanctuary.

In the mists of India's timeless passage through the years
Vishnu descended in Muttra as Lord Krishna;
To mark this earthly journey the Jagannath appears
On his mighty car at the time of the Rajgathra.
A diamond glitters in the wooden head of Vishnu;
Balbadhra and Subadhra ride beside him.
His giant shape is daubed in the sacerdotal hue
Of the Brahmins who attend his every whim.

The pilgrim city is a maze of lanes and secret ways,
Shy courts and many a caravanserai.
From the God's town house up to his country place
Runs a boulevard as wide as the Champs Élysées.

"The Babu, I regret, must not defile our shrine."

My way was barred by a priest whose head was shaven;
And I turned away from the Temple door past a line
Of whining beggars, professional and brazen.

A low caste Hindu, a little better than myself,
Kindly invited me to the roof of his house;
He took out a volume from his library shelf,
Which told the history; and we had our private grouse.
"In these modern times it seems to me very odd,"
Said my low caste friend in a comforting way to me,
"That I am allowed to approach the altar of your God,
While you Lord Vishnu's image may not see."

I told him about the Temple of Laxmi on top of the hill.
We both agreed that things were getting better;
And that all over the world men and women of goodwill.
Were worshipping God in the Spirit and not the Letter.

WILFRED RUSSELL
Flame of the Forest and Other Poems

Kalighat

Under the heavy sunlight all the cripples
of Calcutta form the guard of honour to the gate
of Kali, and the road is red with spat-out betel,
dirty with the dung of cows and goats
dry in the heavy sunlight, trodden hard
by horny feet of poor and unshod people
why hurry between the stalls, the blind, the lepers,
to the dark fetish who protects this city.
Above their shouting nothing else is heard
but the occasional beating of a goat from within

and the sudden drowning rumble, the persistent anger
of the great drum at the time of sacrifice.

The streaming heavy current of poor people
and the pressing heavy weight of the striking,
beating, battering sun.

The court is lined with merchants selling flowers,
incense, images, pictures of the Goddess.
Its floor is grimy from dirty feet and goat-dung
pressed into the cracks between the rough worn stones.
Goats are on sale for the Goddess, and her children
carry their offerings, climbing the foot-worn steps or
watch the place where, in the courtyard's centre,
the executioner beheads a bleating victim
calmly, without fuss or useless ritual.
In one clean stroke the pinioned head is severed.
A stray bitch and her puppies quickly come
to lick the blood that spatters the dirty pavement.
The body kicks a little to the persistent fury of the drum,
then goat and drum are dumb.
There is only the noise of many poor and gentle people,
chattering laughing and shouting, as they walk
barefoot over the courtyard to the shrine,
where suddenly all is solemn and still.

In the half-darkness little oil-lamps shine
around the black body of Kali dressed in silk,
garlanded many times, scented and jewelled—
a fierce black fetish with a golden tongue
pouring like a river from her mouth,
a river of gold, pouring over the people, over
the blood and dirt of the courtyard to where the dirty
sluggish water of Tolly's Nullah laves the faithful
at the poor ghat. (That here the lovely Ganga

should come to this, that this black mud should be
their purity, to wash off sins from the soul,
and should speak to the poor people of Calcutta
of the cool clean swell of the sea!)

"I teach them not to reject or renounce the world that
        befalls them,"
the black image of Kali seems to say,
"these dark people, these men thin and spare,
these plump rolling matrons, these crying children, these
        women
slender and shapely under poor cotton saris.

"I teach them not to reject, not to turn away,
but to accept, to take the thorn with the rose,
death with life, hatred with love, and night with day."

A.L. BASHAM

Architecture

In treating of the beauty of these towns, I must premise that I have sometimes been astonished to hear the contemptuous manner in which Europeans in the Indies speak of these and other places. They complain that the buildings are inferior in beauty to those of the Western world, forgetting that different climates require different styles of architecture; that what is useful and proper at Paris, London, or Amsterdam, would be entirely out of place at Delhi; insomuch that if it were possible for any one of those great capitals to change place with the metropolis of the Indies, it would become necessary to throw down the greater part of the city, and to rebuild it on a totally different plan. Without doubt, the cities of *Europe* may boast great beauties; these, however, are of an appropriate character, suited to a cold climate. Thus Delhi also may possess beauties adapted to a warm climate. The heat is so intense in Hindoustan, that no one, not even the King, wears stockings; the only cover for the feet being babouches, or slippers, while the head is protected by a small turban, of the finest and most delicate materials. The other garments are proportionably light. During the summer season, it is scarcely possible to keep the hand on the wall of an apartment, or the head on a pillow. For more than six successive months, everybody lies in the open air without covering — the common people in the streets, the merchants and persons of condition sometimes in their courts or gardens, and sometimes on their terraces, which are first carefully watered. Now, only suppose the streets of S. Jaques or S. Denis transported hither, with their close houses and endless stories; would they be habitable? or would it be possible to sleep in them during the night, when the absence of wind increases the heat almost to suffocation? Suppose one just returned on horseback, half dead with heat and dust, and drenched, as usual, in perspiration; and then imagine the luxury of squeezing up a narrow dark staircase to the fourth or fifth story, there to remain almost choked with heat. In the *Indies*, there is no such troublesome task to perform. You have only to swallow quickly a draught of fresh water, or lemonade; to undress; wash face, hands, and feet, and then immediately drop upon a sofa in some shady place, where one or two servants fan you with their great *pankhas* or fans. But I shall now endeavour to give you an accurate description of *Delhi,* that you may judge for yourselves how far it has a claim to the apellation of a beautiful city.

FRANCIS BERNIER (1620-88)
Travels in the Moghul Empire (1656-68)
translated by A. CONSTABLE

Fatehpur: The Romantic City

Akbar built the city as a small personal tribute to himself. The vanity of Indian potentates had a way of running to brand new cities. Witness Jai Singh's Jaipur, five miles from the existing and perfectly satisfactory town of Amber; Jodha's Jodhpur, an hour's walk from Mandor; the Udaipur of Udai Singh next door to Arh. An expensive form of royal vanity; but one for which the modern tourist should be grateful. There is nothing more picturesque than a deserted city, nothing more mournfully romantic. These deserted cities of Northern India are particularly romantic because, being relatively modern, they are all in an excellent state of preservation. For a building that is intact, but deserted, is much more romantic, more picturesquely melancholy than a deserted ruin. One expects a ruin to be deserted, nobody, it is obvious, could possibly live in Pompeii, or among the roofless remains of an English abbey. But in a building that is intact one expects to find inhabitants. When such a building is deserted, we are mournfully surprised; and the contrast between its emptiness and intactness strikes us as being strange and suggestive.

Fatehpur is less than four hundred years old, and, so far as the principal buildings are concerned, it is in a state of perfect preservation. The red sandstone which Akbar used in the building of his city is a hard, weather-resisting rock. The sculpture, the mouldings are still clean-edged and sharp. There has been no blurring of outlines, no crumbling, no leprous decay. Akbar's red city stands today in the condition in which he left it — and stands empty, untenanted even by the monkeys which inhabit so many of India's deserted palaces and temples.

To those whom the dry and sterile elegance of Shah Jahan's Agra has left unsatisfied, the architecture of Fatehpur

Sikri will seem refreshing. For the greatest of the alien Mohammedan emperors was a patron of the indigenous Hindu art of India, and the architecture of his capital is marked by something of the genuine Hindu vigour and wealth of imagination. The *liwan* or covered portion of the mosque is particularly fine. It is divided up into three square chambers, in line and communicating; and the characteristically Hindu ceilings of these chambers are supported by a number of very tall Hindu columns. The building is superb in proportion and detail, and is certainly one of the finest pieces of interior architecture on a large scale to be seen in Upper India. And yet, such is the prestige of expensive material that poor uninteresting buildings, wholly lacking in grandeur or originality, like the Pearl Mosque at Agra, the pavilions by the lake at Ajmere, are much more widely celebrated. They are of marble; Fatehpur is only of sandstone.

ALDOUS HUXLEY (1894-1963)
Jesting Pilate

Taj-Mahal

The Taj-Mahal was built by Emperor Shahjahan (1627-57) in memory of his dearly loved queen, Mumtaz, who died in childbirth.

This you knew, O Emperor Shahjahan,
That youth, glory and riches all pass away
In the stream of Time.
Might the sorrow of his heart
Be made deathless,
That was the desire of the Emperor.

Let the pomp of regal power
Vanish like the last glow of the sunset sky,
But may one deep sigh
Make tender the heavens,
This was your wish.
The lustre of all your diamonds and pearls
Is like the rainbow,
Spreading enchantment over the distant sky;
If that lustre dims, let it vanish,
But may this Taj-Mahal glisten bright
Like a tear drop on the cheek of Time.
Oh mind of Man,
You have no time to look backwards,
You hurry along the stream of life from port to port,
Taking up burdens at one
And laying them down at the other.
At the whisper of the south wind,
The spring flowers that fill the skirt of the forest,
Are scattered to dust
At the approach of twilight.
There is no time to linger.
Therefore in the wintry night the Kunda
Blossoms anew to adorn tearful autumn's tray of delight.
O Heart, you must leave all your gatherings by the wayside,
At the end of the day,
At the end of the night
There is no time to linger and to look backward.
And so, Emperor, your anxious heart
Had desired to steal the heart of Time
Through Beauty's enchantment.
Flinging that garland round her neck,
Have you given to death that is formless,
A form immortal.

There is no time to mourn in the busy flow of the years,
Therefore you have prisoned your restless cry
With the silent net of stern marble.
The love-names you used to call your beloved
On moon-light nights in the privacy of your chamber,
Those whispering love-calls you have here left behind
In the ear of the Infinite.
The tearful tenderness of love has blossomed
In these quiet stones as the flowers of Beauty.
O Poet-Emperor, this dream-picture of your heart,
This new "Cloud-Messenger",
Is soaring in songs and rhythms toward that Unseen,
Where your beloved has become one
With the glow of early dawn,
The tender sigh of the weary eventide,
The ethereal loveliness of the Chameli in the Moonlight,
And the shoreless region beyond all words
Whence the hungering eye returns baffled
From its quest.
Your messenger of Beauty.
Eluding the watchman of Time,
Proclaims eternally: "I have not forgotten,
I have not forgotten, O beloved."

You have passed away, O Emperor.
Your empire has vanished like a dream
And your throne lies in the dust.
The memory of your warriors
Under whose tramp the earth once shuddered,
Is borne on the dust-laden winds of Delhi.
Your musicians sing no more,
The strains of the *nahabat* mingle no more
With the ripples of the Jumna.
The jingling music of the princesses' anklets

Which died down amidst the forsaken ruins,
Reappears in the cry of the crickets
And resounds in the darkness of the night.
Still your messenger, untired and unfailing,
Ignoring the rise and fall of empires,
The rhythm of life and death,
Proclaims through the ages
With the voice of the eternal-bereaved:
"I have not forgotten, I have not forgotten,
O beloved."

*

Who gives you life, O Stone?
Who provides you,
Year by year, with the nectar of Immortality?
You hold up to the heavens eternally
This Joy-flower of earth,
And round you blows all the year
The sad breath of parting Spring.
The tear-dipped songs that died away
At end of the night of union,
Lit by the dim candle, are still echoing
Ceaselessly in your heart,
O stone, deathless Stone!
From his torn heart,
The bereaved Emperor brought out the jewel of separation
And laid it in the hand of the Universe,
For all to behold.
The royal guards are not there to keep watch;
All the heavens embrace her;
The sky imprints on her gently
One silent kiss of Eternity.
The first rays of the morning sun
Throw their crimson glow upon her,

And the pale rays of the moon,
With a sad smile of parting,
Make her tender!

O Empress! through Beauty's enchantment
The memory of your love has become sublime.
That memory, incorporeal and ethereal,
Taking form,
Merges the Emperor's love with the Love universal,
And spreads beyond you to the whole world
In the imperishable light of life!
From the secrecy of the royal chamber
You have brought your glorious crown
And placed it on the heads of all lovers,
From dwellers in palaces to those in the meanest huts.
The memory of your love has sanctified them all.
The Emperor has taken leave of his own royal deed.
Today, the eternal sorrow of the mind of Man,
Embracing this marble Beauty,
Is seeking its realisation night and morn!

RABINDRANATH TAGORE (1861-1941)
The Flight of Swans
translated by AUROBINDO BOSE

Kashmir

You have no doubt discovered before this time that I am charmed with *Kachemire*. In truth, the kingdom surpasses in beauty all that my warm imagination had anticipated. It is probably unequalled by any country of the same extent, and should be, as in former ages, the seat of sovereign authority, extending its dominion over all the circumjacent mountains, even as far as *Tartary* and over the whole of *Hindoustan,* to the island of *Ceylon.* It is not indeed without reason that the *Mogols* call *Kachemire* the terrestrial paradise of the *Indies,* or that *Ekbar* was so unremitting in his efforts to wrest the sceptre from the hand of its native Princes. His son *Jehan Guyre* became so enamoured of this little kingdom as to make it the place of his favourite abode, and he often declared that he would rather be deprived of every other province of his mighty empire than lose *Kachemire.*

*

But what may be considered peculiar of *Kachemire,* and the staple commodity, that which particularly promotes the trade of the country and fills it with wealth, is the prodigious quantity of shawls which they manufacture, and which gives occupation even to the little children. These shawls are about an ell and a half long, and an ell broad, ornamented at both ends with a sort of embroidery, made in the loom, a foot in width. The *Mogols* and *Indians,* women as well as men, wear them in winter round their heads, passing them over the left shoulder as a mantle. There are two sorts manufactured: one kind with the wool of the country, finer and more delicate than that of *Spain;* the other kind with the wool, or rather hair (called *touz*) found on the breast of a species of wild goat which inhabits *Great Tibet.* The *touz* shawls are much more esteemed than those made with the native wool. I have seen some, made purposely for the *Omrahs,* which cost one hundred and fifty *roupies;* but I cannot learn that the others have ever sold for more than fifty. They are very apt, however, to be worm-eaten, unless frequently unfolded and aired. The fur of the beaver is not so soft and fine as the hair from these goats....

The people of *Kachemire* are proverbial for their clear

complexions and fine forms. They are as well made as
Europeans, and their faces have neither the *Tartar* flat nose
nor the small pig-eyes that distinguish the natives of
Kacheguer, and which generally mark those of *Great Tibet*.
The women especially are very handsome; and it is from this
country that nearly every individual, when first admitted to
the court of the *Great Mogol*, selects wives or concubines,
that his children may be whiter than the *Indians* and pass
for genuine *Mogols*. Unquestionably there must be beautiful
women among the higher classes, if we may judge by those
of the lower orders seen in the streets and in the shops.
When at *Lahor* I had recourse to a little artifice, often
practised by the *Mogols* to obtain a sight of these hidden
treasures; the women of that town being the finest brunettes
in all the *Indies*, and justly renowned for their fine and
slender shapes. I followed the steps of some elephants,
particularly one richly harnessed, and was sure to be gratified
with the sight I was in search of, because the ladies no sooner
hear the tinkling of the silver bells suspended from both
sides of the elephant than they all put their heads to the
windows. This is a stratagem with which I often amused
myself in *Kachemire*, until a more satisfactory method of
seeing the fair sex was devised by an old pedagogue, well
known in the town, with whom I read the *Persian* poets. I
purchased a large quantity of sweetmeats, and accompanied
him to more than fifteen houses, to which he had freedom
of access. He pretended I was his kinsman lately arrived
from *Persia*, rich and eager to marry. As soon as we entered
a house, he distributed my sweetmeats among the children,
and then everybody was sure to flock around us, the married
women and the single girls, young and old, with the twofold
object of being seen and receiving a share of the present.
The indulgence of my curiosity drew many *roupies* out of
my purse; but it left no doubt on my mind that there are

as handsome faces in *Kachemire* as in any part of *Europe*.

FRANCIS BERNIER (1620-88)
Travels in the Moghul Empire (1656-68)
translated by A. CONSTABLE

The Towers of Silence, Bombay

But look, at the entrance of a prosperous house, and a little further on, near the door of a miserable, broken-down dwelling, there, on one side and another, is quite a large gathering of people, grave, bearded men, all clad in white, silent, seated on old wooden benches that encumber the road.

"These are the relations and friends of the two dead men," my guide whispers in my ear. "They alone will presently accompany the body. The parents and wives will remain at the home of the dead, drowned in tears, sobs and prayers. As for the white robes that seem to attract your attention, it is the customary mourning worn by our men. The women wear black, as you do in Europe.

Slowly the first procession sets out — a white litter, hermetically sealed, carried on the shoulders of eight white-gloved bearers, while those who are to walk fall in line behind it, their hands clasped on their foreheads, with the most edifying signs of compassion. Inwardly I am amazed at the singular mixture of idealism and superstition in the members of this sect, who have a horoscope cast at their birth, who abstain from smoking, for fear of profaning the fire, and who, in order to purify themselves, drink the urine of a bull mixed with water that has been drawn by moonlight. Now we are climbing up the slope of Malabar Hill, the adorable little rise of palms that crowns the peninsula of Bombay, strewn with palaces and gay villas among clumps of acacias and coconut, banana and mimosa trees. Further on, emerging from the dense tropical foliage, there are five massive, grey towers, five smooth, round turrets, each one pierced by a single opening, a black, grilled gate, beneath which, by stooping, two men can enter from the front.

The Towers of Silence, the horrible and magnificent cemetery of the Parsees! ... Why must this sunny, dreamy corner, this flowery paradise, this perfumed air, this riot of colours conceal the fearful spectacle of this quarry-to-be and the place of decay?

The bearers of the white litter have entered a shady lane which leads to one of the five towers. Above their heads wheel birds of prey, great and small, eagles, kites and buzzards, which in a few minutes will seize with their grey beaks the leavings of the vultures' feast.

The vultures! I can distinguish them now on their funeral perch. At the sound of steps they stretch out their skinny necks; bending greedily towards the approaching prey, they gobble joyously on the top of the tower and swing their eager, gluttonous heads heavily from left to right.

But a hand is placed on my shoulder.

"We must stop here. You can go no further. Look; from this little knoll you can see the black wicket open and the vultures fling themselves into the interior to accomplish the work of destruction prescribed by the Zend-Avesta."

*

Ah, what a sinister vision! That clicking lock, half-open wicket, those bearers bending down and slipping in, carrying a long, white object ... A few minutes ... Then a second click. The funereal men have accomplished their task, they are returning among the living. And now there is a furious commotion which I cannot see but which I hear; a battle of hooked beaks, a concert of harsh, discordant cries.

"Come," says the guide, "in twenty minutes it will all be over. Besides, what is the use of remaining? You could not understand. Our religion, you see, forbids us to destroy our dead by Water, Earth or Fire — that is, to soil the three elements by the impure contact of our corpses. So we leave it to the vultures, to the sun, to the waters of heaven to destroy our 'vestments of flesh and bone' and return them to the earth."

"So you, who are speaking to me at this moment, in such choice language, with so clear an intelligence, you, an Irâni òf the upper class, almost or better than a European, you will be torn, slashed shred from shred by these hideous creatures?"

"I as well as the others ... As well as this second one whose procession is approaching ... As well as those that will come here tomorrow and the day after. Thus teaches Zarathustra. And besides, do you not think that, as between the worms of the tomb and the vultures of the open air, it is all one in the end?"

And beneath the sapphire sky of India, under these vivid, luxuriant palms, surrounded by these rare flowers and these penetrating perfumes, it seems to me that this gold-bespectacled Parsee has just paraphrased, without knowing it, the great thought of Schpenhauer, summing up the vicious circle of the human race:

"Death is the Reservoir of Life; Life is the Reservoir of Death."

ROBERT CHAUVELOT
Mysterious India
translated by E.S. BROOKS

The Mirror Rooms of Amber

They are wonderfully rich, these mirror rooms at Amber. Their elaborateness surpasses that even of the famous mirror room at Bagheria, near Palermo. But whereas the Sicilian room is nothing more than the old-fashioned glass-and-gilding merry-go-round made stationary, the Indian rooms are a marvel of cool and elegant refinement. True, this form of decoration does not lend itself to the adornment of large areas of wall or ceiling; it is too intricate for that. But fortunately the rooms in Indian palaces are seldom large. In a country where it rains with a punctual regularity and only at one season of the year, large rooms of assembly are unnecessary. Crowds are accommodated and ceremonials of state performed more conveniently out of doors than in. The Hall of Audience in an Indian palace is a small pillared pavilion placed at one end on an open courtyard. The king sat in the pavilion, his courtiers and petitioners thronged the open space. Every room in the palace was a private room, a place of intimacy. One must not come to India expecting to find grandiose specimens of interior architecture. There are no long colonnaded vistas, no galleries receding interminably according to all the laws of perspective, no colossal staircases, no vaults so high that at night the lamplight can hardly reach them. Here in India, there are only small rooms adorned with the elaborate decoration that is meant to be looked at from close to and in detail. Such are the mirror rooms at Amber.

ALDOUS HUXLEY (1894-1963)
Jesting Pilate

Jaipur

Young beside Petra, but a rose-red city
Caught in a dance that carries time away:
Each facing row of houses is a spray
Of single roses with no parallel wonder
In our own time; heads up, with measured splendour,
They hold before our eyes, like a bouquet,
Wide vistas of green hills — these everyday
Houses and shops that tread in dignity.

Beside the jewelled Palace of the Winds,
Beneath the swaying palaces that bear
White blossom nodding nodding in the air,
Terrace on terrace, crowned by cupolas:
How gracefully they wrought, those agile minds,
On flower-like stems domes light as primulas.

Those Rajput rulers in their alien day
Surrounded by their silk nobility
Kept jewelled women in captivity,
Who played within these walls their formal play
Of robing, love, fruition and decay —
And sometimes even wept to speak a line
Or felt authentic shivers down the spine
Seeing a pointed slipper turn their way.

Were they quite happy in their limited pale
Between the bathing-pools, the orange-trees?
Or did they turn from laughter to the street
And stare through window-slits at dusty feet
And vivid turbans of a jostling, male
Far world, and wonder at its ribaldries?

R.N. CURREY
Indian Landscape (1947)

Chitore

It was almost midnight, as the moon grew near full, when we looked for the first time on the fortress of Chitore. The lights in the village at the foot had been extinguished, and the hill with its great length stood dark and isolated against the sky. Almost directly above the black cleft of the cow's mouth stood the Tower of Victory of Kumbha Rana, like a finger pointing upwards in witness of past glory. And even in the darkness we could see the gentle curving lines of the walls following the contour of hillside, with its three miles of length and one of breadth. Silently we sat on a low stone a mile off and drank in the scene. Even thus may Padmini have caught her first glimpse of this city of her fate!

It is not a connected story, this for which Chitore is famous. The wild romance of which her annals are so full is a series of gleams and flashes, lasting through hundreds of years. Like watching from the plain the escalade of some rocky summit is the effort of one who strives to picture the past of Chitore. Again and again do the banners of the clansmen appear amidst trees and crags, only again and again to be lost to sight. Wherever the mists of history lift, there are revealed the old-time ideals of the courage and pride of woman and the glory of man. Chitore is no mere chronological record; she is an eternal symbol, the heart's heart of one phase of the Indian genius.

Architecturally the splendour of the city justifies her pride. The rock on which she stands slopes inwards from all sides, with the result that there are innumerable tanks and a water supply practically unlimited. Within the walls are the remains of what has been virtually two cities, one to the north-east, the ancient capital of the time before Bappa Raoul, and one more modern which grew up between his accession in A.D. 728 and the evacuation under Akbar in 1568.

The old manor-grange, on the veranda Bappa Raoul, in the eighth century, administered justice, scarcely comports with our modern notions of a palace. In front of it, not far away, is a Tower of Victory, now crumbling to pieces, and everywhere the living rock of the original foundation is close at hand. The life of the garrison within this fortress must have been strangley like that of a camp.

Long and narrow, like some lean grey lion crouching for the spring, lies walled Chitore on its craggy hill. And the newly-arrived traveller watching it may see it tonight, as the returning escort may have seen it when Padmini's marriage procession halted for the last time on the homeward way, more than seven centuries ago. Then, as now, the long heavy walls curved lovingly, like the canvas of a tent, about the city. Little can the "lotus fair" Padmini have slept that night, the last of the long journey from her father's distant stronghold. Rather must she have gazed on through hour after hour of waking dreamfulness, counting the tale of the turrets and bastions of the fortress that tomorrow she would enter as bride and queen. Within her was the confidence of the Indian wife, who thinks of herself as beginning what is only a new chapter in an old story, as recovering a thread that was held but a while ago, and dropped at death. Not for the first time were they to take up tomorrow the tale of life together — it was an ancient comradeship of the soul. Did no vision of the future make Padmini shrink and pause, in the glory of this her great homecoming? Had the bard whispered no word above her cradle of the tragedy of greatness that lay before her? Did she know that as long as winds would wail over Chitore they would sing her name, that with her would every stone and every building be associated in the world's memory till the end of time? To her, what would be was but the following of the path of Rajput honour. Was it not always said that, in the hour of birth, the eyes of a boy were set upon a knife, and those of a girl upon a lamp — for the man must leave life by way of the sword and woman by that of fire?

SISTER NIVEDITA
Studies from an Eastern Home (1913)

Gardens of Srinagar

If the Kashmiri gardens are beautiful, that is the work, not so much of man as of nature. The formal beds are full of xinnias and scarlet cannas. The turf is fresh and green. The huge chenar trees go up onto the pale bright sky; their white trunks shine between the leaves, which the autumn has turned to a rusty vermilion. Behind them are the steep bare hills, crested already with snow. Their colour, where the sun strikes them, is a kind of silvery-glaucous gold and, in the shadows, a deep intense indigo. Below, on the other side, stretches the Dal Lake, with the isolated fort-crowned hill of Hari-Parbat on the further shore. The sun shines out of a flawless sky, but the air is cool against the face. "It is a nipping and an eager air"; for we are at more than five thousand feet above the sea. The Great Moguls regarded Kashmir as the earthly paradise. And a paradise to one coming fresh from the earthly hell of the Punjab in summer it must indeed have seemed. The visitor from temperate lands finds it less paradisiacal because more familiar. The lakes and mountains remind us of Switzerland and Italy, and in the level valley, with its interminable poplar avenues, its waterways, and soggy fields, we find ourselves thinking of

France, of Holland even. Our ecstasies of admiration are
reserved for the unfamiliar tropics.

ALDOUS HUXLEY (1894-1963)
Jesting Pilate

The Victoria Memorial, Calcutta

Can the city forgive the arrogant men who built
this turgid ice-cake fantasy upon
her saving grace? The city can. She takes
to herself all that is built, all that is in her,
and it becomes a part of her. This white
'marble is lovely in the sun at dawn
and at evening takes a light from the orange sky
as a blessing, and the pigeons on its terrace
make mention of the truth behind the lie
of the hard righteousness of those who rule.

Here come people — peasants from the fields
and streams of all Bengal, paying their price, inspecting
portraits of western worthies, arms, and all
the paraphernalia of dead glory round the desk
where once the little old woman wrote who ruled
    so firmly this dominion.

What do they
understand of this past as dead as Akbar?
Who knows what they understand? It is there for them,
the peasants and the people of the suburbs,
as a palace of wonders which poor may visit
on holidays, with their women's anklets jangling,

where they may freely squat upon the terrace
and chew their *channa* in the winter sun.

It is as it is for them, and no association
mar what they see. They have nothing to forgive.
For they know, better than those who built this place,
though they are not able to express it,
that life is impossible without love,
love so deep as to be almost unfelt,
and that the purpose of living is to live.

A.L. BASHAM

Pastoral

A Lover's Calendar
Summer

Pitiless heat from heaven pours
By day, but nights are cool;
Continual bathing gently lowers
The water in the pool;
The evening brings a charming peace:
For summer-time is here
When love that never knows surcease
Is less imperious, dear.

Yet love can never fall asleep;
For he is waked today
By songs that all their sweetness keep
And lutes that softly play,
By fans with sandal-water wet
That bring us drowsy rest,
By strings of pearls that gently fret
Full many a lovely breast.

The sunbeams like fires are hot
That on the altar wake;
The enmity is quite, forgot
Of peacock and of snake;
The peacock spares his ancient foe,
For pluck and hunger fail;

He hides his burning head below
The shadow of his tail.

Beneath the garland of the rays
That leave no corner cool,
The water vanishes in haze
And leaves a muddy pool;
The cobra does not hunt for food
Nor heed the frog at all
Who finds beneath the serpent's hood
A sheltering parasol.

Dear maiden of the graceful song,
To you may summer's power
Bring moonbeams clear and garlands long
And breath of trumpet-flower,
Bring lakes that countless lilies dot,
Refreshing water-sprays,
Sweet friends at evening, and a spot
Cool after burning days.

The Rains

The rain advances like a king
In awful majesty;
Hear, dearest, how his thunders ring
Like royal drums, and see
His lightning-banners wave; a cloud
For elephant he rides,
And finds his welcome from the crowd
Of lovers and of brides.

The clouds, a mighty army, march

With drumlike thundering
And stretch upon the rainbow's arch
The lightning's flashing string;
The cruel arrows of the rain
Smite them who love, apart
From whom they love, with stinging pain,
And pierce them to the heart.

The forest seems to show its glee
In flowering nipa plants;
In waving twigs of many a tree
Wind-swept, it seems to dance;
Its ketak-blossom's opening sheath
Is like a smile put on
To greet the rain's reviving breath,
Now pain and heat are gone.

To you, dear, may the cloudy time
Bring all that you desire,
Bring every pleasure, perfect, prime,
To set a bride on fire;
May rain whereby life wakes and shines
Where there is power of life,
The unchanging friend of clinging vines,
Shower blessing on my wife.

Autumn

The autumn comes, a maiden fair
In slenderness and grace,
With nodding rice-stems in her hair
And lilies in her face.

In flowers of grasses she is clad;
And as she moves along,
Birds greet her with their cooing glad
Like bracelets' tinkling song.

A diadem adorns the night
Of multitudinous stars;
Her silken robe is white moonlight,
Set free from cloudy bars;
And on her face (the radiant moon)
Bewitching smiles are shown:
She seems a slender maid, who soon
Will be a woman grown.

Over the rice-fields, laden plants
Are shivering to the breeze;
While in his brisk caresses dance
The blossom-burdened trees;
He ruffles every lily-pond
Where blossoms kiss and part,
And stirs with lover's fancies fond
The young man's eager heart.

Winter

The bloom of tenderer flowers is past
And lilies droop forlorn,
For winter-time is come at last,
Rich with its ripened corn;
Yet for the wealth of blossoms lost
Some hardier flowers appear
That bid defiance to the frost
Of sterner days, my dear.

The vines, remembering summer, shiver
In frosty winds, and gain
A fuller life from mere endeavour
To live through all that pain;
Yet in the struggle and acquest
They turn as pale and wan
As lonely women who have missed
Known love, now lost and gone.

Then may these winter days show forth
To you each known delight,
Bring all that women count as worth
Pure happiness and bright;
While villages, with bustling cry,
Bring home the ripened corn,
And herons wheel through wintry sky,
Forget sad thoughts forlorn.

Early Spring

Now, dearest, lend a heedful ear
And listen while I sing
Delights to every maiden dear,
The charms of early spring:
When earth is dotted with the heaps
Of corn, when heron-scream
Is rare but sweet, when passion leaps
And paints a livelier dream.

When all must cheerfully applaud
A blazing open fire;
Or if they need must go abroad,

The sun is their desire;
When everybody hopes to find
The frosty chill allayed
By garments warm, a window-blind
Shut, and a sweet young maid.

Then may the days of early spring
For you be rich and full
With love's proud, soft philandering
And many a candy-pull,
With sweetest rice and sugar-cane:
And may you float above
The absent grieving and the pain
Of separated love.

Spring

A stalwart soldier comes, the spring,
Who bears the bow of love;
And on that bow, the lustrous string
Is made of bees, that move
With malice as they speed the shaft
Of blossoming mango-flower
At us, dear, who have never laughed
At love, nor scorned his power.

Their blossom-burden weights the trees;
The winds in fragrance move;
The lakes are bright with lotuses,
The women bright with love;
The days are soft, the evenings clear
And charming; everything

That moves and lives and blossoms, dear,
Is sweeter in the spring.

The groves are beautifully bright
For many and many a mile
With jasmine-flowers that are as white
As loving woman's smile:
The resolution of a saint
Might well be tried by this;
.Far more, young hearts that fancies paint
With dreams of loving bliss.

KALIDASA (*c.* A.D. 400-500)
The Seasons
translated by A.W. RYDER

The Dawn

I

The moon behind the western mount is sinking;
The eastern sun is heralded by dawn;
From heaven's twin lights, their fall and glory linking,
Brave lessons of submission may be drawn.

Night-blooming lilies, when the moon is hidden,
Have naught but memories of beauty left.
Hard, hard to bear! Her lot whom heaven has bidden
To live alone, of love and lover reft.

On jujube-trees the blushing dewdrops falter;
The peacock wakes and leaves the cottage thatch;
A deer is rising near the hoof-marked altar,

And stretching, stands, the day's new life to catch.

The moon that topped the loftiest mountain ranges,
That slew the darkness in the midmost sky,
Is fallen from heaven, and all her glory changes:
So high to rise, so low at last to lie!

> KALIDASA (c. A.D. 400-500)
> *Shakuntala*
> translated by A.W. RYDER

II

The night was almost over. Dawn was about to break. The moon was sinking into the western sea like a goblet emptied by Queen Night. The pollen of lotuses had been converted into cold paste by the dew, and the bees were getting stuck in it. The soft chatter of skylarks was revealing women at their rendezvous. The huts of ascetics were slowly awakening, full of scholarly expectations. Mendicants were chanting poetic tales. The lamps had become so thin and emaciated that they were unable to bear the weight of the night. They had become dull because their oil had been consumed, as clever people become slack when their affections are exhausted. They had only the bowls left, as noblemen, deprived of their estates, have only their bodies left. In the boudoirs, flowers had withered. The bees, no longer tempted by honey, had vanished. Damsels were getting up. Bracelets jingled on their tremulous, slender arms while the apartments were lighted up by the flashing of their lustrous teeth.

> SUBANDHU (late 6th cent. A.D.)
> *Vasavadatta*

India by Day

They tell me your brown plains
Come to enthral those who stay awhile!
What of that jungle scrub
Of dried bamboo? Ah! You may smile!
What magic holds you now?
What secret in the mighty banyan tree?
The tamarind? Your everlasting browns, monotony?
Where is that vast enchantment that they see?
Great stretches broken here
And there with boulders old and grey,
With flowers all thorns and prickly
Cactus bush, in what was once a pathway!
Your torrid skies are high,
Your birds are shrill, and scavengers are they;
There are no mistle thrushes
To sing to you, in this long blistering May!
Your river-beds are empty
The mighty river fades beneath
The mightier sun ... and leaves its dead self
Straggling, in rocks and crevices, with pebbles
As a wreath! The secret of thy magic
I would wrest from thee, thou tyrant!
Would'st thou then burn me too
And scar me ever, as thine own?

E.M. JONES
Poems of South India (1935)

Sunset

See, my belovèd, how the sun
With beams that o'er the water shake
From western skies has now begun
A bridge of gold across the lake.

Upon the very tree-tops sway
The peacocks; even yet they hold
And drink the dying light of day,
Until their fans are molten gold.

The water-lily closes, but
With wonderful reluctancy;
As if it troubled her to shut
Her door of welcome to the bee.

The steeds that draw the sun's bright car,
With bended neck and falling plume
And drooping mane, are seen afar
To bury day in ocean's gloom.

The sun is down, and heaven sleeps:
Thus every path of glory ends;
As high as are the scalèd steeps,
The downward way as low descends.

KALIDASA (c. A.D. 400-500)
The Birth of the War-God
translated by A.W. RYDER

Night

The twilight glow is fading far
And stains the west with blood-red light,
As when a reeking scimitar
Slants upward on a field of fight.

And vision fails above, below,
Around, before us, at our back;
The womb of night envelops slow
The world with darknes vast and black.

Must while the world is dazed with light,
The smiling moon begins to rise
And, being teased by eager night,
Betrays the secrets of the skies.

Moon-fingers move the black, black hair
Of night into its proper place,
Who shuts her eyes, the lilies fair,
As he sets kisses on her face.

KALIDASA (c. A.D. 400-500)
The Birth of the War-God
translated by A.W. RYDER

Spring

It was the season of spring — that intoxicates with its song
and scent. The mango-buds were opening, and swarms
of bees settled on them, humming softly. The lakes around

the city echoed with the joyous cries of swans thrilled by the
expanding lotuses. Travellers heard with delight the festive
songs sung in every street. The *dhak* trees were in full bloom.
The sweet humming of black-bees among jasmine-buds sounded
like Cupid's trumpet-call of victory. The swarms of bees
clustering round bunches of white flowers looked like sapphires
woven with pearls in a necklace. The trumpet-flower seemed
to be the hook with which the God of Love was fishing among
the restless hearts of men.

SUBANDHU (late 6th cent, A.D.)
Vasavadatta

Indian Landscape

Across this rolling wilderness,
The heavy clouds are scuttling free,
The breeze is blowing keen and strong
And swirls around us, you and me.
In this great loneliness and waste,
This wond'rous, mighty solitude,
We are now one with nature ... love,
And atune to her magic mood.
Just across the rising hillock
The granite quarry looms,
Old, battered and grey and weathered,
Deep, stark, as one of Nature's tombs,
Standing so bare and so sombre,
Beneath the evening's stormy sky,
As chaste as the snow and barren,
Rough-hewn and cut her old slabs lie;
But with thy presence all is light,

All gloom and fear is lost to me,
This wilderness is sun and flowers
While I am standing here with thee!

E.M. JONES
Poems of South India (1935)

The Bursting of the Monsoons

The sky was grey and leaden: the Moon was dull and pale;
Suspended high, the dust-clouds, in canopying veil,
O'erlooked wide fields and hamlets of India's arid plains —
Sun-backed and scorch'd and yellow — a thirsting, for the
    Rains.
The atmosphere was stifling: the air was still as death,
As the parched *jheels* emitted their foul and charnel breath.
Storm-clouded the horizon: a flash across the sky,
A boom of far-off thunder, and a breeze like a distant sigh:
'Tis the dirge of a dying summer: the music of the gods;
Dead leaves rise up and caper: the Melantolia nods:
Tall trees to life awaken: the top-most branches sway
And the long grass is waving along the zephyr way.
A mantle of red shadow envelops and around —
The trees, the grass, the hamlets, as the storm-clouds
    forward bound.
Of a sudden, comes a whirlwind, dancing, spinning rapidly;
Then gust on gust bursts quick, incessant, mad, rushing
    furiously.
A crash — and the Monsoon's on us, in torrents
    everywhere,
With the bellowing roar of thunder, and lightning, flare
    on flare.

The tempest's now abated: a hush falls o'er the scene;
Then myriad birds start chatt'ring and the grass again is
    green,

*

The fields like vast, still mirrors, in sheets of water lie,
The frogs, in droning chorus, sign hoarse their lullaby,
Each tank and pool is flooded: great rivers burst their
    banks:
King Summer's reign is ended: the Monsoon sovereign
    ranks.

L.H. NIBLETT
India in Fable, Verse and Story (1938)

The Rains

I

The rainy season had arrived. Rivers overflowed their banks. Peacocks danced at eventide. The rain quelled the expanse of dust as a great ascetic quells the tide of passion. The *chataka* birds were happy. Lightning shone like a bejewelled boat of Love in the pleasure-pool of the sky; it was like a garland for the gate of the palace of paradise; like a lustrous girdle for some heavenly beauty; like a row of nail-marks left upon the cloud by its lover, the departing day.

The rain was like a chess player, while yellow and green frogs were like chessmen jumping in the enclosures of the irrigated fields. Hailstones flashed like pears from the necklaces of heavenly birds. By and by, the rainy season yielded to autumn, the season of bright dawns; of parrots rummaging

among rice-stalks; of fugitive clouds. In autumn the lakes
echoed with the sound of herons. The frogs were silent and
the snakes shrivelled up. At night the stars were unusually
bright and the moon was like a pale beauty.

SUBANDHU (late 6th cent. A.D.)
Vasavadatta

II

The first shower was smelly and undramatic. Now there is
a new India — damp and grey, and but for the unusual
animals I might think myself in England. The full Monsoon
broke violently, and upon my undefended form. I was under
a little shelter in the garden, sowing seeds in boxes with the
assistance of two aged men and a little boy. I saw black
clouds and felt some spots of rain. This went on for a quarter
of an hour, so that I got accustomed to it, and then a wheel
of water swept horizontally over the ground. The aged men
clung to each other for support. I don't know what happened
to the boy. I bowed this way and that as the torrent veered,
wet through of course, but anxious not to be blown away
like the roof of palm leaves over our head. When the storm
decreased or rather became perpendicular, I set out for the
Palace, large boats of mud forming on either foot. A rescue
expedition, consisting of an umbrella blew inside out and
the servant fell down.

Since then there have been some more fine storms, with
lightning very ornamental and close. The birds fly about
with large pieces of paper in their mouths. They are late,
like everyone else, in their preparations against the rough
weather, and hope to make a nest straight off, but the wind
blows the paper round their heads like a shawl, and they
grow alarmed and drop it. The temperature is now variable,
becomes very hot between the storms, but on the whole
things have improved. I feel much more alert and able to

concentrate. The heat made me feel so stupid and sleepy, though I kept perfectly well.

E.M. FORSTER
The Hill of Devi

The Banyan Tree

A noble banyan tree stands by the side of the Jaunpur road, where it leaves the Civil Lines. Under the dense foliage lingers a kind of ecclesiastical darkness, and the rooted and already massive offshoots from the parent branches are the cathedral pillars. But the shoots which have not yet reached the ground, but hang in the dim air like the ends of aimlessly trailing cables, have an aspect strangely sinister and unholy. They hang there, motionless; and the cathedral of the banyan grove is transformed into a Piranesian prison.

The banyan is like the Hindu family. Its scions remain, even in maturity, attached to the parent tree. The national tree of England is the oak, and English families — once, no doubt, as banyan-like as the Indian — are coming to resemble handfuls of scattered acorns that grow up at a distance from their tree of origin. Those who have had, in India or on the continent of Europe, any experience of the really united banyan family, can only feel thankful at the turn our social botany is taking.

ALDOUS HUXLEY (1894-1963)
Jesting Pilate

The Lotus

Love came to Flora asking for a flower
That would of flowers be undisputed queen,
The lily and the rose, long, long had been
Rivals for that high honour. Bards of power
Had sung their claims. "The rose can never tower
Like the pale lily with her Juno mien" —
"But is the lily lovelier?" Thus between
Flower-factions rang the strife in Psyche's bower.
"Give me a flower delicious as the rose
And stately as the lily in her pride" —
"But of what colour?" — "Rose-red," Love first chose,
Then prayed, — "No, lily-white, — or, both provide;"
And Flora gave the lotus, "rose-red" dyed,
And "lily-white," — the queenliest flower that blows.

TORU DUTT (1856-1877)

The Dog

Every morning my devoted dog
Waits silently by the chair
Till I have greeted him with a touch.
Receiving this slight recognition
His whole body thrills with joy.
Among all dumb creatures,
He alone, piercing the veil of good and bad,
Has seen Man in his entirety —
A being for whom he can give life gladly,

To whom he can pour out love without reason,
From a dim awareness that gropes its way
Towards the world of consciousness.
When I see the self-offering of this mute heart,
Pleading its own need,
I cannot imagine what unique value
His simple wisdom has found in Man.
With his wordless look of pathetic bewilderment,
What he comprehends he cannot put into words;
But to me he reveals the true significance of Man
In the scheme of Creation.

RABINDRANATH TAGORE (1861-1941)
Wings of Death

Beasts and Man

The beasts are very wise,
Their mouths are clean of lies,
They talk one to the other,
Bullock to bullock's brother,
Resting after their labours,
Each in stall with his neighbours.
But man with goad and whip
Breaks up their fellowship,
shouts in their silky ears
Filling their souls with fears.
When he has ploughed the land,
He says: "They understand."
But the beasts in stall together,
Freed from the yoke and tether,

Say as the torn flanks smoke:
"Nay, 'twas the whip that spoke."

RUDYARD KIPLING (1865-1936)
Rudyard Kipling's Verse

Pigs and Buffaloes

Dark children of the mere and marsh,
Wallow and waste and lea,
Outcaste they wait at the village gate
With folk of low degree.

Their pasture is in no man's land,
Their food the cattle's scorn;
Their rest is mire and their desire
The thicket and the thorn.

But woe to those that break their sleep,
And woe to those that dare
To rouse the herd-bull from his keep,
The wild boar from his lair!

RUDYARD KIPLING (1865-1936)
Rudyard Kipling's Verse

The Sacred Cows

Srinagar owns a large population of sacred cows and bulls that wander vaguely through the streets, picking up such vegetable garbage, grass, and fallen leaves as they can find. They are small beasts — the half of good-sized English cattle — and marvellously mild. Red rags mean nothing to these little bulls, they can be trusted in china shops — even in nurseries. Liberty, under feeding, and unlimited access to the females of their species account, no doubt, for this surprising gentleness.

But, though harmless, these Hindu totems are passively a nuisance. They will not attack you as you walk or drive along the streets, but neither will they get out of your way. They stand there, meditatively ruminating, in the middle of the road, and no shouting, no ringing of bells or hooting of horns will send them away. Not until you are right on top of them will they move. The fact is, of course, that they know their own sacredness. They have learned by long experience that they can stand in the road as much as they like and that, however furiously the klaxon sounds, nothing will ever happen to them. Nothing; for Kashmir, though its inhabitants are mostly Mohammedans, is ruled by a pious Hindu dynasty. Up till a few years ago a man who killed a cow was sentenced to death. Under a milder dispensation he now gets only a matter of seven years' penal servitude. A salutary fear of cows is rooted in the breast of every Kashmiri chauffeur. And the totems know it. With a majestic impertinence they stroll along the middle of the roads. When one is a god, one does not disturb oneself for the convenience of mere man, however importunate.

*

It was late in the afternoon when we drove past the Court of Justice. The day's business was over and the sweepers were at work, making clean for the morrow. Outside one of the doors of the building stood a row of brimming waste-paper baskets, and from these, as from mangers, two or three sacred bulls were slowly and majestically feeding. When the baskets were empty officious hands from within replenished them with a fresh supply of torn and scribbled paper. The bulls browsed on; it was a literary feast.

Watching them at their meal, I understood why it is that Indian bulls are so strangely mild. On a diet of waste-paper, it would be difficult for them to be anything but disciples of Gandhi, devotees of non-violence and *ahimsa*. I also understood why it is that Indian cows yield so little milk and, further, why the cattle of either sex are so often afflicted with hiccoughs. Before I came to India, I had never heard a bull hiccoughing. It is a loud and terrifying sound. Hearing behind me that explosive combination of a bellow and a bark, I have often started in alarm, thinking I was on the point of being attacked. But looking round, I would find that it was only one of the mild, dyspeptic totems of the Hindus, gorged with waste-paper and painfully, uncontrollably belching as it walked.

ALDOUS HUXLEY (1894-1963)
Jesting Pilate

The Indian Palm Squirrel

One of the Hindu gods
(At the moment I can't quite give a
Name to the actual one; I *think* it was Shiva,

But it makes no special odds —
Shiva or one of that set),
For his own particular pet
Chose you.

And I can't think why he did,
For of all the bungalow creatures
I most dislike your low-bred impudent features;
And I find your virtue hid
By the maddening noise you make
When your raucous tribe gives tongue;
And you eat, if I don't mistake.
Your young.

Shiva mayhap extolled
Your teeth like a row of razors;
I wish he had seen my clothes — my beautiful blazers
Nibbled and gnawed and holed;
And the carpets are riddled to rags
To feather your needless nest,
And so are my flannel bags,
You pest!

And you ruin the roof, what's more;
And it gives me a nasty feeling
When your horrible offspring fall with a flop from the
      ceiling
And sprawl half-dead on the floor;
Nay, nay — obscure and dark
Was the Great One's choice, chipmunk ...
And I wish your bit of the Ark
Had sunk.

HILTON BROWN
The Gold and the Grey (1930-35)

Indian Village Life

It would be an experience, I think a pleasant one, for any
Westerner to wander into the home of an Indian peasant
in some unfrequented little village, for here he will see no more
the individualist aloofness of modern European civilisation, but
here he will get the warmth of a real and loving welcome as
soon as he may knock at the door. And here he may see a simple
life beautifully lived. For here, when the cock crows at dawn,
are to be seen, gliding in and out of little earthen homes, fair
souls in earthly forms with earthen pitchers poised on their
heads, going to or returning from the village well or stream.
Here in any peasant home could be heard the mothers of the
land, singing sweet hymns as they churn the curds for butter.
When their men return from a dip in the holy waters and from
their prayers to the bright-eyed Sun, their food is ready. Sitting
within the precincts of the kitchen sacred undefiled they eat
their humble loaf of bread, they drink a glass of that cool
invigorating whey, which builds up their bodies and keeps their
minds so clear, and proceed to till their soil. The women busy
themselves in the home. They clean and sweep the house, they
tend their children — each act a sacred rite smilingly undertaken
in the serene spirit of faith in God and executed with patient
love. The middle of the morning sees them well advanced with
preparations for the meal at noon. They have done their
shopping. More often they are self-supporting, for their men
grow all the necessities of food in their plot of land, the women
reap the harvest and turn it into food. When the food is ready,
these mothers, wives, sisters, take it to their kinsfolk in the
fields. Perhaps it is a hot sunny day. It usually is. Then you may
see them sitting under the shade of a banyan feeding their loved
ones with anxious care. The women then take their meal, for
in her sacred role of hostess woman must first feed her guest

the man. The men, fed to satiety, sleep till the burning Sun has passed overhead well into the west. When the cool air blows, they ply their plough till the dusk announces it is time to drive the cattle home. The women have either sat near the fields helping their men in various ways or returned home to sit with their sister of the spinning-wheel to spin the yarn out of which is woven the cloth from which their garments are made. The evening meal is set to cook in the afternoon. The tired and hungry peasants find it ready on their return from the fields. They wash, they pray, they eat, and having nourished their bodies they all repair either to the village church, mosque or temple to say formal prayers to the God whom they have informally mentioned all day, or sit listening in their homes or at the cross-roads to a recitation of some old romance or epic tale till it is time to retire to a well-earned rest.

Such has been the daily round of Indian village life in ancient times, and such it is today — simple hard, yet not altogether devoid of that intense beauty which only depth of thought expressed in the worship of Divine law can create.

The princes live to another code; different, however, only with the difference which wealth and riches bring, in no way else different at all. With them the ritual of food has been embellished with all the elegance and the splendour that refined thought can give. A kitchen is an important place in regal palaces and keeps open all day. Should you steal into one, you may shake hands with the greatest cooks of the land, or if you are lucky, and it is the day before a banquet, you may find the prince himself and the princesses of the royal house, having cast off the false cloak of vain dignity, busy cooking food for the hundred guests or more who are to sup with them at night. A hundred dishes are being cooked, spiced with all the spices that the fertile slopes of Indian hills supply. All follow the directions of their lord while he has his soul in each of the thousand pans and sits with vigilant care watching the operations. Withdraw from the royal kitchen, however, into the rooms of state where the food is to be dispensed. Here on a festival you will find seated a hundred guests or more (on an average day only a few less), rich officers of state, familiars of the palace, poor beggars whom the prince has probably picked up outside the palace gates, for most princes from ancient times till today have followed the custom of never dining alone and inviting any stranger to their fare who passes by the palace walls. The hands of the guests are washed. The prayers are said. The meal begins. The menu is large. There are ten curries or twenty, often one dish cooked in different ways. Each guest receives a big round tray on which plates are laid. The priest leads and the guests obey the gesture for a formal beginning. The prince serves with his own royal hands the rich and the poor alike. The meal is over. The plates are cleared away, the hands of the guests are washed, fragrant hookahs lit and betel leaves distributed to crown the taste of various food with the aroma of the sweetest flavour. The lutes are strung, soft music rises from the harps and sweet dancers dance a classic dance. Each guest receives a song after his heart's desire and life seems one long starry night of pleasure.

A culture in which kings cook and queens peel potatoes, in which each prince and peasant makes the good things of life and enjoys them only when he knows they conduce to the building of his higher nature, sounds like the culture of a land of dreams or of a fairy-tale. And yet it exists. Yes, it exists even in the heart of the individualist machine-ridden world of today. It exists, thank God, in India, where man and nature still rule the day and the machine has not yet wrought its ravages. The littleness and frivolity that are the bane of India's townsfolk may in some ways have robbed it of that simplicity which is the truth-loving peasant, or of that refinement which is the person of a native prince, but thank God that the ritual of food has, under the influence of that noble ideal of God as the Divine Mother dispensing food to a hungry humanity, been always relegated in India to women, and thank God that that glorious order of humanity which goes by the name of Indian womanhood has lived, through all the rigours of history, the guardian of that traditional etiquette and that beautiful ritual of the Indian home which still makes a day of Indian life the consummation of a Perfect Experience.

MULK RAJ ANAND
Curries and Other Indian Dishes

None Lives for Ever

None lives for ever, brother, and
nothing lasts for long. Keep that in
mind and rejoice.
Our life is not the one old burden,
our path is not the one long journey.
One sole poet has not to sign one
aged song.
The flower fades and dies; but he
who wears the flower has not to
mourn for it for ever.
Brother, keep that in mind and rejoice.

There must come a full pause to weave perfection into
music.
Life droops towards its sunset to be drowned in the
golden shadows.
Love must be called from its play to drink sorrow and
be borne to the heaven of tears.

Brother, keep that in mind and rejoice.

We hasten to gather our flowers lest they are plundered
    by the passing winds.
It quickens our blood and brightens our eyes to snatch
    kisses that would vanish if we delayed.
Our life is eager, our desires are keen, for time tolls the
    bell of parting.
Brother, keep that in mind and rejoice.
There is not time for us to clasp a thing and crush it and
    fling it away to the dust.
The hours trip rapidly away, hiding their dreams in their
    skirts.
Our life is short; it yields but a few days for love.
Were it for work and drudgery it would be endlessly long.
Brother, keep that in mind and rejoice.

Beauty is sweet to us, because she dances to the same
    fleeting tune with our lives.
Knowledge is precious to us, because we shall never have
    time to complete it.
All is done and finished in the eternal Heaven.
But earth's flowers of illusion are kept eternally fresh by
    death.
Brother, keep that in mind and rejoice.

RABINDRANATH TAGORE (1861-1941)
The Gardener

People Great and Small

"Brahmans for their lore have honour; Kshattriyas for
    their bravery;
Vaisyas for their hard-earned treasure; Sudras for
    humility."

NARAYANA
Hitopadesa (12th cent. A.D.)
(The Book of Good Counsels)
translated by SIR EDWIN ARNOLD

Buddha Saw

All things spoke peace and plenty, and the Prince
Saw and rejoiced. But, looking deep, he saw
The thorns which grow upon this rose of life;
How the swart peasant sweated for his wage,
Toiling for leave to live; and how he urged
The great-eyed oxen through the flaming hours,
Goading their velvet flanks; then marked he, too,
How lizard fed on ant, and snake on him,
And kite on both; and how the fish-hawk robbed
The fish-tiger of that which it had seized;
The shrike chasing the *bulbul*, which did hunt
The jewelled butterflies; till everywhere
Each slew a slayer and in turn was slain,
Life living upon death. So the fair show
Veiled one vast, savage, grim conspiracy
Of mutual murder, from the worm to man,
Who himself kills his fellow; seeing which —
The hungry ploughman and his labouring kine,
Their dewlaps blistered with the bitter yoke,
The rage to live which makes all living strife —
The Prince Siddârtha sighed. "Is this," he said,
"That happy earth they brought me forth to see?
How salt with sweat the peasant's bread! how hard
The oxen's service! in the brake how fierce
The war of weak and strong! i' th' air what plots!

No refuge e'en in water. Go aside
A space, and let me muse on what ye show."
So saying the good Lord Buddha seated him
Under a jambu-tree, with ankles crossed —
As holy statues sit — and first began
To meditate this deep disease of life,
What its far source and whence its remedy.

*

"Oh! suffering world;
Oh! known and unknown of my common flesh,
Caught in this common net of death and woe,
And life which binds to both! I see, I feel
The vastness of the agony of earth,
The vainness of its joys, the mockery
Of all its best, the anguish of its worst;
Since pleasures end in pain, and youth in age,
And love in loss, and life in hateful death,
And death in unknown lives which will but yoke
Men to their wheel again to whirl the round
Of false delights and woes that are not false.
Me too this lure hath cheated, so it seemed
Lovely to live, and life a sunlit stream
For ever flowing in a changeless peace;
Whereas the foolish ripple of the flood
Dances so lightly down by bloom and lawn
Only to pour its crystal quicklier
Into the foul salt sea. The veil is rent
Which blinded me! I am as all these men
Who cry upon their gods and are not heard,
Or are not heeded — yet there must be aid!
For them and me and all there must be help!
Perchance the gods have need of help themselves,
Being so feeble that when sad lips cry

They cannot save! I would not let one cry
Whom I could save! How can it be that Brahm
Would make a world and keep it miserable,
Since, if, all-powerful, he leaves it so,
He is not good, and if not powerful,
He is not God? — Channa! lead home again!
It is enough! mine eyes have seen enough!"

SIR EDWIN ARNOLD (1832-1904)
The Light of Asia

Asoka Proclaims

This saith king Priyadarsi, Beloved of the Gods [Asoka]. Twenty-six years after my coronation, I have declared the following species of animals exempt from slaughter, viz. parrots, mainas, ruddy geese, wild geese, nandimuk-has, gelatas, bats, queen-ants, terrapins, boneless fish, vedaveyakas, gangapuputakas, skate-fish, tortoises and porcupines, leaf-hares, twelve-antler stags, bulls set at liberty, household vermin, rhinoceroses, white pigeons, village pigeons and all the quadrupeds which are neither useful nor edible.

Those she-goats, ewes and sows, which are either pregnant or milch, are not to be slaughtered, nor their young ones which are less than six months old. Cocks are not to be caponed. Husks containing living beings should not be burnt. Forests must not be burnt either uselessly or in order to destroy living beings. The living must not be fed with the living.

At the three Chaturmasis and at the full-moon of the month of Tishya, for three days in each case, viz. the fourteenth and fifteenth of one fortnight and the first of the next, and invariably on every fast day, fish is exempt from slaughter and should not be sold. And on the same days, not only these but also other species of beings should not be killed in the elephant-forest and in the fishermen's preserves.

On the eighth of each fortnight and on the fourteenth and fifteenth, on the Tishya and Punarvasu days, on the three Chaturmasi days and on every auspicious day, bulls are not to be castrated. And he-goats, rams, boars, and such other animals as are usually castrated should not be castrated on those days. Horses and bullocks should not be branded on the Tishya and Punarvasu days, on the Chaturmasis and during the fortnights associated with the Chaturmasis.

Up to the time when I completed twenty-six years after my coronation, the release of prisoners has been ordered by me for twenty-five times during the period in question.

Inscriptions of Asoka (269-232 B. C.)
Pillar Edict 5
translated by D.C. SIRCAR

Kalidasa

An ancient heathen poet, loving more
God's creatures, and His women, and His flowers
Than we who boast of consecrated powers;
Still lavishing his unexhausted store
Of love's deep, simple wisdom, healing o'er
The world's old sorrows, India's griefs and ours;
That healing love he found in palace towers,
On mountain, plain, and dark, sea-belted shore,
In songs of holy Raghu's kingly line
Or sweet Shakuntala in pious grove,
In hearts that met where starry jasmines twine

Or hearts that from long, lovelorn absence strove
Together. Still his words of wisdom shine:
All's well with man, when man and woman love.

A.W. RYDER

Portrait of Akbar
(1556-1609)

My father used to hold discourse with learned men of all persuasions, particularly with the Pandits and the intelligent persons of Hindustán. Though he was illiterate, yet from constantly conversing with learned and clever persons, his language was so polished, that no one could discover from his conversation that he was entirely uneducated. He understood even the elegancies of poetry and prose so well, that it is impossible to conceive anyone more proficient. The following is a description of his person. He was of middling stature, but with a tendency to be tall, wheat-colour complexion, rather inclining to dark than fair, black eyes and eyebrows, stout body, open forehead and chest, long arms and hands. There was a fleshy wart, about the size of a small pea, on the left side of his nose, which appeared exceedingly beautiful, and which was considered very auspicious by physiognomists, who said that it was the sign of immense riches and increasing prosperity. He had a very loud voice, and a very elegant and pleasant way of speech. His manners and habits were quite different from those of other persons, and his visage was full of godly dignity.

Memoirs of Emperor Jahangir
translated by ELLIOT AND DOWSON

Kabir
(1440-1518)

I

Kabir's songs are of this kind: outbirths at once of rapture and of charity. Written in the popular Hindi, not in the literary tongue, they were deliberately addressed — like the vernacular poetry of Jacopone da Todi and Richard Rolle — to the people rather than to the professionally religious class; and all must be struck by the constant employment in them of imagery drawn from the common life, the universal experience. It is by the simplest metaphors, by constant appeals to needs, passions, relations which all men understand — the bridegroom and bride, the guru and disciple, the pilgrim, the farmer, the migrant bird — that he drives home his intense conviction of the reality of the soul's intercourse with the Transcendent. There are in his universe no fences between the "natural" and "supernatural" worlds; everything is a part of the creative Play of God, and therefore — even in its humblest details — capable of revealing the Player's mind.

*

Kabir belongs to that small group of supreme mystics — amongst whom St. Augustine, Ruysbroeck, and the Sufi poet Jalalu'ddin Rumi are perhaps the chief — who have achieved that which we might call the synthetic vision of God. These have resolved the perpetual opposition between the personal and impersonal, the transcendent and immanent, static and dynamic aspects of the Divine Nature; between the Absolute of philosophy and the "sure true Friend" of devotional religion. They have done this, not by taking these apparently incompatible_concepts one after the other; but by ascending to a height of spiritual intuition at which they are, as Ruysbroeck said, "melted and merged in the Unity," and perceived as the completing opposites of a perfect Whole. This proceeding entails for them — and both Kabir and Ruysbroeck expressly acknowledge it — a universe of three orders: Becoming, Being and that which is "More than Being," i.e. God. God is here felt to be not the final abstraction, but the one actuality. He inspires, supports, indeed inhabits, both the durational, conditioned, finite world of Becoming and the unconditioned, non-successional, infinite world of Being; yet utterly transcends them both. He is the omnipresent Reality, the 'All-pervading" within Whom "the worlds are being told beads." In His personal aspect He is the "beloved Fakir," teaching and companioning each soul. Considered as Immanent Spirit, He is "the Mind within the mind." But all these are at best partial aspects of His nature, mutually corrective: as the Persons in the Christian doctrine of the Trinity — to which this theological diagram bears a striking resemblance — represent different and compensating experiences of the Divine Unity within which they are resumed. As Ruysbroeck discerned a plane of reality upon which "we can speak no more of Father, Son, and Holy Spirit, but only of One Being, the very substance of the Divine Persons"; so Kabir says that "beyond both the limited *and* the limitless is He, the Pure Being."

EVELYN UNDERHILL

II

Turning away from the world I have forgotten both caste and lineage;

My weaving is now in the infinite silence.
I have now no quarrel with any one;

I have given up both the Pandits and the Mullas.
I weave clothes and I wear them myself;
Where I see no pride there I sing God's praises.
What the Pandits and the Mullas prescribed for me,
I have received no advantage from, and have abandoned.
My heart being pure I have seen the Lord;·
Kabir having searched and searched himself, hath found
    God within him.

KABIR (1440-1518)
translated by M.A. MACAULIFFE

Tulsi Das
(1532-1623)

The importance of Tulsi Das in the history of India cannot be over-rated. Putting the literary merits of his work out of the question, the fact of its universal acceptance by all classes, from Bhagalpur to the Panjab and from the Himalaya to the Narmada, is surely worthy of note. "The book is in everyone's hands, from the court to the cottage, and is read or heard and appreciated alike by every class of the Hindu community, whether high or low, rich or poor, young or old." It has been interwoven into the life, character, and speech of the Hindu population for more than three hundred years, and is not only loved and admired by them for its poetic beauty, but it is reverenced by them as their Scriptures. It is the Bible of a hundred millions of people and is looked upon by them as much inspired as the Bible is considered inspired by the English clergyman. Pandits may talk of the Vedas and of the Upanisads, and a few may even study them; others may say they pin their faith on the Puranas; but to the vast majority of the people of Hindustan, learned and unlearned alike, their sole form of conduct is the so-called *Tulsi-krit Ramayan*. It is indeed fortunate for Hindustan that this is so, for it has saved the country from the tantric obscenities of Shaivism. Ramanand was the original saviour of Upper India from the fate which has befallen Bengal, but Tulsi Das was the great apostle who carried his doctrine east and west and made it an abiding faith.

The religion he preached was a simple and sublime one, a perfect faith in the name of God. But what is most remarkable in it, in an age of immorality when the bonds of Hindu society were loosened and the Moghul empire being consolidated, was its stern morality in every sense of the word. Tulsi was the great preacher of one's duty towards one's neighbour. Valmiki praised Bharat's sense of duty, Lachhman's brotherly affection, and Sita's wifely devotion, but Tulsi taught them as an example.

SIR G.A. GRIERSON
Notes on Tulsi Das

Ram and Sita

They who love not Ram and Sita
Should be abandoned as if they were millions of enemies,
   however much we love them.
Prahlad abandoned his father, Bibhishan his brother Rawan,
   and Bharat his mother,
Bali his guru, the women of Brij their husbands, and their
   lives were all happier for having done so.

The opinion of all holly saints is that relations with and
  love of God are alone true.
Of what avail is the eye-salve which causeth the eyes to
  burst; what more can I say?
Saith Tulsi Das, that spouse is worshipful, that son is
  dearer than life,
Who is attached to Ram; he is my real friend in this world.

TULSI DAS
translated by M.A. MACAULIFFE

The Virtues are One's Family

Make wisdom thy mother, contentment thy father,
Truth thy brother — this is best.
People talk, but talking is of no avail.
The measure of Thy might, O God, cannot be obtained.
Modesty and attention are my two parents-in-law;
Good works I have accepted as my spouse;
Union with saints hath been my auspicious time for
Marriage, and separation from the world my wedding.
Saith Nanak, from such a union sprung truth as my
  offspring.

NANAK (1469-1538)
translated by M.A. MACAULIFFE

So Have I Lived

I have known want and woe and fear;
I have known this world to be a House of Pain,
  of sad bereavement and decay;
I have known a father's grief for his dead sons;
I have loved life but dreaded life itself;
I have seen merit unrewarded go;
I have seen golden garlands worn round pariah donkeys'
  necks;
I have seen a royal charger gall his back with a pack pony's
  load;
I have seen fools drink *sherbet* of rose-water and candy
  loaf;
I have seen the wise suck their own heart's blood;
I have seen a poet, a courtier at the court, strut peacock-
  like;
I have seen a poet, loved of the people, beg for a pittance
  from the King;
I have been a helpless witness of man killing man in civil
  strife and mutiny;
I have watched an Empire falling to decay and dying;
I have watched an Emperor taken captive and exiled to
  an alien land;
I have felt old foundations shifting as on sand and crashing.
So have I lived and passed my days.
How can I bring myself to say that God exists,
God the Bounteous Giver, God the Beneficent?
For God's possible for those who lead happy sheltered
  lives,
And know God's grace and his loving care.

MIRZA GHALIB (1797-1869)
translated by J.L. KAUL

If it Lay in My Will

Enough of this sun-and-moon-neighbouring glory —
Enough of this office of heralding dawn!
Unblessed are to me the abodes of the planets,
A lowly earth-dwelling is more than these heights;
No heaven is my home, but a tenantless void,
Dawn's skirt of the hundred-fold rent is my shroud;
To live and die daily my fate, to be poured
The morning-draught first by the cupbearer Death.
Worthless this service, this splendour, this dignity,
— Better take darkness than shine for one hour!

No star would I be, if it lay in my will,
But a gleaming white pearl in the water's deep bed;
And then, if too fearful the strife of the waves,
Leave ocean behind, and adorn some fair neck;
To shine as the pendant of beauty is bliss,
As a gem in the crown of an Emperor's consort!
A fragment of stone, when its destiny smiled,
Could be set in the ring on the finger of Solomon.
But of all such in this world the glory must perish,
Must perish the jewel whose worth is a ransom;
To live, is to have no acquaintance of death:
The thing that can feel death's demand, has no life.

If death be the end, let me rather, adorning
That earth-realm, be changed to a flower-falled dewdrop,
Or speck in the bridal gold-dust on some forehead,
Or spark that the sighs of some troubled heart waft.
Or why should I not be the teardrop that rolls
On the long lashes fringing the eyes of a lady
Whose lord, in chain armour enmeshed, has departed
To battle, by love of his country compelled —

A woman whose face is a picture where hope
And despair are in combat, whose silence shames speech,
Whose patience is built on her husband's firm will,
Whose looks from their modesty borrow their eloquence;
— At the hour of farewell when the rosy cheek pales
And the sorrow of parting makes beauty more beautiful.
There, though she locked up her heart, would I gleam,
One waterdrop spilled from her eye's brimming cup,
To find in the dust an immortal new life,
And teach to the world the long passion of love.

IQBAL (1873-1938)
Poems from Iqbal
translated by V.G. KIERNAN

Vivekananda

(1863-1902)

A Hindu Missionary in the West

Indian philosophy has in recent years had a deep and growing fascination for many minds, though up to the present time its expònents in this country have been entirely Western in their thought and training, with the result that very little is really known of the deeper mysteries of the Vedanta wisdom, and that little only by a select few. Not many have the courage or the intuition to seek in heavy translations, made greatly in the interests of philologists, for that sublime knowledge which they really reveal to an able exponent brought up in all the traditions of the East.

It was therefore with interest and not without some curiosity, writes a correspondent, that I proceeded to interview an exponent entirely novel to Western people, in the person of the Swami Vivekananda, an actual Indian Yogi, who has boldly undertaken to visit the Western world to expound the traditional teaching which has been handed down by ascetics and Yogis through many ages, and who in pursuance of this object, delivered a lecture last night in the Princes' Hall.

The Swami Vivekananda is a striking figure with his turban (or mitre-shaped black cloth cap) and his calm but kindly features.

On my inquiring as to the significance, if any, of his name, the Swami said: — "Of the name by which I am now known (Swami Vivekananda), the first word is descriptive of a Sannyâsin, or one who formally renounces the world, and the second is the title I assumed — as is customary with all Sannyâsins — on my renunciation of the world; it signifies, literally, the bliss of discrimination."

"And what induced you to forsake the ordinary course of the world, Swami?" I asked.

"I had a deep interest in religion and philosophy from my childhood," he replied, "and our books teach renunciation as the highest ideal to which man can aspire. It only needed the meeting with a great Teacher — Ramakrishna Paramahamsa — to kindle in me the final determination to follow the path he himself had trod, as in him I found my highest ideal realised."

"Then did he found a sect, which you now represent?"

"No," replied the Swami quickly. "No, his whole life was spent in breaking down the barriers of sectarianism and dogma. He formed no sect. Quite the reverse. He advocated and strove to establish absolute freedom of thought. He was a great Yogi."

"Then you are connected with no society or sect in this country? Neither Theosophical nor Christian Scientist, nor any other?"

"None whatever!" said the Swami in clear and impressive tones. (His face lights up like that of a child, it is so simple, straightforward and honest.) "My teaching is my own interpretation of our ancient books, in the light which my Master shed upon them. I claim no supernatural authority. Whatever in my teaching may appeal to the highest intelligence and be accepted by thinking men, the adoption of that will be my reward." "All religions," he continued, "have for their object the teaching either of devotion, knowledge, or Yoga, in a concrete form. Now, the philosophy of Vedanta is the abstract science which embraces all these methods, and this it is that I teach, leaving each one to apply it to his own concrete form. I refer each individual to his own experiences, and where reference is made to books, the latter are procurable, and may be studied by each one for himself. Above all, I teach no authority proceeding from hidden beings speaking through visible agents, any more than I claim learning from hidden books or manuscripts. I am the exponent of no occult societies, nor do I believe that good can come of such bodies. Truth stands on its own authority, and truth can bear the light of day."

"Then you do not propose to form any society, Swami?" I suggested.

"None; no society whatever. I teach only the Self, hidden in the heart of every individual and common to all. A handful of strong men knowing that Self and living in Its light would revolutionise the world, even today, as has been the case by single strong men before, each in his day." "Have you just arrived from India?" I inquired — for the Swami is suggestive of Eastern suns.

"No," he replied, "I represented the Hindu religion at the Parliament of Religions held at Chicago in 1893. Since then I have been travelling and lecturing in the United States. The American people have proved most interested audiences and sympathetic friends, and my work there has so taken root that I must shortly return to that country?"

"And what is your attitude towards the Western religions, Swami?"

"I propound a philosophy which can serve as a basis to every possible religious system in the world, and my attitude towards all of them is one of extreme sympathy — my teaching is antagonistic to none. I direct my attention to the individual, to make him strong, to teach him that he himself is divine, and I call upon men to make themselves conscious of this divinity within. That is really the ideal — conscious or unconscious — of every religion."

"And what shape will your activities take in this country."

"My hope is to imbue individuals with the teachings to which I have referred, and to encourage them to express them to others in their own way; let them modify them as they will; I do not teach them as dogmas; truth at length must inevitably prevail.

"The actual machinery through which I work is in the hands of one or two friends. On October 22nd, they have arranged for me to deliver an address to a British audience at Princes' Hall, Piccadilly, at 8.30 p.m. The event is being advertised. The subject will be on the key of my philosophy — 'Self-Knowledge.' Afterwards I am prepared to follow any course that opens — to attend meetings in people's drawing-rooms or elsewhere, to answer letters, or discuss personally. In a mercenary age I may venture to remark that none of my activities are undertaken for a pecuniary reward."

I then took my leave from one of the most original of men that I have had the honour of meeting.

The Westminster Gazette
23 October 1895

I Have Loved This World

I

I have never put trust in my deeds
But only in my self —
For I know the relentless waves of eternal Time
Will wash those deeds away.
Morning and night,
Filling my soul's chalice with divine nectar,
I have drunk it.
The love I have cherished every moment
Has been garnered in that cup —
The burden of sorrow has not cracked it,
Nor the dust blackened its handicraft.
When I leave the stage of life,
I know that season after season
The flowers shall bear witness
How I have loved this world.
This love, this gift of life
Alone is true;
When I depart,
This undying truth shall confute death.

RABINDRANATH TAGORE (1861-1941)
Wings of Death

II

O Poet,
Take your last ablution
In the limpid waters of the emergent night.
This toiling earth has served you,
Has nourished you,
But do not cling to her.

She has no hesitation to take away
What once she gave you.
The reward that you received at the outer gate —
Do not clutch it to your heart.
The gilding of the coin will wear away with time,
Revealing the stain within.
If you have cultivated the fruit in your orchard,
Let it find its end dropping to the earth.
The season of flowers is ended —
So let also end
Your being swayed by the breath of human flattery.

While marching forward,
Do not turn back and stretch out your hands.
In life,
What you gave truly,
Insult it not by asking for a price.
Let your begging bowl be your last offering,
Like withered leaves that greet the Spring.

That for which you are waiting
With hope in your heart,
Is not glory —
It is the silent call of dawn to the new life;
It is the crown of morning light
On the brow of the newly awakened.

RABINDRANATH TAGORE (1861-1941)
Wings of Death

Muhammad Ali Jinnah
(1876-1948)

Sayyid Ahmad Khan proclaimed the separateness of Muslims and reconciled them to the West. Iqbal gave them a dynamic faith and a sense of mission. Once more they looked forward. But the further they looked, the more widely the path diverged from their fellow Indians. Then came Muhammad Ali Jinnah (1876-1948) to provide political form to this movement of life and spirit. Ahmad was the philosopher, Iqbal the prophet, and Jinnah the statesman-creator of Pakistan. A lawyer from western India of impeccable Western dress and taste, the young Jinnah began as a Muslim Nationalist supporter of Congress. He was disillusioned by Gandhi's non-co-operation campaigns, but as late as 1937 he contemplated co-operation with the Congress in coalition ministries. It was only when the Congress leaders made it clear that for them cooperation meant absorption that his opposition became unrelenting. From then onward he was implacable. He saw no choice for Muslims between absorption into Hinduism or separation. Therefore separation it had to be. He adopted the Pakistan concept in 1940 and pursued his goal with remorseless logic and flawless skill. By 1945 no Indian settlement was possible without Jinnah's consent.

This maker of a nation was slight in build and precise in manner. He was the reverse of a demagogue or a fanatic, yet he could fan fanaticism and arouse popular passion. He was so little in touch with his own culture that he could not speak Urdu. He despised the mob and hated disorder. His disdain for the people whom he led and the implicit devotion with which they repaid him remind one of the Protestant Parnell leading the Catholic Irish towards Home Rule. In both cases

there was a formal manner and icy aloofness; in Jinnah there
was also a fund of cold logic, a quietude of manner, and a
Western sartorial elegance which suggested anything rather
than the fiery conviction of a prophet. But behind this daunting
and uninspiring facade lay keen ambition, pride of achievement,
an iron will, and a certain icy passion. Most men in anger
are heated and confused; Jinnah was colder and clearer than
ever. Such men are formidable when aroused because they are
implacable and remorseless. From the day that the Congress
broke faith with the League (as he considered) after the
elections of 1937, his political passion was continuous. And
it was remorseless against the Muslim Nationalists, whom he
regarded as traitors and whose leader had penned the fatal
message. This was the man who controlled the Muslims even
more fully than Gandhi controlled the Congress. In both cases
there were dissenting minorities and in both cases they were
powerless.

PERCIVAL SPEAR
India

The First Shock

Though I thus began to make both ends meet, I got the
first shock of my life about this time. I had heard what
a British officer was like, but up to now had never been face
to face with one.

My brother had been secretary and adviser to the late
Ranasaheb of Porbandar before he was installed on his *gadi,*
and hanging over his head at this time was the charge of
having given wrong advice when in that office. The matter
had gone to the Political Agent who was prejudiced against

my brother. Now I had known this officer when in England, and he may be said to have been fairly friendly to me. My brother thought that I should avail myself of the friendship and, putting in a good word on his behalf, try to disabuse the Political Agent of his prejudice. I did not at all like this idea. I should not, I thought try to take advantage of a trifling acquaintance in England. If my brother was really at fault, what use was my recommendation? If he was innocent, he should submit a petition in the proper course and, confident of his innocence, face the result. My brother did not relish this advice. "You do not know Kathiawad," he said, "and you have yet to know the world. Only influence counts here. It is not proper for you, a brother to shirk your duty, when you can clearly put in a good word about me to an officer you know."

I could not refuse him, so I went to the officer much against my will. I knew I had no right to approach him and was fully conscious that I was compromising my self-respect. But I sought an appointment and got it. I reminded him of the old acquaintance, but I immediately saw that Kathiawad was different from England; that an officer on leave was not the same as an officer on duty. The Political Agent owned the acquaintance, but the reminder seemed to stiffen him. "Surely you have not come here to abuse that acquaintance, have you?" appeared to be the meaning of that stiffnes, and seemed to be written on his brow. Nevertheles I opened my case. The *sahib* was impatient. "Your brother is an intriguer. I want to hear nothing more from you. I have no time. If your brother has anything to say, let him apply through the proper channel." The answer was enough, was perhaps deserved. But selfishness is blind. I went on with my story. The *sahib* got up and said: "You must go now."

"But please hear me out," said I. That made him more angry. He called his peon and ordered him to show me the door. I was still hesitating when the peon came in, placed his hands on my shoulders and put me out of the room.

The *sahib* went away as also the peon, and I departed, fretting and fuming. I at once wrote out and sent over a note to this effect: "You have insulted me. You have assaulted me through your peon. If you make no amends, I shall have to proceed against you."

Quick came the answer through his *sowar:*

"You were rude to me. I asked you to go and you would not. I had no option but to order my peon to show you the door. Even after he asked you to leave the office, you did not do so. He therefore had to use just enough force to send you out. You are at liberty to proceed as you wish."

With this answer in my pocket, I came home crestfallen, and told my brother all that had happened. He was grieved, but was at a loss as to how to console me. He spoke to his vakil friends. For I did not know how to proceed against the *sahib*. Sir Pherozeshah Mehta happened to be in Rajkot at this time, having come down from Bombay for some case. But how could a junior barrister like me dare to see him? So I sent him the papers of my case, through the vakil who had engaged him, and begged for his advice. "Tell Gandhi," he said, "such things are the common experience of many vakils and barristers. He is still fresh from England, and hot-blooded. He does not know British officers. If he would earn something and have an easy time here, let him tear up the note and pocket the insult. He will gain nothing by proceeding against the *sahib,* and on the contrary will very likely ruin himself. Tell him he has yet to know life."

The advice was as bitter as poison to me, but I had to swallow it. I pocketed the insult, but also profited by it. "Never again shall I place myself in such a false position, never again shall I try to exploit friendship in this way," said I to myself, and since then I have never been guilty of a breach of that determination. This shock changed the course of my life.

MAHATMA GANDHI (1869-1948)
My Experiments with Truth

Truth is God

I do not regard God as a person. Truth for me is God, and God's Law and God are not different things or facts, in the sense that an earthly king and his law are different. Because God is an Idea, Law Himself. Therefore, it is impossible to conceive God as breaking the Law. He, therefore, does not rule our actions and withdraw Himself. When we say He rules our actions, we are simply using human language and we try to limit Him. Otherwise, He and His Law abide everywhere and govern everything. Therefore, I do not think that He answers in every detail every request of ours, but there is no doubt that He rules our action and I literally believe that not a blade of grass grows or moves without His will.

MAHATMA GANDHI (1869-1948)
Young India

The Imperfect Mahatma

One great reason for the misunderstanding lies in my being considered almost a perfect man. Friends who know my partiality for the Bhagavad-Gita have thrown relevant verses at me, and shown how my threat to commit suicide contradicts the teaching which I am attempting to live. All these mentors of mine seem to forget that I am but a seeker after Truth. I claim to have found the way to it. I claim to be making a ceaseless effort to find it. But I admit that I have not yet found it. To find Truth completely is to realise oneself and one's destiny, i.e. to become perfect. I am painfully conscious of my imperfection, and therein lies all the strength I possess, because it is a rare thing for a man to know his own limitations.

MAHATMA GANDHI (1869-1948)
Young India

The Variety and Unity of India

The diversity of India is tremendous; it is obvious; it lies on the surface and anybody can see it. It concerns itself with physical appearances as well as with certain mental habits and traits. There is little in common, to outward seeming, between the Pathan of the North-West and the Tamil in the far South. Their racial stocks are not the same, though there may be common strands running through them; they differ in face and figure, food and clothing, and, of course language. In the North-Western Frontier Province there is already the breath of Central Asia, and many a custom there, as in Kashmire, reminds one of the countries on the other side of the Himalayas. Pathan popular dances are singularly like Russian Cossack dancing. Yet, with all these differences, there is no mistaking the impress of India on the Pathan, as this is obvious on the Tamil. This is not surprising, for these border lands, and indeed Afghanistan also, were united with India for thousands of years. The old Turkish and other races who inhabited Afghanistan and parts of Central Asia before the advent of Islam were largely Buddhists, and earlier still, during the period of the Epics, Hindus. The frontier area was one of the principal centres of old Indian culture and it abounds still with ruins of monuments and monasteries and, especially, of the great university of Taxila, which was at the height of its fame two thousand years ago, attracting students from all over India as well as different parts of Asia. Changes of religion made a difference but could not change entirely the mental backgrounds which the people of those areas had developed.

The Pathan and the Tamil are two extreme examples; the others lie somewhere in between. All of them have their distinctive features, all of them have still more the distinguishing mark of India. It is fascinating to find how the Bengalis, the Marathas, the Gujratis, the Tamils, the Andhras, the Oriyas, the Assamese, the Canarese, the Malayalis, the Sindhis, the Punjabis, the Pathans, the Kashmiris, the Rajputs, and the great central block comprising the Hindustani-speaking people, have retained their peculiar characteristics for hundreds of years, have still more or less the same virtues and failings of which old tradition or record tells us, and yet have been throughout these ages distinctively Indian, with the same national heritage and the same set of moral and mental qualities. There was something living and dynamic about this heritage which showed itself in ways of living and a philosophical attitude to life and its problems. Ancient India, like ancient China, was a world in itself, a culture and a civilisation which gave shape to all things. Foreign influences poured in and often influenced that culture and were absorbed. Disruptive tendencies gave rise immediately to an attempt to find a synthesis. Some kind of a dream of unity has occupied the mind of India since the dawn of civilisation. That unity was not conceived as something imposed from outside, a standardisation of externals or even of beliefs. It was something deeper and, within its fold, the widest tolerance of belief and custom was practised and every variety acknowledged and even encouraged.

Differences, big or small, can always be noticed even within a national group, however closely bound together it may be. The essential unity of that group becomes apparent when it is compared to another national group, though often the differences between two adjoining groups fade out or intermingle near the frontiers, and modern developments are tending to produce a certain uniformity everywhere. In ancient and mediaevel times, the idea of the modern nation was non-existent, and feudal, religious, racial, or cultural bonds had more importance. Yet I think that at almost any time in recorded history an Indian would have felt more or less at home in any part of India, and would have felt as a stranger and alien in any other country. He would certainly have felt less of a stranger in countries which had partly adopted his culture or religion. Those who professed a religion of non-Indian origin or, coming to India, settled down there, became distinctively Indian in the course of a few generations, such as Christians, Jews, Parsees, Moslems. Indian converts to some of these religions never ceased to be Indians on account of a change of their faith. They were looked upon in other countries as Indians and foreigners, even though there might have been a community of faith between them.

J.L. NEHRU (1889-1964)
The Discovery of India

A Noble Man

In good fortune not elated, in ill-fortune not dismayed,
Ever eloquent in council, never in the fight affrayed —
Proudly emulous of honour, steadfastly on wisdom set;
Perfect virtues in the nature of a noble soul are met.
Whoso hath them, gem and glory of the three wide worlds
    is he;
Happy mother she that bore him, she who nursed him
    on her knee.

*

Noble hearts are golden vases — close the bond true
    metals make;
Easily the smith may weld them, harder far it is to break.
Evil hearts are earthen vessels — at a touch they crack
    a-twain,
And what craftsman's ready cunning can unite the shards
    again?

*

Anger comes to noble natures, but leaves there no strife
    or storm:
Plunge a lighted torch beneath it, and the ocean grows
    not warm.

NARAYANA
Hitopadesa (12th cent. A.D.)
(The Book of Good Counsels)
translated by SIR EDWIN ARNOLD

Leader

Whoso hath the gift of giving wisely, equitably, well;
Whoso, learning all men's secrets, unto none his own will
    till:

Whoso, ever cold and courtly, utters nothing that offends,
Such an one may rule his fellows unto Earth's extremest
    ends.

> NARAYANA
> *Hitopadesa* (12th cent. A.D.)
> *(The Book of Good Counsels)*
> translated by SIR EDWIN ARNOLD

Good Men

Fruit-laden bend down to earth;
The water-pregnant clouds hang low;
Good men are not puffed up by power —
The unselfish are by nature so.

A good man never lets grief get the upper hand.
The mountains are calm even in a tempest.

> KALIDASA (*c.* A.D. 400-500)
> *Shakuntala*
> translated by A.W. RYDER

Maiden's Love

Here stands the eager lover, and you pale
For fear lest he disdain a love so kind:
The seeker may find fortune, or may fail;
But how could fortune, seeking, fail to find?

The ardent lover comes, and yet you fear

Lest he disdain love's tribute, were it brought,
The hope of which has led his footsteps here —
Pearls need not seek, for they themselves are sought.

Though deeply longing, maids are coy
And bid their wooers wait;
Though eager for united joy
In love, they hesitate.

Love cannot torture them, nor move
Their hearts to sudden mating;
Perhaps they even torture love
By their procrastinating.

KALIDASA (c. A.D. 400-500)
Shakuntala
translated by A.W. RYDER

The Young Bride

The boat is sailing upstream
And darkness descends on the horizon.
O girl-bride! To which village do you sail?
The festival flute has filled the twilight sky
With tender melodies of the *multan*.
Your girl-companions have dressed you
In robes of crimson,
Secretly drying their tears.

The ripple of the waves
Seems to babble to the winds:
"Countless brides have sailed this way,
Gazing at yonder bank."

The Lord of Destiny did not utter a word,
His eyes rested upon the bride
Trembling with fear and bashfulness,
And as helmsman took his seat
Invisible on the barque.

From the known to the unknown sails the girl-bride,
Swaying between tears and smiles.
Leaving one home she has to find a new
In the heart of the unknown.
Look, yonder village waits for you!
Make haste to reach it before night-fall.
Through what countless centuries
Have not apprehensive brides
Crowded that landing place.

Generation after generation,
This eternal stream of the transitory, the fugitive,
Has written its history, leaving on record
The nameless deeds of the forgotten.
Age after age has been threaded together
By the stream of life,
Which left no mark behind.
If one received pain,
No wound is there to show it —
Death, the great healer, having blotted it out.

Therefore the twilight
Has spread hope on your path,
And whispered in your ears:
"She alone is happy
Who has filled her heart with love.
Cruel unhappiness
And parting lie ahead;
And yet your days will be full

And without regrets, if you can say:
'With light did I kindle my life,
With my all have I loved.'"

RABINDRANATH TAGORE (1861-1941)
The Herald of Spring
translated by AUROBINDO BOSE

On Becoming a Wife

My child, when you have entered your husband's home,
Obey your elders; and be very kind
To rivals; never be perversely blind
And angry with your husband, even though he
Should prove less faithful than a man might be;
Be as courteous to servants as you may,
Not puffed with pride in this your happy day:
Thus does a maiden grow into a wife;
But self-willed women are the curse of life.

KALIDASA (*c.* A.D. 400-500)
Shakuntala
translated by A.W. RYDER

Woman

Woman, you are blest!
You have your home, your household work —
In the midst of it you keep a little gap
Through which you hear the cry of the weak.

You bring your offering of service
And pour out your love.
Woman! you hear day and night the call
of the goddess of life,
Who in her mind bears the power of serving.
You have taken upon yourself the Creator's work
And are His helper.
You open the way to recovery
And ever renew the out-worn world;
For the unfortunate, the luckless,
Your patience is endless —
Their helplessness calls out your mercy.
Again and again, the callous, the intolerant
Insult you;
Wiping your tears away
You forgive them.
With bowed head, at ingratitude's door,
Night and day you suffer wounds.
The hapless and useless one,
Whom the goddess of life throws as waste away,
You lift up,
And the heat of his humiliation
You cool with soothing hands.

To him you give worship as to a god
And your nursing care!
Quietly, bravely, in beauty's form,
You carry within you
The preserving force of the universe,
And for the fallen, the broken, the deformed,
The gracious touch of the Lovely One!

RABINDRANATH TAGORE (1861-1941)
Recovery

The Peasants

The dwarf barefooted, chanting
Behind the oxen by the lake,
Stepping lightly and lazily among the thorn trees
Dusky and dazed with sunlight, half awake;

The women breaking stones upon the highway,
Walking erect with burdens on their heads,
One body growing in another body,
Creation touching verminous straw beds.

Across scorched hills and trampled crops
The soldiers straggle by,
History staggers in their wake.
The peasants watch them die.

ALUN LEWIS

The Indian Fortune-Teller

He comes with mystic air
In flowing turmeric robes
With strings and strings of beads
And ear-rings on his lobes.
"I tell it Master's fortune,"
He says in accents mild,
"You'll have it too much money
And plenty wife and child."

He places on my palm
A dirty string of dice

And tells me all my past
As he heard it from the *Syce**.

He speaks of great promotion
Of lucky stars and bad
He tells me where I'll go
And just when I'll be "had".

He gives the same old yarn
And tells me very soon,
I'll be pompous General
On the "thirty-first" of June!

L. H. NIBLETT
India in Fable, Verse and Story

The Beggar

He comes —
Breaking the heart into pieces, ruefully regretting on the
    road.
Stomach and back are one.
He walks on his crutches,
For a handful of grain to satisfy his hunger
He spreads out his torn old handbag.
Breaking the heart into pieces, ruefully regretting on the
    road.
He had two children with him, always spreading their
    hands.
They rub their stomachs with the left hand,
Spread out to get a little sympathy is the right hand.

---

* Syce=groom

Jama Masjid, Delhi

Jaigarh and Amer Valley

Manikarnika Ghat, Varanasi

Ceremonial Elephant, Kerala

Moharram — Tazia

Sangam, Allahabad

Surya Namaskar — Yogasana

Baburnama

Stone Carvings, Mahabalipuram

Jaisalmer Temple

When the lips are dried with hunger,
What can cruel fate do or the giver?
They are satisfied with drops of fear
They are licking left-overs, while standing on the road,
The dogs are also bent upon snatching that.

NIRALA
translated by N. N. BANERJI

A Tamil Coolie Girl

Wrapped in your cloth of scarlet,
And bodice of vivid blue,
Jangling bangles glittering
In every dazzling hue.

Your head is tilted proudly,
Your hair is a glossy sheen,
You walk with an air of greatness,
No coolie, but some young queen.

Primitive are you ... simple,
And of knowledge you have none,
Whence comes this air of royalty,
As you walk in scorching sun?

What mystery are you I wonder?
Ignorant and young and slow,
Yet dignified and charming,
As on your way you go.

E. M. JONES
Poems of South India (1935)

The Patwari and Patel

Historian of the Ryot, he who keeps
The books which show to whom each field belongs,
Its mortgages and transfers; who in heaps
Of figures chronicles its rights and wrongs
Of fortune when the harvest fails, or when
A child is born or dies; Historian and
Accountant, one whose honesty of pen
Means much to all who cultivate the land;
A registrar of births and deaths and tillage —
Is the Patwari of the Indian village.

You know him by his spectacles and air
Of education, and he looks well fed.
That is the old Patel, with snow-white hair
And grand old face; he is the village head —
Collects the dues of Government, and rules
The roost on lines and laws which never change.
To him new-fangled notions, such as Schools
And Vaccination, are as ogres strange:
Yet must he feed their maw; his aim and work are
To make all things go smooth and please the Sirkar.

LUNKAH
Whiffs (1891)

Humour and Sentiment

Women

"Nearest to the King is dearest, be thy merit low or high;
Women, creeping plants, and princes, twice round that
which groweth nigh."

NARAYANA
Hitopadesa (12th cent. A.D.)
(*The Book of Good Counsels*)
translated by SIR EDWIN ARNOLD

Knowledge of Women

A monk who has left his mother and father and all
worldly ties, determines to walk about alone and wise,
to abstain from sexual pleasures, and to ask for a secluded
place where to lodge.

With clever pretences women make up to him, however
foolish they be; they know how to contrive that some monks
will become intimate with them.

They will often sit down at his side; they always put on
fine clothes; they will show him the lower part of their body,
and the armpit, when lifting up their arms, so that he will
follow them about.

And occasionally a woman will tempt him to a comfortable

couch or bed. But he should know these things to be as many traps under various disguises.

*

When a monk breaks the law, dotes on a woman, and is absorbed by that passion, she afterwards scolds him, lifts her foot, and tramples on his head.

"O monk, if you will not live with me as a woman who has still her hair, I shall tear it out; but do not live separated from me."

But when they have captured him, they send him on all sorts of errands: "Look for the bodkin to carve the bottle-gourd, fetch some nice fruits.

"Bring wood to cook the vegetables, or that we may light a fire at night; paint my feet, come and meanwhile rub my back!

"Look after my clothes, bring food and drink, get me some perfume, a broom, a barber to shave my head!

"Give me the collyrium-box, my ornaments, the lute, Lôdhra-powder, a Lôdhra-flower, the Vênupalâsika-lute, a pill!

"A Utpalakushta, Tagara-powder, and aloe pounded together with Usira, oil for anointing the face, baskets of bamboo wickerwork to put my things in!

"Reach me the lip-salve, fetch the umbrella and slippers, the knife to cut the string, have my robe dyed bluish!

"Give me the pot to cook the vegetables in, Myrobalans, the jar to fetch water in, the stick to paint the mark upon the forehead, the pin to apply collyrium to the eyelids, or the fan when it is hot!

"Fetch me the pincers, the comb, the ribbon to bind up the hair, reach me the looking-glass, put the toothbrush near me!

"Fetch me areca-nut and betel, needle and thread, the chamber-pot, the winnowing basket, the mortar, the pot for liquefying natron!

"Give me the vessel used in worshipping the gods, the water-pot. Friend, dig a privy. Fetch the bow for our son, the bullock for the Srâmanêra!

"The small pot, the drum, and the ball of cloth for the boy to play with. Sramana, the rainy season is at hand, look after the house and the stores!

"Fetch the chair with woven twine seat, the wooden shoes to walk on!" Pregnant women order their husbands about like slaves to fulfil their cravings.

When a son, the reward of their wedded life, is born, the mother bids the father to hold the baby, or to give it her. Thus some supporters of their sons have to carry burdens like camels.

Getting up in the night they lull the baby asleep like nurses; and though they are ashamed of themselves, they wash the clothes like washermen.

This has been done by many men who for the sake of pleasures have stooped so low; they become the equals of slaves, animals, servants, beasts of burden — mere nobodies.

One should not mind the entreaties of women, but abstain from their friendship and company. These pleasures which are derived therefrom are called causes of blamable actions.

Jaina Sutras (*Sutrakritanga*) (*c.* 300 B.C.)
translated by H. JACOBI

Two Types of Women

There is a country called Trigarta. In it lived three householders with much accumulated capital; they were brothers, and their names were Dhanaka, Dhanayaka, and Dhunyaka. During their lifetime Indra sent no rain for twelve years: the grain drooped; plants failed to seed; trees bore no fruit; the clouds were barren; rivers dwindled; swamps were mere mudholes; many springs went dry; bulbs, roots, and fruit grew scarce; story-telling declined; social pleasures fell into disuse; robber bands multiplied; anthropophagy appeared; human skulls, white as cranes, rolled underfoot; thirsty crows migrated in clouds; cities, villages, towns, and other settlements decayed.

When these householders had exhausted their store of grain, and had eaten in turn the goats and sheep, the drove of buffalo, the herd of cows, the maidservants, the manservants, the children, the eldest and the middle wife, they agreed to eat next day the youngest wife, Dhumini. But Dhunyaka, the youngest brother, unable to eat his darling, fled with her that same night. Carrying her when she grew weary, he plunged into a forest. Relieving her hunger and thirst with his own flesh and blood, he carried her, until in mid-journey he encountered a man writhing on the forest floor, with hands and feet and ears and nose cut off. This man too he charitably took on his shoulder, and in a forest nook abounding in bulbs, roots, and deer he laboriously thatched a hut of leaves where he lived a long time. He treated the pitiful mutilations with oil of almonds and sesame, and shared his own meat and vegetables equally.

One day, when the wounds were healed and vigour had returned, when Dhunyaka had gone to hunt deer, Dhumini approached the man with sexual desire, and for all his upbraiding, forced him to satisfy her. When her husband returned and asked for water, she tossed him the bucket and rope, saying: "Draw your own drink; my head aches." Then, as he drew water from the well, she gave him a quick push from behind.

She put the cripple on her shoulder and wandered from land to land, winning the name of a devoted wife and a variety of honours. Finally she settled down in immense affluence through the favour of His Majesty of Avanti. Presently she learned that her husband, accidentally discovered and rescued by thirsty merchants, was roaming Avanti, begging his bread. So Dhumini deposed that he was the wretch who had mutilated her lord, and had that saintly character condemned by the unwitting king to torture and death.

But when Dhunyaka was being led to execution, his arms bound behind his back — since a prolongation of life was predestined, he cheerfully said to the functionary: "If the beggar whom I am supposed to have mutilated is prepared to speak ill of me, my punishment is deserved." "No harm in trying," said the officer, summoned the cripple, and presented him. That upright fellow wept profusely, fell at the saintly feet, and gave a true relation of the man's charity and the woman's vile behaviour. The king, enraged, disfigured the trollop's face and appointed her cook for the dogs, while Dhunyaka became the recipient of his favour. And that is why I say that woman's heart may be callous.

*

In the Dravidian country is a city called Kanchi, where lived Shaktikumara, the multi-millionaire son of a merchant. As he approached the age of eighteen, he anxiously reflected: "There is no true happiness for a man without a wife, or with a wife who lacks the appropriate virtues. Now how could I find a virtuous wife?"

So, diffident of the problematical satisfaction in a wife recommended by others, he became a fortune-teller, tucked a measure of rice in his garment's hem, and roamed the earth. Now those who had daughters exhibited their daughters to him as a man who could interpret stigmata. But whatever the stigmata, he would say whenever he saw a girl of his own caste: "My good girl, can you feed me properly with this measure of rice?" As a result, he wandered from house to house, ridiculed and rejected.

In a city on the right bank of the Kaveri in the Shibi country, he one day inspected a maiden presented by her nurse. She was meagrely begemmed, for she with her parents had run through a great property, though still possessing a dilapidated mansion. When he set eyes on her, he thought: "In the case of this girl, not a single member is too fat or too thin, too short or too long, lacking in symmetry or purity of outline. The fingers have a tinge of pink; the hands are marked with many stigmata of fortune — the barley-corn, the fish, the lotus, the bowl, and others. The ankle joints are even; the feet plump, not stringy. The calves have a classic curve; and the knees slip almost unobserved into the swell of the thighs. The hips are balanced, regular, sweetly set, and shaped like chariot wheels. The navel has elegance, flatness, and depth; the lower body is adorned with three plicatures. The breasts, with emergent nipples, give a broad-based beauty to the entire chest. The graceful arms are marked with the lines that promise money, grain, and numerous sons; the nails have a glossy polish like a jewel; the fingers are straight, tapering, pink; there is a daintiness in the slope of the shoulder, and an absence of knobbiness at the joints. The slender neck shows the conchshell's curve. The lip has a slight pout and an even colour; the charming chin does not retreat; the cheek is full and firm; the brows unite to form a black, soft, wavy line; the nose resembles a half-blown sesamum blossom; the great, gentle eyes have a sweet and modest glance, yet flashing with three colours — pure black, white, and the pigmented part; the brow charms like the crescent moon; the curls are bewitching as a mine of sapphires; each lovely ear has double decoration, its ring and the winsome line of a drooping lotus stem: the whole face is like a lily. Her hair is abundant, long, curly (not kinky), not fading even at the end, of a smooth glossy black throughout, and fragrant.

"Such is her person; the character must correspond.

Besides, I have her. So I will apply my test and marry her. For endless regrets are the certain portion of the heedless." So, with an affectionate glance, he said to her: "My dear young lady, are you by any chance competent to convert this measure of rice into an adequate meal for me?"

Hereupon the girl signalled with her eyes to the old serving-woman, who took the measure of grain from his hand, washed the girl's feet, and seated her in a spot, carefully sprinkled and swept, before the house door. The girl trampled the fragrant rice, dried it a little at a time, turned it repeatedly in the sun, put it on a hard, level spot, struck it very gently with hollow stalk, and extracted the kernels without crushing the husks. "Mother," she said to the nurse, "jewellers find a use for these husks, which serve to polish gems. Take them these, and with the pennies earned buy firewood — solid sticks, neither too moist nor too dry — a modest kettle, and two saucers."

When this had been done, in a shallow, wide-mouthed, pot-bellied mortar of *urjoon* wood, with a long, heavy acacia pestle, plated with iron at the head, smooth in the body, and with a perceptible tenuity in the waist, she caused the grains to rise and fall with the busy grace and skill of her arm; repeatedly made them hop and sink with her fingers; stripped them of awns in the winnowing sieve; rinsed them a number of times; then — having paid honour to the fireplace — dropped them into quintessential boiled water. As the grains softened, hopped, and swelled, she collected the fire, fitted the lid to the kettle, and strained off the scum. Then she patted with the ladle; stirred a little at a time; and making sure that the clots were cooking evenly, set the kettle upside down. Next, she sprinkled with water such fagots as were only scorched and sent the charred, but no longer burning, sticks to the retailers with the command: "For the pennies you get for these, buy as much as you can in vegetables, butter, curds, oil, emblic, and tamarind."

When the nurse had done this, she provided a couple of *hors d'oeuvres;* then, remarking that the scummy broth should be set in a new saucer planted in moist sand, she cooled it with a gentle breeze from a palm-leaf fan, added sufficient salt, and let the smoke from the wood fire scent it; she also ground the emblic fine to bring out its odour, sweet as a lotus; next, by the lips of the nurse, she invited him to take a bath. This he did thoroughly, receiving oil and emblic from her after she too had bathed.

After his bath, he seated himself on a plank set on the pavement (sprinkled and swept), and fingered the two saucers of liquid served on the quarter of a greenish white plantain leaf clipped from a tree in the courtyard. Then she set the rice gruel before him. He drank, relaxed, felt happy; and satisfaction pervaded his frame. Next, she served him two ladlefuls of rice, and brought a little butter, soup, and a relish. The following course was the rest of the rice, with curds, powdered spices, and fragrant, refreshing buttermilk and clotted cheese.

The man enjoyed his meal to the last morsel, then asked for water. She let it spout a continuous stream from a new pitcher; it was rich with the odour of incense, perfumed with fresh trumpet flowers, fragrant with full-blown lotuses. He set the saucer to his lips. His eyelashes were tinged and granulated by clinging drops, cool as snow; his ears took delight in the trickling sound of the stream; his cheek tingled and thrilled at the delicious contact; his nostrils expanded to the rushing gush of fragrance; his sense of taste was entranced by the exquisite flavour: he drank the pure water in great gulps. Then, in obedience to a nod, the maiden gave him a gargle from another vessel. Finally, the old nurse cleared the table; and on the pavement, freshly cleansed with cow dung, he dozed for a time, wrapped in his ragged cloak. Greatly pleased, he married the girl with all due ceremony and took her home.

After marriage, however, he neglected her and kept a mistress, whom the wife also treated as a dear friend. Her husband she served as a god, indefatigable in personal attention, indomitable in household duty, winning the devotion of domestics by inexhaustible considerateness. Subjugated by her merits, the husband subordinated the entire household to her, made her sole mistress of life and person, and thus enjoyed virtue, money, and love. And that, I may say, is how good wives please the soul.

DANDIN (*c.* A.D. 600-700)
The Ten Princes
translated by A.W. RYDER

A Courtesan's Mother

At this point the mother lifted her hands, touched the earth with hair dappled with grey, lifted her head, and spoke: "Holy sir, this your maid servant acquaints you with my own wrongdoing. And this wrongdoing of mine lay in the performance of my obvious duty. For obvious duty is as follows for the mother of a *fille de joie:* care of her daughter's person from the hour of birth; nourishment by a diet so regulated as to develop stateliness, vigour, complexion, intelligence, while harmonising the humours, gastric calefaction, and secretions; not permitting her to see too much even of her father after the fifth year; festive ritual on birthdays and holy days; instruction in the arts of flirtation, both major and minor; thorough training in dance, song, instrumental music, acting, painting, also judgment of foods, perfumes, flowers, not forgetting writing and graceful speech; a conversational acquaintance with grammar, with logical inference and conclusion; profound skill in money-making, sport, and betting on cockfights or chess; assiduous use of go-betweens in the passages of coquetry; display of numerous well-dressed attendants at religious or secular celebrations; careful selection of teachers to ensure success at unpremeditated vocal and other exhibitions; advertising on a national scale by a staff of trained specialists; publicity for beautymarks through astrologers and such; eulogistic mention in gatherings of men about town of her beauty, character, accomplishments, charm, and sweetness by hangers-on, gay dogs, buffoons, female religionists, and others; raising her price considerably when she has become an object of desire to young gentlemen; surrender to a lover of independent fortune, a philogynist or one intoxicated by seeing her charms, a gentleman eminent for rank, figure, youth, money, vigour, purity, generosity, cleverness, gallantry, art, character, and sweetness of disposition; delivery, with gracious exaggeration of value received, to one less affluent, but highly virtuous and cultivated (the alternative is levying on his natural guardians, after informal union with such a gentleman); collection of bad debts by vamping judge and jury; mothering a lover's daughter; abstraction by ingenious tricks of money left in an admirer's possession after payment for periodical pleasures; steady quarrelling with a defaulter or miser; stimulation of the spirit of generosity in an overthrifty adorer by the incentive of jealousy; repulse of the impecunious by biting speeches, by public taunts, by cutting his daughters, and by other embarrassing habits, as well as by simple contempt; continued clinging to the open-handed, the chivalrous, the blameless, the wealthy, with full consideration of the interrelated chances of money and misery.

"Besides, a courtesan should show readiness indeed, but no devotion to a lover; and, even if fond of him, she should not disobey mother or grandmother. In spite of all, the girl disregards her God-given vocation and has spent a whole month of amusement — at her own expense! — with a Brahman youth, a fellow from nowhere whose face is his fortune. Her snippiness has offended several perfectly solvent admirers and has pauperised her own family. And when I scolded her and told her: 'This is no kind of a scheme. This isn't pretty,' she was angry and took to the woods. And if she is obstinate, this whole family will stay right here and starve to death. There is nothing else to do." And the mother wept.

DANDIN (*c.* A.D. 600-799)
The Ten Princes
translated by A.W. RYDER

Those Men are Fools!

Those men are fools, it seems to me,
Who trust to women or to gold;
For gold and girls, 'tis plain to see,
Are false as virgin snakes and cold.

Love not a woman; if you ever do,
She mocks at you, and plays the gay deceiver:
Yet if she loves you, you may love her too;
But if she doesn't, leave her.

Too true it is that
A courtesan will laugh and cry for gold;
She trusts you not, but waits your trustful hour.
If virtue and a name are yours, then hold!
Avoid her as you would a graveyard flower.

And again:
As fickle as the billows of the sea,

Glowing no longer than the evening sky,
A woman takes your gold, then leaves you free;
You're worthless, like cosmetics, when you're dry.

Yes, women are indeed fickle.
One man perhaps may hold her heart in trust,
She lures another with coquettish eyes,
Sports with another in unseemly lust,
Another yet her body satisfies.

As some one has well said:
On mountain-tops no lotuses are grown;
The horse's yoke no ass will ever bear;
Rice never springs from seeds of barley sown;
A courtesan is not an honest fair.

SHUDRAKA (4th cent. A.D.)
The Little Clay Cart
translated by A.W. RYDER

Hunting, Gambling, Girls and Alcohol

"Your majesty, there is nothing so beneficial as hunting. It gives the legs magnificent exercise; and long-winded speed might prove very handy after a defeat. It dries up the phlegmatic humour; thus promoting digestion, the sole foundation of health. By reducing fat, it makes the body vigorous, sinewy, agile. It gives power to endure cold, heat, wind, rain, hunger, thirst. It interprets the mental activities of living beings from their physical expression. It supplements scanty crops with the flesh of deer, buffaloes, wild oxen, and other game. It makes land routes secure by killing such creatures as wolves and tigers. It explores mountainous or forested regions, with their varied resources. It wins the confidence of jungle tribes. It fosters energy, thus impressing hostile armies. These advantages deserve a high rating.

"Or take gambling. It develops an unexampled magnanimity, since you drop a pile of money like a straw. With its alternations of winning and losing, it liberates you from servile joy or despondency. It nourishes impetuosity, the basis of all manliness. It compels a continuous exercise of quick intelligence in detecting tricks (very difficult to perceive) with dice, sleight of hand, the board, and other equipment. Demanding exclusive attention, it gives superb training in mental concentration. It makes for delight in audacity, the companion of brisk resolution; for ability to hold one's own while rubbing up with the toughest customers; for the cultivation of self-reliance; for getting a living without stinginess.

"Or again, take the society of good-looking girls. That makes money and virtue worth having. That means genuine manly pride; skill in thought-reading; conduct untainted by sordid greed; training in all the social arts; quickness of wit and speech because you must be forever devising means to get what you lack, to keep what you get, to enjoy what you keep, to dream of what you enjoy, to pacify the peevish, and so on; public deference for your well-groomed person and stunning clothes; social acceptability; great respect from servants; smiling address; dignity; gallantry; the winning, through children, of salvation on earth and salvation in heaven.

"Then again, take alcohol. This fortifies the charm of youth through steady use of spirituous antidotes to numerous diseases. It neutralises all misfortunes by increasing self-esteem. It kindles sexual desire and improves the capacity for pleasure. It drowns the consciousness of sin, so counteracting morbidity.

By removing the fetters of reticence, it conduces to mutual confidence. By repressing envy, it makes for pure joy. It encourages continual enjoyment of music and other sense-impressions; the acquisition of countless and varied friendships; unrivalled beauty of person; unparalleled graces; martial spirit, resulting from the loss of fear and depression."

DANDIN (c. A.D. 600-700)
The Ten Princes
translated by A.W. RYDER

Women

Remembered she will bring remorse;
Seen she makes the mind unclear;
Touched she nearly drives one mad!
Why call such a creature dear?

Whirlpool of doubts, home of immodesty, harbour of cruel deeds, treasury of faults, made of deceit, a mine of double dealing, blocking the door of heaven, the gate of hell, a casket of illusions, why was woman created of poison and nectar, the snare of all things living?

BHARTRIHARI (c. 600 A.D.)
Sringar-Satakam
(Verses on Sex)
translated by A.L. BASHAM

Let No One Be a Girl

Let no one be born,
But if one must
Let no one be a girl.
If one must be a girl
Then may she never fall in love,
If she must fall in love,
Free her from her family
O make me sure of him until I end.
Should I meet my lover
And his love flow strongly
Like currents of a river,
Let his darling heart
Be free of other girls.
If he yields to other loves,
Let him know his mind and heart ...

VIDYAPATI (early 15th cent. A.D.)
translated by D. BHATTACHARYA

The Blind Men and the Elephant

In olden times, in this very city of Savatthi, there was a certain king. And that king ordered a certain man: "Come, my man, assemble in one place all the men in Savatthi who are blind from birth." "Yes, your majesty," said that man to that king. And when, in obedience to the king's command, he had laid hands on all the men in Savatthi who were blind from birth, he approached that king. And having approached, he said this to that king: "Your majesty, the blind from birth in Savatthi are assembled for you." "Very well! Now let the blind men feel of the elephant." "Yes your majesty," said that man to the king. And in obedience to the king's command he let the blind men feel of the elephant, saying: "This, O blind men, is what an elephant is like."

Some of the blind men he let feel of the elephant's head, saying: "This, O blind men, is what an elephant is like." Some of the blind men he let feel of the elephant's ears, saying: "This, O blind men, is what an elephant is like." Some of the blind men he let feel of the elephant's tusks, saying: "This, O blind men, is what an elephant is like." Others he let feel of the trunk, saying the same. Others he let feel of the belly, others of the legs, others of the back, others of the ·tail, saying to each and to all: "This, O blind men, is what an elephant is like."

Now when that man had let the blind men feel of the elephant, he approached that king. And having approached, he said this to that king: "Your majesty, those blind men have felt of the elephant; do as you think fit."

Then that king approached those blind men. And having approached, he said this to those blind men: "Blind men, have you felt of the elephant?" "Yes, your majesty, we have felt of the elephant." "Tell me, blind men, what is an elephant like?"

The blind men who had felt of the elephant's head, said: "Your majesty, an elephant is like a water-pot." The blind men who had felt of the elephant's ears, said: "Your majesty, an elephant is like a winnowing-basket." The blind men who had felt of the elephant's tusks, said: "Your majesty, an elephant is like a plough-share." Those who had felt of the trunk, said: "An elephant is like a plough-pole." Those who had felt of the belly, said: "An elephant is like a granary." Those who had felt of the legs, said: "An elephant is like pillars." Those who had felt of the back, said: "An elephant is like a mortar." The blind men who had felt of the elephant's tail, said: "Your majesty, an elephant is like a fan."

And they fought among themselves with their fists, saying: "This is what an elephant is like, that is not what an elephant is like;" "This is not what an elephant is like, that is what an elephant is like." And thereat that king was delighted.

"Precisely so, O monks, the heretics, the wandering ascetics, are blind, without eyes; know not good, know not evil; know not right, know not wrong. Knowing not good, knowing not evil, knowing not right, knowing not wrong, they quarrel and brawl and wrangle and strike one another with the daggers of their tongues, saying: 'This is right, that is not right;' 'This is not right, that is right.'"

UDANA (*c.* 100 A.D.)
translated by E.W. BURLINGAME

Wealth and Success

Beware of Lakshmi [Goddess of Wealth], my son. She is fickle and her ways are but little understood. When acquired she is hard to keep. Even though held fast by the cords of heroism, she escapes. Though guarded by elephants she flees away. She does not regard race, she does not follow the fortune of a family, does not consider character, does not count intelligence, does not court righteousness, does not honour generosity. She has no use for sacred learning, she does not understand truth, she does not value discrimination. Like the hazy outline of an aerial city, she vanishes as soon as we look upon her. She dwells on the edge of a sword, as if perpetually engaged in learning cruelty. Like a creeper, she is a parasite; like a river, she is full of bubbles; like the sun's rays on a cloudy day, she rests now on one thing and now on another. She regards the virtuous as impure, she despises the lofty as unpropitious, she looks upon the gentle as worthless. She avoids a hero like a thorn, leaps over a courteous man as if he were a snake, shuns the giver of charities as nightmare. She keeps away from the temperate and mocks at the wise. Her ways are full of jugglery and contradiction. Though creating a fever she also produces a chill; though rising from water she increases thirst; though of earthly mould she is invisible; though attached to the highest, she really loves only the base. For the poisonous weeds of desire she is like a fostering shower; for the deer of the senses, she is like the hunter's alluring song; for the picture of virtue she is like a polluting cloud of smoke. Lakshmi is the cataract filming over the light of wisdom, the lair of the serpent of sin, the watch-tower for the monster of pride, the prologue of the drama of deception. Under her influence the heart of a king becomes the abode of shameful thoughts.

And remember, my dear Chandrapida, that success is a very uncertain commodity. Sometimes kings are puffed up by their achievements, and their natures are poisoned as if by an accumulation of diseases. Moreover, kings are liable to be tortured by the senses which, though only five in number, turn into a thousand. Pierced by the arrows of Cupid, kings, already sunk in luxury, are struck down and writhe in their agony. To make things worse, they are deceived and misled by rogues who hang around them. These evil companions describe gambling as a relaxation, adultery as a sign of cleverness, drinking as a necessary pleasure, neglect of the family as freedom from bonds. To them contempt for a *guru's* words is a sign of originality, disregard of the gods is freedom, flattery is forethought, recklessness is enterprise and lack of discrimination is impartiality. Guided by such boon companions, and cheated by their sweet words, kings become conceited and blind. Though subject to all the limitations of ordinary mortals, they regard themselves as divine beings.

They esteem their glance as a favour and their words as a glorious blessing to others. Burdened by the pride of their imaginary greatness, they neglect the gods, slight their teachers, and make fun of the learned as fools wasting their opportunities of pleasure in useless labour. They accept a counsellor's skill only in deception and appoint as their family priests only those charlatans who indulge in magical rites and the like.

BANABHATTA (early 7th cent. A.D.)
Kadambari

On the Conduct of a Wife

In the event of any misconduct on the part of her husband, she should not blame him excessively, though she be a little displeased. She should not use abusive language towards him, but rebuke him with conciliatory words, whether he be in the company of friends or alone. Moreover, she should not be a scold, for, says Gonardiya "There is no cause of dislike on the part of a husband so great as this characteristic in a wife." Lastly, she should avoid bad expressions, sulky looks, speaking aside, standing in the doorway, and looking at passers-by, conversing in pleasure groves, and remaining in a lonely place for a long time; and finally she should always keep her body, her teeth, her hair, and everything belonging to her tidy, sweet, and clean.

VATSYAYANA (*c.* A.D. 400-500)
Kama Sutra
translated by SIR RICHARD BURTON

The Mem Sahebs in India

After bathing, and eating the morning meal, he dressed in his full regimentals, and went to pay his respects to the Adjutant Saheb and the Commanding Officer. He took me with him. I rather dreaded this, as I had never yet seen a Saheb, and imagined they were terrible to look on, and of great stature — I thought at least seven feet high.

In those days there were but few Sahebs in Oude — only one or two Saheb Residents in Lucknow, where I had never been. In the villages in my country, most curious ideas existed about them: anyone who had chanced to see a Saheb told the most absurd stories of them. In fact, nothing then could be said that would not have been believed. It was reported they were born from an egg which grew on a tree. This idea still exists in remote villages. Had a Mem Saheb come suddenly into some of our villages, if she was young and handsome, she would have been considered as a kind of fairy, and most probably have been worshipped; but should the Mem Saheb have been old and ugly, the whole village would have run away, and have hid in the jungle, considering the apparition as a *yaddoo gurin* (a witch). Therefore my dread of seeing a Saheb for the first time in my life is not to be wondered at.

I remember, when I was at a *mela* (fair) at the Taj Mahal at Agra, hearing the opinion of some country-people who had come from afar off to see the Taj, about the Saheb *log*. An old woman said she had always been told they were born from eggs, which came on a tree, in a far-off island, but that morning she had seen a Saheb with a *puri* by his side, who she declared was covered with feathers of the most beautiful colours, that her face was as white as milk, and that the Saheb had to keep his hand on her shoulders to prevent her flying away. This she had seen with her own eyes, and it was all true. I am not so ignorant as all this now, but at the time I first came to Agra, I should have believed it. I afterwards frequently saw this Saheb driving his lady about, and she wore a tippet made of peacock's feathers, which the old woman thought were wings.

Autobiography of Subadar Sita Ram 1861
translated by NORGATE

Travel not with a Fool

If the traveller meet not
With his better or his equal,
Let him make his lonely journey strong:
With a fool there is no fellowship.

"These sons are mine, this wealth is mine,"
The fool torments himself to think,
When he himself is not his own:
Much less the sons, much less the wealth.

The fool who knows he is a fool,
A pandit is at least in this;
But the fool who thinks himself a pandit,
He is called a fool indeed.

Dhammapada (70. B.C.)
(Hymns of the Faith)
translated from the Pali by A.J. EDMUNDS

Virtue for its own Sake

As it is said in the *Ugrapariprccha*: "And after giving, one should not feel regret." From weakness of completion comes weakness of the act itself; from regret comes also destruction of merit, as well as of sin, that is the meaning. And do not "blaze abroad thy goodly deed." For in many ways the Lord declares that merit must be hidden and that sin is to be revealed; for then what is revealed dwindles away; sin dwindles just by the remorse, and merit by the satisfaction. There is no offence when a disinterested person proclaims it for the sake of all beings; as in the *Ratnamegha* the instance of the physician explains the harmlessness of self-exultation. Again, if one desires to guard his merit,

> From honour and from gain recoil,
> Exalted thoughts for ever shun;
> The Bodhisat steadfast in faith
> In the good law must have no doubt.

SANTIDEVA
Siksha-Samuccaya
translated by C. BENDALL and W.H.D. ROUSE

The Bunneah

> Whatever the name or the badge on us,
> Chaprasi, or ryot, or what —
> The Bunneah, fat, oleaginous,
> Or lean, is lord of the lot:
> The means of our eating and drinking,

Of money for marriage and feast;
We sign in his books without blinking,
And often not caring the least.
We know that he cheats, and the rate of
His interest no one can tell;
It's fifty long years since the date of
The loan he made for our well —
Two hundred rupees to my father —
We have paid him six hundred, and still
When I cross him he's apt to be rather
Persistent about that old bill.

This is why we are all so dependent,
And why when he comes into Court
I must swear against any defendant.
O friends, it is miserable sport!
But why does the Sirkar believe us?
Sometimes though he fails, and I laugh.
Yet the old game goes on: he deceives us —
Writes a bond for so much, and gives half.

It's the same with the Rajahs, folk chatter,
The Bunneahs are getting the land;
With them though it wouldn't much matter,
If it weren't for the Sirkar's strong hand.
The Sahibs have got Courts for collecting
The debts of the Bunneah, and so
(Confound such mistaken protecting!)
The Rajahs can't cut them too low.

The Sahib says, "You people are funny;
You talk in that fashion, and yet
You make for the Bunneah his money
By recklessly plunging in debt."
Funny people! The Sahibs are still funnier.

Is not debt our old custom? Yes, yes.
Then how can we do without Bunneah?
That's a riddle I never can guess.

LUNKAH
Whiffs (1891)

Poverty

This is my sorrow. They whom I
Would greet as guests, now pass me by.
"This is a poor man's house," they cry.

As flitting bees, the season o'er,
Desert the elephant, whose store
Of ichor spent, attracts no more,

Believe me, friend. My sorrow does not spring
From simple loss of gold;
For fortune is a fickle, changing thing,
Whose favours do not hold;
But he whose sometime wealth has taken wing,
Finds bosom-friends grow cold.

A poor man is a man ashamed; from shame
Springs want of dignity and worthy fame;
Such want gives rise to insults hard to bear;
Thence comes despondency; and thence, despair;
Despair breeds folly; death is folly's fruit. —
Ah! the lack of money is all evil's root!

The poor man's kinsmen do not heed his will;
The friends who loved him once, now stand afar;
His sorrows multiply; his strength is nil;

Behold his character's bright-shining star
Fades like the waning moon; and deeds of ill
That others do, are counted to him still.

No man holds converse with him; none will greet
With due respect the poor man when they meet.
Where rich men hold a feast, if he draws near,
He meets with scornful looks for looks of cheer.
Where vulgar throngs are gathered, 'tis the same;
His scanty raiment wakes his heartfelt shame.
Five are the deadly sins we knew before;
Alas! I find the sixth is — to be poor.

SHUDRAKA (4th cent. A.D.)
The Little Clay Cart
translated by A.W. RYDER

Man and Woman

At morn, as soon as I open my eyes,
I see scattered helter-skelter
Papers, note-books, torn envelopes;
No order, no commas, no semi-colons!
I rummage through them in vain
And never find what I seek.

Here is the world of Man
Stamped with his ingrained indolence!

Suddenly, the hand of Woman intervenes —
And instantly all disorder disappears!
All that was shameless confusion
Her hand transforms into beauty;

All that was torn is mended,
All that was soiled is cleansed,
And nowhere linger the hidden nests of useless rubbish!

Amid my own untidiness I think in wonder:
In the heart of Creation
Flow these two streams of Man and Woman.
Man gathers round him rubbish;
Woman comes and constantly cleanses it away.

RABINDRANATH TAGORE (1861-1941)
Wings of Death

Manners and Customs

Hospitality

I

$\mathcal{T}$hose foolish householders who constantly seek to live on the food of others, become, in consequence of that baseness, after death the cattle of those who give them food.

A guest who is sent by the setting sun in the evening, must not be driven away by a householder; whether he has come at supper-time or at an inopportune moment, he must not stay in the house without entertainment.

. Let him not eat any dainty food which he does not offer his guest; the hospitable reception of guests procures wealth, fame, long life, and heavenly bliss.

Let him offer to his guests seats, rooms, beds, attendance on departure and honour while they stay, to the most distinguished in the best form, to the lower ones in a lower form, to equals in an equal manner.

The Laws of Manu (A.D. 100-200)
III. 104-107
translated by G. BUEHLER

II

Bar thy door not to the stranger, be he friend or be he foe,
For the tree will shade the woodman while his axe doth lay it low.

233

Greeting fair, and room to rest; fire, and water from the
    well —
Simple gifts — are given freely in the house where good
    men dwell, —

Young, or bent with many winters; rich, or poor, whate'er
    thy guest,
Honour him for thine own honour — better is he than
    the best.

Pity them that ask thy pity: who art thou to stint thy
    hoard,
When the holy moon shines equal on the leper and the
    lord!

When thy gate is roughly fastened, and the asker turns
    away,
Thence he bears thy good deeds with him, and his sins
    on thee doth lay.

In the house the husband ruleth; men the Brahman 'teacher'
    call;
Agni is the Twice-born's Master — but the guest is lord
    of all.

NARAYANA
Hitopadesa (12th cent. A.D.)
(*The Book of Good Counsels*)
translated by SIR EDWIN ARNOLD

Good Manners

Say the sages, nine things name not: Age, domestic joys
and woes,
Counsel, sickness, shame, alms, penance; neither poverty
disclose.
Better for the proud of spirit, death, than life with losses
told;
Fire consents to be extinguished, but submits not to be
cold.

NARAYANA
Hitopadesa (12th cent. A.D.)
(*The Book of Good Counsels*)
translated by SIR EDWIN ARNOLD

Manners and Etiquette

One must not sit down on a couch or seat which a
superior occupies; and he who occupies a couch or seat
shall rise to meet a superior, and afterwards salute him.

For the vital airs of a young man mount upwards to leave
his body when an elder approaches; but by rising to meet him
and saluting he recovers them.

He who habitually salutes and constantly pays reverence
to the aged obtains an increase of four things, viz. length of
life, knowledge, fame, and strength.

After the word of salutation, a Brâhmana who greets an
elder must pronounce his name, saying, "I am N. N."

To those persons who, when a name is pronounced, do
not understand the meaning of the salutation, a wise man

should say, "It is I"; and he should address in the same manner all women.

In saluting he should pronounce after his name the word *bhoh;* for the sages have declared that the nature of *bhoh* is the same as that of all proper names.

A Brâhmana should thus be saluted in return, "May'st thou be long-lived, O gentle one!" and the vowel "a" must be added at the end of the name of the person addressed, the syllable preceding it being drawn out to the length of three *moras.*

A Brâhmana who does not know the form of returning a salutation, must not be saluted by a learned man; as a Sûdra, even so is he.

Let him ask a Brâhmana, on meeting him, after his health, with the word *kusala,* a Kshatriya with the word *anámaya,* a Vaisya with the word *kshema,* and a Sûdra with the word *anárogya.*

He who has been initiated to perform a Srauta sacrifice must not be addressed by his name, even though he be a younger man; he who knows the sacred law must use in speaking to such a man the particle *bhoh* and the pronoun *bhavat* your worship.

But to a female who is the wife of another man, and not a blood-relation, he must say, "Lady" (*bhavati*) or "Beloved sister!"

To his maternal and paternal uncles, fathers-in-law, officiating priests, and other venerable persons, he must say, "I am N. N.," and rise to meet them, even though they be younger than himself.

A maternal aunt, the wife of a maternal uncle, a mother-in-law, and a paternal aunt must be honoured like the wife of one's teacher; they are equal to the wife of one's teacher.

The feet of the wife of one's brother, if she be of the same caste (*varna*), must be clasped every day; but the feet of wives of other paternal and maternal relatives need only be embraced on one's return from a journey.

Towards a sister of one's father and of one's mother, and towards one's own elder sister, one must behave as towards one's mother; but the mother is more venerable than they.

Fellow-citizens are called friends and equals though one be ten years older than the other, men practising the same fine art though one be five years older than the other, Srotriyas though three years intervene between their ages, but blood-relations only if the difference of age be very small.

Know that a Brâhmana of ten years and Kshatriya of a hundred years stand to each other in the relation of father and son; but between those two the Brâhmana is the father.

Wealth, kindred, age, the due performance of rites, and fifthly, sacred learning are titles to respect: but each later-named cause is more weighty than the preceding ones.

*

The teacher, the father, the mother, and an elder brother must not be treated with disrespect, especially by a Brâhmana, though one be grievously offended by them.

The teacher is the image of Brahman, the father the image of Prajapâti the lord of created beings, the mother the image of the earth, and an elder full brother the image of oneself.

The Laws of Manu (A.D. 100-200)
II 119-36, 225-26
translated by G. BUEHLER

Of the Manners of Indians

The Indians all live frugally, especially when in camp. They dislike a great undisciplined multitude, and consequently they observe good order. Theft is of very rare occurrence. Megasthenês says that those who were in the camp of Sandrakottos, wherein lay 400,000 men, found that the thefts reported on any one day did not exceed the value of two hundred drachmae, and this among a people who have no written laws, but are ignorant of writing, and must therefore in all the business of life trust to memory. They live, nevertheless, happily enough, being simple in their manners and frugal. They never drink wine except at sacrifices. Their beverage is a liquor composed from rice instead of barley, and their food is principally a rice-pottage. The simplicity of their laws and their contracts is proved by the fact that they seldom go to law. They have no suits about pledges or deposits, nor do they require either seals or witnesses, but make their deposits and confide in each other. Their houses and property they generally leave unguarded. These things indicate that they possess good, sober sense; but other things they do which one cannot approve: for instance, that they eat always alone, and that they have no fixed hours when meals are to be taken by all in common, but each one eats when he feels inclined. The contrary custom would be better for the ends of social and civil life.

MEGASTHENES (302 B.C.)
translated by J.W. McCRINDLE

Rules of Conduct

One should obey one's mother and father and likewise one's elders. One should be steadfast in one's kindness towards living beings. One should speak the truth. In this way, one should propound these attributes of Dharma.

In the same way, the pupil should honour his teacher and this practice should be established by one in the proper manner among one's relations. This is an ancient rule and the principle is long standing. One should act in this way.

This record is written by the scribe named Chapala.

Thus saith the Beloved of the Gods.

You should act as instructed by the Beloved of the Gods. You should order the Rajjukas and the Rajjukas in their turn shall order the people of the countryside as well as the local officers called Rashtrika in the following words: "Mother and father are to be obeyed. And similarly elders are to be obeyed. Living beings should be treated with kindness. Truth must be spoken. These attributes of Dharma are to be propounded." Thus you should order in the words of the Beloved of the Gods.

You should order in the same way the elephant-riders, scribes, charioteers and teachers of the Brahmana community in the following words: "You should instruct your pupils in accordance with what is the ancient usage. This instruction should be obeyed. Whatever honour is enjoyed by the teacher lies really in this. Then again, the principle underlying these instructions should be established in the proper manner among the teacher's female relations by the male relatives he may have. This principle should also be established by them among their own pupils according to the old usage. You should thus guide and instruct your pupils in the proper way, so that the said principle grows among them abundantly."

Inscriptions of Asoka (269-232 B.C.)
Minor Rock Edict 2
translated by D.C. SIRCAR

Rules of Etiquette among the Hindus

Hindus have several ways of greeting each other. In some provinces they put the right hand on the heart; in others they simply stretch it out to the acquaintance they are meeting, for they never greet a person whom they do not know, unless he be of very high rank. When two Hindu acquaintances meet, they generally say a few meaningless words to each other such as, "You-so-and-so you here? That's all right!" "And I-so-and-so here I am." Then each goes on his way.

They have also borrowed the *salaam* from the Mohamedans; but this they never use except to strangers. The *salaam* consists in touching the forehead with the right hand, and bowing at the same time, with more or less emphasis, according to the rank of the person they are greeting. In the case of a person of very high rank they sometimes touch the ground with both hands and then raise them to their foreheads, or else they come close to him and touch his feet three times.

Hindus who do not belong to the Brahmin caste greet Brahmins by performing *namaskara*, which consists in joining both hands, touching the forehead, and then putting them above the head. This mode of salutation, which is only offered to a superior, is accompanied by these two words, "*Saranam, ayya!*" which means "Respectful greeting my lord"; upon which the Brahmin extends his right hand, partially open, as if he expects to receive something from the person who is paying him this mark of respect, and gravely answers to the Latin "*Benefaxit tibi Deus!*" or to our "God bless you!" It is a mysterious compound expression, made up of three words which convey good wishes. Only Brahmins and gurus have the right to give the *asirvadam* or to pronounce the sacred word over those who treat them with respect or give them presents. Some persons, when saluting a Brahmin, content themselves with raising their clasped hands as far as their chest.

Another very respectful manner of greeting is to extend both hands towards the feet of him whom you wish to honour, or to seize his knees while you throw yourself at his feet. This is a very common mode of greeting between a son and a father, or between a younger and an elder brother, on meeting after a long separation. The same humble attitude is also adopted when asking for pardon or for a favour; and only when the object is attained does the postulant relax his hold on the feet of the person whom he is addressing.

When a Hindu is about to make a ceremonious visit to members of his family who live at a distance, he makes a halt when he gets near the place and sends someone to warn his relatives that he is coming. The relatives then start at once to fetch him, and conduct him to their home, often with much ceremony, and accompanied by music. It is not customary either to shake hands or to kiss each other on these occasions. A man who publicly kisses a woman, even if she be his wife, commits the grossest breach of social decorum. A brother would not think of taking such a liberty with a sister, or a son with his mother. Only on a visit of condolence do they make a pretence of doing so to the person to whom the visit is paid; and this form of salute, in which the lips do not really touch the face, is only permissible between persons of the same sex.

Women bow respectfully to men without speaking or looking at them. Children salute their parents in the same manner and stand upright before them, with their arms crossed on their chests. Whenever relatives or very great friends meet after a long separation, they clasp each other in their arms and take hold of each other's chin, shedding tears of joy.

Hindus who visit or meet each other after a long absence have, like ourselves, a set of commonplace phrases which they make use of for want of anything better. But in most cases the ideas they express are diametrically opposed to ours. Thus, for instance, if we Europeans were speaking to a friend or acquaintance, we should think he would be pleased if we congratulated him on his appearance of good health, his increased stoutness, or his good complexion, etc. If we think him altered for the worse, we take care not to let him see that we notice it, for fear it might pain him.

A Hindu, on the contrary, when he meets a friend no matter how strong and well he may be looking, never fails to offer him the following greeting: "How sadly you have altered since I last saw you! How thin and worn you look! I fear you must be very ill," and other equally consoling remarks. It would offend a Hindu deeply if you were to say he was looking well on first meeting him. Anyone who was so ill advised as to make so indiscreet a remark would certainly be suspected of feeling jealous, envious, and regretful at the signs of health which were the theme of his unfortunate compliments.

In the same way, you must never congratulate a Hindu on his good luck; you must not say that he has pretty children a lovely house, beautiful gardens, fine flocks and herds, or that everything that he undertakes turns out well, or that he is happy or lucky, etc.; he would be sure to think that envy prompted compliments of this kind. Long ago, before I knew anything about Hindu etiquette, I was walking one day at the edge of a large tank or lake where some men were fishing with nets. I stood still to watch them, and seeing that they landed a quantity of fish each time the nets were let down, I thought I might congratulate them on their good luck. But my civility had a most unlooked for result, for these worthy people gathered up their nets and their fish without a word, and looking at me very indignantly, promptly went off, grumbling to each other under their breath: "What have we done to this Feringhi guru that he comes here and is so jealous of us?"

Just as we French and English do, but contrary to the Spanish and Portuguese custom, the Hindus, in quitting an apartment with a visitor, always allow him to walk first. The object is to avoid turning one's back upon a guest, and he, in turn, in order not to appear wanting in politeness, walks, sideways until both have passed the threshold. When leaving the presence of a prince or any great personage, it is customary, for the same reason, to walk backwards until one is out of his presence; and this is also why a servant, when accompanying his master on foot or on horseback, never walks in front of him.

It is considered good manners in India to blow your nose with your fingers; and there is nothing impolite in audibly getting rid of flatulency. Persons of all ranks, indeed, seem to rather encourage this habit, as according to them it is sure sign of a good digestion. It is certainly an original, if somewhat disgusting spectacle to a European, to see a large number of Brahmins coming away from a feast indulging in a sort of competition as to who shall give vent to the loudest eructations, calling out at the same time, with emphatic gravity, "*Narayana*" as if to thank Vishnu for his favours.

After sneezing a Hindu never fails to exclaim, "*Rama*! *Rama*!" and no doubt there is some superstition attached to this pious ejaculation. Again, when a Brahmin yawns, he snaps his fingers to the right and left to scare away evil spirits and giants.

To tread on anyone's foot, even by accident, demands an immediate apology. This is done by stretching out both hands towards the feet of the offended person. A box on the ear is not considered a graver affront than a blow given with the fist, or a kick with the bare foot; but a blow on the head, should it knock off the turban, is a very gross insult. By far the greatest indignity of all, however, is to be struck with one of the shoes or sandals that Hindus wear. Whoever submitted to such an insult without insisting on receiving satisfaction, would be excluded from his caste. The mere threat of such an insult is often sufficient to provoke a criminal prosecution.

It is a mark of respect when women turn their backs on men whom they hold in high esteem. At any rate, they must turn away their faces or cover them with their saris. Again, when they leave the house, propriety requires them to proceed on their way without paying any attention to the passers-by; and if they see a man they are expected to bow their heads and look in the opposite direction. There are a good many, however, who are not always quite so modest.

*

There are several ceremonious visits which must be paid, such as visits of condolence, visits of *pongul*, and several others of which I shall speak later on. The feast of *pongul* and the following days are mostly celebrated by presents which near relatives make to each other, and which consist of new earthen vessels on which certain designs are traced in lime, also ground rice, fruit, sugar, saffron, etc. Such gifts are conveyed with much solemnity and accompanied by instruments of music. These little attentions are indispensable in the case of certain individuals. For instance, a mother must not neglect giving presents to her married daughter; otherwise the mother-in-law would resent the omission to her dying day.

With them letters of condolence on occasions of mourning can never take the place of a visit, as they so often do with us. Some member of the family must go in person to wail and lament, and perform the other ridiculous ceremonies that are customary on such occasions, even though a journey of fifty miles or more has to be made.

When a Hindu visits a person of importance for the first time he must not omit to take presents with him, which he will offer as a mark of respect, and to show that he comes with friendly intentions. It is generally considered a lack of good manners to appear with empty hands before anyone of superior position, or from whom a favour is expected. Those whose means do not permit of their offering presents of great value may bring such things as sugar, bananas, coconuts, betel, etc.

In conclusion it must be admitted that the laws of etiquette and social politeness are much more clearly laid down, and much better observed by all classes of Hindus, even by the lowest, than they are by people of corresponding social position in Europe.

ABBE J.A. DUBOIS
Hindu Manners, Customs and Ceremonies (1816)
translated by H.K. BEAUCHAMP

Yawning

The idolaters of INDIA observe this custom, that when anyone yawns they crack their fingers, while crying out many times *Ginarami*, that is to say, remember NARAMI, who passes among the idolaters as a great saint. This cracking of the fingers is done, it is said, to prevent any evil spirit entering into the body of the yawner.

J.B. TAVERNIER (1605-1689)
Travels in India
translated by V. BALL

Brahman Marriage
On choosing a bride

In connecting himself with a wife, let him carefully avoid the ten following families, be they ever so great, or rich in kine, horses, sheep, grain, or other property.

Viz. one which neglects the sacred rites, one in which no male children are born, one in which the Veda is not studied, one the members of which have thick hair on the body, those which are subject to haemorrhoids, phthisis, weakness of digestion, epilepsy, or white and black leprosy.

Let him not marry a maiden with reddish hair, nor one who has a redundant member, nor one who is sickly, nor one either with no hair on the body or too much, nor one who is garrulous or has red eyes.

Nor one named after a constellation, a tree, or a river, nor one bearing the name of a low caste, or of a mountain, nor one named after a bird, a snake, or a slave, nor one whose name inspires terror.

Let him wed a female free from bodily defects, who has an agreeable name, the graceful gait of a Hamsa or of an elephant, a moderate quantity of hair on the body and on the head, small teeth, and soft limbs.

But a prudent man should not marry a maiden who has no brother, nor one whose father is not known, through fear lest in the former case she be made an appointed daughter and in the latter lest he should commit sin.

Eight kinds of Marriages

Now listen to the brief description of the following eight marriage-rites used by the four castes varna which partly secure benefits and partly produce evil both in this life and after death.

They are the rite of Brahman, that of the gods (Daiva), that of the Rishis (Arsha), that of Pragâpati, that of the Asuras, that of the Gandharvas, that of the Râkshasas, and that of the Pisâkas.

Which is lawful for each caste (varna) and which are the virtues or faults of each rite, all this I will declare to you, as well as their good and evil results with respect to the offspring.

One may know that the first six according to the order followed above are lawful for a Brâhmana, the four last for a Kshatriya, and the same four, excepting the Râkshasa rite, for a Vaisya and a Sûdra.

The sages state that the first four are approved in the case of a Brâhmana, one, the Râkshasa rite in the case of a Kshatriya, and Asura marriage in that of a Vaisya and of a Sûdra.

But in these Institutes of the sacred law three of the five last are declared to be lawful and two unlawful; the Paisâka and the Asura rites must never be used.

For Kshatriyas those before-mentioned two rites, the Gandharva and the Râkshasa, whether separate or mixed, are permitted by the sacred tradition.

The gift of a daughter, after decking her with costly garments and honouring her by presents of jewels, to a man learned in the Veda and of good conduct, whom the father himself invites, is called the Brâhma rite.

The gift of a daughter who has been decked with ornaments, to a priest who duly officiates at a sacrifice, during the course of its performance, they call the Daiva rite.

When the father gives away his daughter according to rule, after receiving from the bridegroom, for the fulfilment of the sacred law, a cow and a bull or two pairs, that is named the Arsha rite.

The gift of a daughter by her father after he has addressed the couple with the text, "May both of you perform together your duties," and has shown honour to the bridegroom, is called in the Smriti the Prâgâpatya rite.

When the bridegroom receives a maiden, after having given as much wealth as he can afford, to the kinsmen and to the bride herself, according to his own will, that is called the Asura rite.

The voluntary union of a maiden and her lover one must know to be the Gândharva rite, which springs from desire and has sexual intercourse for its purpose.

The forcible abduction of a maiden from her home, while she cries out and weeps, after her kinsmen have been slain or wounded and their houses broken open, is called the Râkshasa rite.

When a man by stealth seduces a girl who is sleeping, intoxicated, or disordered in intellect, that is the eighth, the most base and sinful rite of the Pisâkas.

Honour of Women

Women must be honoured and adorned by their fathers, brothers, husbands, and brothers-in-law, who desire their own welfare.

Where women are honoured, there the gods are pleased; but where they are not honoured, no sacred rite yields rewards.

Where the female relations live in grief, the family soon wholly perishes; but that family where they are not unhappy ever prospers.

The Laws of Manu (A.D. 100-200)
III. 6-11, 20-34, 55-57
translated by G. BUEHLER

Polyandry in Ladakh

Before leaving the subject of marriage, we must say a little more about the customs of polyandry, as Ladakh is one of the few countries remaining where it still obtains. Various economic reasons have been urged for this unusual procedure. The foremost is that it arose in order to keep down the population in a land where sustenance of the body is so hardly won from the dry soil, and the difficulty of transport necessitates any small community being self-contained. A second is that where the nomadic life prevailed, it was inconvenient to trail many women and children around. But a *Ladaki* himself will tell the questioner that the custom is of royal institution, and is for the stabilising of property. If each of several sons possessed wife and family, how could they all be supported on one landhold? Certainly the component parts, after dividing into three or more shares, would not be sufficient for any one family. This, therefore, is a different way of stating the first reason alleged, and the present method of tenure is much more economical. The wife is brought for the elder son, and, as a matter of fact, only one more brother is likely to share the lady's favours. The third son is probably given to the Church, and any more pass into other families as *makpas*. The *makpa* leaves his father's home and gods, as we have seen, adopts those of the heiress to whom he is wedded, and, when either of his parents dies, he is not allowed even to touch the corpse, though he may officiate fully in the case of the dead bodies of his bride's parents. As our Buddhist serving-man put it: "My daughter is of no profit to my corpse, save to say 'Father, Father!' and weep, and throw a little barley behind me, but she must not touch me." So does the marriage tie really become firmer than the relation between parents and offspring. In upper Ladakh, therefore, more than two brothers rarely share one wife, as it is impossible, practically, for more than that number to avoid quarrelling. If the eldest son approves of this second bridegroom, and thinks that they will be able to share their wife peaceably, the younger man is included in the wedding ceremony. The white head-dress is given to him also by the chief bridegroom, and the marriage-tie is as binding on him as on his elder brother. In lower Ladakh, however, where more of the men-folk are away from home trading or travelling, the link is said to be bearable between as many as five brothers. The house and the land and all the children belong to the eldest brother, whether the latter are his begetting or his brothers', and the younger inherits all if the former predeceases him. Hence the word for uncle is always *Aba Chungun*, "little father."

A.R. HEBER and K.M. HEBER
In Himalayan Tibet (1926)

The Pilgrimage to Mecca

"The Pilgrimage to Mecca" is commanded by Mahumud to his followers at least once during their lifetime, provided the obstacles are not insurmountable. Indulgences are made for the sick, or individual poverty. All who have the means at command, whatever may be their distance from the place, are expected to perform the Hadje themselves if possible; or, if prevented by any circumstances they cannot control, they are required to pay the expenses of other persons willing to be their proxies.

Whatever information I have acquired on the subject of this pilgrimage has been gleaned from frequent conversations with Meer Hadjee Shaah, who, as I have before remarked, performed the Hadje from Hindoostaun to Mecca, at three different periods of his eventful life.

If the fatigues, privations, and difficulties of the pilgrimage to Mecca be considered, the distance from Hindoostaun must indeed render the Hadje a formidable undertaking; yet, the piously disposed of both sexes yearn for the opportunity of fulfilling the injunctions of their Lawgiver, and at the same time, gratifying their laudable feelings of sympathy and curiosity — their sympathy, as regards the religious veneration for the place and its purposes; their curiosity, to witness with their own eyes those places rendered sacred by the words of the Khoraun in one instance, and also for the deposits contained in the several tombs of prophets, whom they have been taught to reverence and respect as the servants of God.

Every year may be witnessed in India the Mussulmauns of both sexes forming themselves in Kauflaahs (parties of pilgrims) to pursue their march on this joyous expedition, believing, as they do, that they are fulfilling a sacred duty. The number of women is comparatively few, and those chiefly from the middling and lower classes of the people, whose expenses are generally paid by the rich females. The great obstacle to the higher classes performing the pilgrimage themselves is, that the person must at times be necessarily exposed to the view of the males. The lower orders are less scrupulous in this respect, who, whilst on the pilgrimage, wear a hooded cloak of white calico, by which the person is tolerably well secreted, so that the aged and youthful have but one appearance; the better sort of people, however, cannot reconcile themselves to go abroad, unless they could be permitted to have their covered conveyances, which in this case is impossible.

The qualifications necessary for all to possess, ere they can be deemed fit subjects for the Hadje, are, as I learn, the following:

"They must be true Mussulmauns in their faith; that is, believe in one only true God, and that Mahumud is His Prophet.

"They must strictly obey the duties commanded by Mahumud; that is, prayer five times daily, the fast of Rumzaun, etc.

"They must be free from the world; that is, all their debts must be paid, and their family so well provided for, according to their station, that no one dependent on them may be in want of the necessaries of life during the absence of the pilgrim from his home and country.

"They must abstain from all fermented or intoxicating liquors, and also from all things forbidden to be eaten by the law (which is strictly on the Mosaic principle).

"They must freely forgive their enemies; and if they have given any one cause of offence, they must humble themselves, and seek to be forgiven.

"They must repent of every evil they have committed, either in thought, word, or deed, against God or their neighbour."

Thus prepared, the pious Mussulmaun sets out on his supposed duty, with faith in its efficacy, and reliance on the goodness of Divine providence to prosper him in the arduous undertaking.

MRS. B. MIR HASSAN ALI
Observations on the Mussulmauns of India (1832)

The Circumcision of a Muslim Boy

Circumcision (khatna, sunnat, in Sind *sathra, toharu*) should be performed between the ages of seven and twelve or fourteen, but it is lawful to do it seven days after birth. Akbar prohibited the rite before the age of twelve, and it was then to be optional with the boy.

On the appointed day friends are invited and entertained. For a few days before the rite the boy is rubbed with Haldi or turmeric and made to sit in state (known in south India as *manja baithna*). He is dressed in red or yellow clothes, decorated with flowers, and *Missi* or dentifrice is rubbed on his teeth, this being the only occasion on which males use it. He is then carried in procession round the town. Others postpone the dinner and the procession till after the operation. The boy is seated on a large new earthen pot inverted, or on a chair with a red handkerchief spread over it. A couple of hours before he has been dosed with the electuary known as *Ma'jûn*, made from hemp and used as an anodyne. Some friends hold the boy firmly and the barber performs the operation with a sharp razor. When it is over the boy is told to call out three times "Din," "The Faith." To divert his attention he is made to slap the operator for causing him so much pain. One of the relatives chews betel and squirts the red spittle on the wound to make him believe that there has been no flow of blood. While the operation is in progress the Brahûi mother puts a handmill on her head, a kinswoman a Koran, and they stand facing west and praying till all is over; in the Mari tribe the mother stands in the centre of a group of singing women having in her hands an upper millstone over which are sprinkled red earth and rice, and on these an iron ring, a green head, and a piece of red cloth, all tied together with a red string apparently symbolical of virility. In Sind, while the mother holds a stone on her head, a male relation pours water upon it, and sometimes instead of the mother, the father stands with his feet in water and holds a Koran on his head. Care is taken of the severed foreskin, lest a witch may work evil magic by means of it. Pathans on the north-west frontier bury it in a damp part of the house where the water jars are kept, possibly in the hope that it may grow and increase the virility of the boy. In other parts of the Panjab it is buried, thrown on the house roof, or attached to it by a straw; in Delhi it is tied with a peacock's feather to the boy's left foot, so that no evil shadow may fall upon him and injure him. Some Brahûis bury it under a green tree so that the lad may be fruitful in generation, or they bury it in damp earth, thinking to cool the burning pain of the wound.

After the operation the barber applies a dressing, and the wound heals in the course of a week or so. While the rite is being done, some rice and other gifts are laid close by which are given to the barber, but if the boy was seated on a chair this is not given away. In Sind the father places the fee under the lad's right foot and the friends wave money, which the barber receives, over the boy's head, or he puts his brass saucer in the room and people drop money into it.

JAFAR SHARIF
Islam in India (1832)
translated by G.A. HERKLOTS

Studentship

B ut a student who resides with his teacher must observe the following restrictive rules, duly controlling all his organs, in order to increase his spiritual merit.

Every day, having bathed, and being purified, he must offer libations of water to the gods, sages and manes, worship the images of the gods, and place fuel on the sacred fire.

Let him abstain from honey, meat, perfumes, garlands, substances used for flavouring food, women, all substances turned acid, and from doing injury to living creatures.

From anointing his body, applying collyrium to his eyes, from the use of shoes and of an umbrella or parasol, from sensual desire, anger, covetousness, dancing, singing, and playing musical instruments.

From gambling, idle disputes, backbiting, and lying, from looking at and touching women, and from hurting others.

Let him always sleep alone, let him never waste his manhood; for he who voluntarily wastes his manhood, breaks his vow.

The Laws of Manu (A.D. 100-200)
II. 175-80
translated by G. BUEHLER

Vegetarianism

Q — Were all people to live on non-flesh diet, lions and other carnivorous animals would multiply in such large numbers that they would kill all such useful animals as cows. Your attempt to prevent their slaughter would come to nothing.

A — It is the business of the State to punish or even kill all those men and animals that are injurious (to the community).

Q — Should their flesh (of the animals thus killed) be thrown away?

A — It would do no harm to the world whether it be thrown away, given to dogs or such other carnivorous animals, cremated or even eaten by some meat-eater. But if eaten by a man, it will tend to change his disposition and make him cruel.

The use of all such foods and drinks as are obtained through injuring or killing others or through theft, dishonesty, breach of faith, fraud or hypocrisy is *forbidden*, in other words, they all come under the heading of *forbidden* articles of diet. Whilst the acquisition of foods and drinks through righteous means without injuring or killing any living creature falls in the category of *permissible* articles of diet. This also includes all those articles that give health, and strength, destroy disease, promote intellectual power and energy and prolong life, such as rice, wheat, sugar, milk, butter, fruits, tubers and roots, when properly mixed in due proportion and cooked, and eaten in moderation at proper meal times. The abstinence from the use of all those things that do not agree with one's constitution and are apt to produce disease or other evil effects, and in the use of those that are prescribed for one (by his medical attendant) also constitute adherence to what is called the *permissible diet*.

Q — Is there any harm in eating together, i.e. out of the same dish?

A — Yes, it is harmful, because people differ in their nature and constitutions, etc. from each other. Just as one in eating out of the same dish with a leper is apt to catch the disease, likewise eating with other people is always liable to produce evil results. It can never do any good.

SWAMI DAYANAND (1824-83)
Satyarth Prakash
translated by Dr. C. BHARADWAJA

The Betel-Leaf

This betel is a leaf which resembles that of an orange, but is longer. It is held in great esteem in Hindustán, in many parts of Arabia, and the kingdom of Hormuz; and indeed it deserves its reputation. It is eaten in this way: they bruise a piece of areca nut, which they also call supari, and place it in the mouth; and moistening a leaf of betel or *pán* together with a grain of quick-lime, they rub one on the other; roll them up together, and place them in the mouth. Thus they place as many as four leaves together in their mouths, and chew them. Sometimes they mix camphor with it, and from time to time discharge their spittle, which becomes red from the use of the betel.

This masticatory lightens up the countenance and excites an intoxication like that caused by wine. It relieves hunger, stimulates the organs of digestion, disinfects the breath, and strengthens the teeth. It is impossible to describe, and delicacy forbids me to expatiate on its invigorating and aphrodisiac virtues. The following verses display and confirm only some of its valuable properties.

*

It is probably owing to the stimulating properties of this leaf, and to the aid of this plant, that the king of that country is enabled to entertain so large a seraglio; for it is said that it contains as many as 700 princesses and concubines.

ABDUR-RAZZAK
Persian ambassador to the King of Vijayanagar 1443
translated by ELLIOT AND DOWSON

Betel Chewing

Betel-nut is bitter, hot, sweet, spicy, binding, alkaline —
A demulcent — an astringent — foe to evils intestine;
Giving to the breath a fragrance — to the lips a crimson
  red;
A detergent, and a kindler of Love's flame that lieth dead.
Praise the gods for the good Betel! — these be thirteen
  virtues given.
Hard to meet in one thing blended, even in their happy
  heaven.

NARAYANA
Hitopadesa (12th cent. A.D.)
(*The Book of Good Counsels*)
translated by SIR EDWIN ARNOLD

Keeping up Appearances

To the Westerner all Indians seem old men of
Thermopylae. In the ordinary affairs of life I am a bit
of a Thermopylean myself. But even I am puzzled, disquieted,
and rather exasperated by the Indians. To a thoroughly neat-
minded and efficient man, with a taste for tidiness and strong
views about respectability and the keeping up of appearances,
Indians must be literally maddening.

It would be possible to compile a long and varied list
of what I may call Indian Thermopylean behaviour of Indians
in a single sphere of activity — that of ceremonial. For it
is, I think, in matters of ceremonial and the keeping up of
appearances that Indians most conspicuously fail, in our

Western opinion, "to do anything properly." Nobody who has looked into a temple or witnessed the ceremonies of an Indian marriage can fail to have been struck by the extraordinary "sloppiness" and inefficiency of the symbolical performances. The sublime is constantly alternated with the ridiculous and trivial, and the most monstrous incongruities are freely mingled. The old man of Thermopylae is as busy in the palace as in the temple; and the abodes of Indian potentates are an incredible mixture of the magnificent and the cheap, the grandiose and the ludicrously homely. Cows bask on the front steps; the ante-room is filthy with the droppings of pigeons; beggars doze under the gates, or search one another's heads for lice; in one of the inner courts fifty courtesans from the city are singing interminable songs in honour of the birth of the Maharaja's eleventh grandchild; in the throne room, nobody quite knows why, there stands a brass bedstead with a sham mahogany wardrobe from the Tottenham Court Road beside it; framed colour prints from the Christmas number of *The Graphic* of 1907 alternate along the walls with the most exquisite Rajput and Persian miniatures; in the unswept jewel room, five million pounds' worth of precious stones lies indiscriminately heaped; the paintings are peeling off the walls of the private apartments, a leprosy has attacked the stucco, there is a hole in the carpet; the marble hall of audience is furnished with bamboo chairs, and the Rolls Royces are driven by ragged chauffeurs who blow their noses on the long and wind-blown end of their turbans. As an Englishman belonging to that impecunious but dignified section of the upper middle-class which is in the habit of putting on dress-clothes to eat — with the most studied decorum and out of porcelain and burnished silver — a dinner of dish-water and codfish, mock duck and cabbage, I was always amazed, I was pained and shocked by this failure on the part of Eastern monarchs to keep up appearances, and do what is owing to their position.

*

The Indian's Thermopylisms are due, it seems to me, to entirely different causes. He is careless about keeping up appearances, because appearances seem to him as nothing in comparison with "spiritual reality." He is slack in the performance of anything in the nature of symbolic ceremonial, because the invisible thing symbolised seems to him so much more important than the symbol. He is a Thermopylean, not through excess of "realism" and the aesthetic sense, but through excess of "spirituality." Thus the Maharaja does not trouble to make his surroundings look princely, because he feels that princeliness lies within him, not without. Marriages are made in heaven; therefore it is unnecessary to take trouble about mere marriage ceremonies on earth. And if the soul of every Indian is overflowing with love and respect for Mahatma Gandhi, why should Congress delegates trouble to give that respect the merely physical form of silence and motionlessness?

Such arguments, of course, are never consciously put. But the training of Indians is such that they act as though in obedience to them. They have been taught that this present world is more or less illusory, that the aim of every man should be to break out of the cycle of recurrent birth, that the "soul" is everything and that the highest values are purely "spiritual." Owing to their early inculcation, such beliefs have tended to become almost instinctive, even in the minds of those whose consciously formulated philosophy of life is of an entirely different character. It is obvious that people holding such beliefs will attach the smallest importance to the keeping up of appearances.

ALDOUS HUXLEY (1894-1963)
Jesting Pilate

Amusements and Festivals

Gamester's Lament

The dangling nuts, born where the wind blows the lofty
    tree,
Delight me with their rolling on the board.
The cheering vibhidaka has brought me joy,
Like a draught of soma from Mount Mujavant.

She did not scold me, or lose her temper.
She was kind to my friends and me.
But because of a throw too high by one
I have rejected my loving wife.

Her mother hates me. My wife repels me —
A man in trouble finds no one to pity him.
They say, "I've no more use for a gambler
Than for a worn-out horse put up for sale."

When the conquering die has got his possessions
Others embrace the gamester's wife.
His father, his mother, his brothers say of him:
"We don't know him! Take him as a bondman!"

I think to myself: "I won't go with the others!
I'll stop behind when my friends go to play!"
But then the brown ones raise their voices,
And off I go, like a mistress to her lover.

The gambler goes to the hall of assembly.

"Shall I win?" he wonders. His body trembles.
The dice run counter to his hopes,
And give his opponent the lucky throws.

The dice are armed with hooks and piercing,
They are deceptive, hot and burning.
Like children they give and take again, they
Strike back at their conquerors.
They are sweetened with honey through the
Magic they work on the gambler.

They play in a troop of three times fifty.
Like to god Savitr, they are true to their laws.
They will not bend to the wrath of the mighty,
And even a king bows low before them.

The dice roll down, the dice leap upwards,
Unarmed they withstand the man with arms.
They are heavenly coals, strewn over the board,
And though they are cool they burn up the heart.

The forsaken wife of the gambler sorrows,
And the mother of the son who wanders afar.
In debt, in fear, in need of money,
He goes by night to the house of others.

The gambler grieves when he sees a woman,
Another man's wife, in their pleasant home.
In the morning he yokes the chestnut horses.
In the evening he falls by the hearth, a beggar.

So to the general of your great army,
To him who is king, the chief of your host,
I say, stretching out to him my ten fingers:
"I risk my all! I am speaking the truth!"

"Don't play with dice, but plough your furrow!
Delight in your property, prize it highly,

Look to your cattle and look to your wife,
You gambler!" Thus noble Savitr tells me.

So make friends with us, be kind to us!
Do not force us with your fierce magic!
May your wrath and hatred now come to rest!
May no man fall into the snares of the brown ones!

The Rigveda X. 95
translated by A.L. BASHAM in
The Wonder That Was India

A King's Harem

On a site naturally best fitted for the purpose, the king shall construct his harem, consisting of many compartments, one within the other, enclosed by a parapet and a ditch, and provided with a door.

He shall construct his own residential palace after the model of his treasury-house; or he may have his residential abode in the centre of the delusive chamber, provided with secret passages made into the walls; or in an underground chamber provided with the figures of goddesses and of altars carved on the wooden door-frame, and connected with many underground passages for exit; or in an upper story provided with a staircase hidden in a wall, with a passage for exit made in a hollow pillar, the whole building being so constructed with mechanical contrivance as to be caused to fall down when necessary.

Or considering the danger from his own classmates, such contrivances as the above, mainly intended as safeguards against danger, may be made on occasions of danger or otherwise as he deems fit.

No other kind of fire can burn that harem which is thrice circumambulated from right to left by a fire of human make; nor can there be kindled any other fire. Nor can fire destroy that harem the walls of which are made of mud mixed with ashes produced by lightning and wetted in hail-water.

Poisonous snakes will not dare to enter into such buildings as are provided with jivanti (*Faederia Foetida*), sveta (*Aconitum Ferox*), mushkakapushpa (?), and vandaka (*Epidendrum Tesselatum*), and as are protected by the branches of pejata (?) and of asvattha (*Ficus Relgiosa*).

Cats, peacocks, mongooses, and the spotted deer eat up snakes.

Parrots, minas and Malabar birds shriek when they percieve the smell of snake poison.

The heron (*crauncha*) swoons in the vicinity of poison; the pheasant feels distress; the youthful cuckoo dies; the eyes of the partridge are reddened.

Thus remedies shall be applied against fire and poison.

On one side in the rear of harem, there shall be made for the residence of women compartments provided not only with all kinds of medicines useful in midwifery and diseases, but also with well-known pot-herbs, and a water-reservoir; outside these compartments, the residences of princes and princesses; in front (of the latter building), the toilet-ground, the council-ground, the court, and the offices of the heir-apparent and of superintendents.

In the intervening places between two compartments, the army of the officer in charge of the harem shall be stationed.

When in the interior of the harem, the king shall see the queen only when her personal purity is vouchsafed by an old maidservant. He shall not touch any woman (unless he is apprised of her personal purity); for hidden in the queen's chamber, his own brother slew king Bhadrasena; hiding himself under the bed of his mother, the son killed king Karusa;

mixing fried rice with poison, as though with honey, his own queen poisoned Kasiraja; with an anklet painted with poison, his own queen killed Vairantya; with a gem of her zone bedaubed with poison, his queen killed Sauvira; with a looking-glass painted with poison, his own queen killed Jalutha; and with a weapon hidden under her tuft of hair, his own queen slew Viduratha.

Hence, the king shall always be careful to avoid such lurking dangers. He shall keep away his wives from the society of ascetics with shaved head or braided hair, of buffoons, and of outside prostitutes (dasi). Nor shall women of high birth have occasion to see his wives except appointed midwives.

Prostitutes with personal cleanliness effected by fresh bath and with fresh garments and ornaments shall attend the harem.

Eighty men and fifty women under the guise of fathers and mothers, and aged persons, and eunuchs shall not only ascertain purity and impurity in the life of the inmates of the harem, but also so regulate the affairs as to be conducive to the happiness of the king.

Every person in the harem shall live in the place assigned to him, and shall never move to the place assigned to others. No one of the harem shall at any time keep company with outsider.

The passage of all kinds of commodities from or into the harem shall be restricted and shall, after careful examination be allowed to reach their destination either inside or outside the harem, as indicated by the seal-mark.

KAUTILYA
Arthasâstra (321-300 B.C.)
translated by R. SHAMASASTRY

Deer Hunting

King: Charioteer, the deer has led us a long chase.
  And even now
  His neck in beauty bends
  As backward looks he sends
  At my pursuing car
  That threatens death from far.
  Fear shrinks to half the body small;
  See how he fears the arrow's fall!
  The path he takes is strewed
  With blades of grass half-chewed
  From jaws wide with the stress
  Of fevered weariness.
  He leaps so often and so high,
  He does not seem to run, but fly.

KALIDASA (c. A.D. 400-500)
Shakuntala
translated by A.W. RYDER

The Life of a Cultured Householder

Having thus acquired learning, a man, with the wealth that he may have gained by gift, conquest, purchase, deposit, or inheritance from his ancestors, should become a householder (Grihastha), and pass the life of a citizen. He should take a house in a city or large village, or in the vicinity of good men, or in a place which is the resort of many persons. This abode would be situated near some water, and divided into different compartments for different purposes.

It should be surrounded by a garden, and also contain two rooms, an outer and an inner one. This inner room should be occupied by the females, while the outer room, balmy with rich perfumes, should contain a bed, soft, agreeable to the sight, covered with a clean white cloth, low in the middle part, having garlands and bunches of flowers upon it, and a canopy above it, and two pillows, one at the top, another at the bottom. There should also be a sort of couch, and at the head of this a sort of stool, on which should be placed the fragrant ointments for the night, such as flowers, pots containing collyrium and other fragrant substances, things used for perfuming the mouth, and the bark of the common citron tree. Near the couch, on the ground, there should be a pot for spitting, a box containing ornaments, and also a lute hanging from a peg made of the tooth of an elephant, a board for drawing, a pot containing perfume, some books, and some garlands of the yellow amaranth flowers. Not far from the couch, and on the ground, there should be a round seat, a toy cart, and a board for or playing with dice; outside the outer room there should be cages of birds, and a separate place for spinning, carving and suchlike diversions. In the garden there should be a whirling swing and a common swing, as well as bower of creepers covered with flowers in which a raised parterre should be made for sitting.

Now, the householder, having got up in the morning and performed his necessary duties, should wash his teeth, apply a limited quantity of ointments and perfumes to his body, put some ornaments on his person and collyrium on his eyelids and below his eyes, colour his lips with alacktaka, and look at himself in the glass. Having then eaten betel leaves, with other things that give fragrance to the mouth, he should perform his usual business. He should bathe daily, anoint his body with oil every other day, apply a lathering substance to his body every three days, get his head (including face) shaved every four days and the other parts of his body every five or ten days. All these things should be done without fail, and the sweat of the armpits should also be removed. Meals should be taken in the forenoon, in the afternoon, and again at night, according to Charayana. After breakfast, parrots and other birds should be taught to speak, and the fighting of cocks, quails, and rams should follow. A limited time should be devoted to diversions with Pithamardas, Vitas, and Vidushakas, and then the midday sleep should be taken. After this, the householder, having put on his clothes and ornaments, should, during the afternoon, converse with his friends. In the evening there should be singing, and after that the householder, along with his friend, should await in his room, previously decorated and perfumed, the arrival of the woman that may be attached to him, or he may send a female messenger for her or go to her himself. After her arrival at his house, he and his friends should welcome her and entertain her with a loving and agreeable conversation. Thus end the duties of the day.

The following are the things to be done occasionally as diversions or amusements:

1. Holding festival in honour of different deities
2. Social gatherings of both sexes
3. Drinking parties
4. Picnics
5. Other social diversions

*

In the pleasure room, decorated with flowers, and fragrant with perfumes, attended by his friends and servants, the citizen should receive the woman, who will come bathed and dressed, and will invite her to take refreshment and to drink freely. He should then seat her on his left side, and holding her hair, and touching also the end and knot of her garment, he should gently embrace her with his right arm. They should then carry on an amusing conversation on various subjects, and may also talk suggestively of things which would be considered as coarse, or not to be mentioned generally in society. They may then sing, either with or without gesticulations, and play on musical instruments, talk about the arts, and persuade each other to drink. At last, when the woman is overcome with love and desire, the citizen should dismiss the people that may be with him, giving them flowers, ointments, and betel leaves; and then when the two are left alone, they should proceed as has been already described in the previous chapter.

VATSYAYANA
Kama Sutra (*c.* A.D. 400-500)
translated by SIR RICHARD BURTON

Honeymoon

For the first three days after marriage, the girl and her husband should sleep on the floor, abstain from sexual pleasures, and eat their food without seasoning it either with alkali or salt. For the next seven days they should bathe amidst the sounds of auspicious musical instruments, should decorate themselves, dine together, and pay attention to their relatives as well as to those who may have come to witness their marriage. This is applicable to persons of all castes. On the night of the tenth day the man should begin in a lonely place with soft words, and thus create confidence in the girl. Some authors say that for the purpose of winning her over he should not speak to her for three days, the girl may be discouraged by seeing him spiritless, like a pillar, and, becoming dejected, she may begin to despise him as a eunuch. Vatsayayana says that the man should begin to win her over, and to create confidence in her, but should abstain at first from sexual pleasures. Women being of a tender nature, want tender beginnings, and when they are forcibly approached by men with whom they are but slightly acquainted, they sometimes suddenly become haters of sexual connection, and sometimes even haters of the male sex. The man should therefore approach the girl according to her liking, and should make use of those devices by which he may be able to establish himself more and more in her confidence.

VATSAYAYANA
Kama Sutra (*c.* A.D. 400-500)
translated by SIR RICHARD BURTON

Eclipse-Festival

I have witnessed two solar eclipses which it is scarcely possible I should ever forget. The one I saw from France in the year 1654, the other from *Delhi* in the *Indies* in 1666. The sight of the first eclipse was impressed upon my mind by the childish credulity of the French people, and by their groundless and unreasonable alarm; an alarm so excessive that some brought drugs as charms to defend themselves against the eclipse; some kept themselves closely shut up, and excluded all light either in carefully-barred apartments or in cellars; while thousands flocked to their respective churches; some apprehending and dreading a malign and dangerous influence; others believing that the last day was at hand, and that the eclipse was about to shake the foundations of the world. Such were the absurd notions entertained by our

countrymen, notwithstanding the writings of *Gassendi,*
Roberval, and other celebrated astronomers and philosophers,
which clearly demonstrated that the eclipse was only similar
to many others which had been productive of no mischief;
that this obscuration of the sun was known and predicted,
and was without any other peculiarity than what might be
found in the reveries of ignorant or designing astrologers.

The eclipse of 1666 is also indelibly imprinted on my
memory by the ridiculous errors and strange superstitions of
the *Indians.* At the time fixed for its appearance on the banks
of the *Gemna,* when I saw both shores of the river, for nearly
a league in length, covered with *Gentiles* or idolaters, who
stood in the water up to the waist, their eyes riveted to the
skies, watching the commencement of the eclipse, in order
to plunge and wash themselves at the very instant. The little
boys and girls were quite naked; the men had nothing but
a scarf round their middle, and the married women and girls
of six or seven years of age were covered with a single cloth.
Persons of rank or wealth, such as *Rajas* (*Gentile* sovereign
princes, and generally courtiers in the service and pay of the
king), *Serrafs* or money changers, bankers, jewellers, and
other rich merchants, crossed from the opposite side of the
river with their families, and pitching their tents fixed *kanates*
or screens in the water, within which they and their wives
washed and performed the usual ceremonies without any
exposure. No sooner did these idolaters percieve that the
obscuration of the sun was begun than they all raised a loud
cry, and plunged the whole body under water several times
in quick succession; after which they stood in the river, lifted
their eyes and hands towards the sun, muttered and prayed
with seeming devotion, filling their hands from time to time
with water, which they threw in the direction of the sun,
bowing their heads very low, and moving and turning their
arms and hands, sometimes one way, sometimes another. The

deluded people continue to plunge, mutter, pray, and perform their silly tricks until the end of the eclipse. On retiring they threw pieces of silver at a great distance into the *Gemna*, and gave alms to the *Brahmens*, who failed not to be present at this absurd ceremony. I remarked that every individual on coming out of the water put on new clothes placed on the sand for that purpose, and that several of the most devout left their old garments as presents for the *Brahmens*.

In this manner did I observe from the roof of my house the solemnisation of the grand eclipse-festival, a festival which was kept with the same external observations in the *Indus*, in the *Ganges*, and in the other rivers and *Talabs* (or tanks of the *Indies*), but above all in that one at *Tanaiser*, which contained on that occasion more than one hundred and fifty thousand persons, assembled from all parts of the empire; its waters being considered on the day of an eclipse more holy and meritorious than those of any other.

FRANCIS BERNIER (1620-88)
Travels in the Moghul Empire (1656-68)
translated by A. CONSTABLE

Elephant Fighting

The festivals generally conclude with an amusement unknown in *Europe* — a combat between two elephants; which takes place in the presence of all the people on the sandy space near the river; the King, the principal ladies of the court, and the *Omrahs* viewing the spectacle from different apartments in the fortress.

A wall of earth is raised three or four feet wide and five or six high. The two ponderous beasts meet one another face to face, on opposite sides of the wall, each having a couple of riders, that the place of the man who sits on the shoulders, for the purpose of guiding the elephants with a large iron hook, may immediately be supplied if he should be thrown down. The riders animate the elephants either by soothing words, or by chiding them as cowards, and urge them on with their heels, until the poor creatures approach the wall and are brought to the attack. The shock is tremendous, and it appears surprising that they ever survive the dreadful wounds and blows inflicted with their teeth, their heads, and their trunks. There are frequent pauses during the fight; it is suspended and renewed; and the mud wall being at length thrown down, the stronger or more courageous elephant passed on and attacks his opponent, and, putting him to flight, pursues and fastens upon him with so much obstinacy, that the animals can be separated only by means of *cherkys*, or fireworks, which are made to explode between them; for they are naturally timid, and have a particular dread of fire, which is the reason shy elephants have been used with so very little advantage to armies since the use of fire-arms. The boldest come from *Ceylon*, but none are employed in war which have not been regularly trained, and accustomed for years to the discharge of muskets close to their heads, and the bursting of crackers between their legs.

The fight of these noble creatures is attended with much cruelty. It frequently happens that some of the riders are trodden underfoot, and killed on the spot, the elephant having always cunning enough to feel the importance of dismounting the rider of his adversary, whom he therefore endeavours to strike down with his trunk. So imminent is the danger considered, that on the day of combat the unhappy men take the same formal leave of their wives and children as if condemned to death. They are somewhat consoled by the reflection that if their lives should be preserved, and the King be pleased with their conduct, not only will their pay be augmented, but a sack of *Peyssas* (equal to fifty francs) will be presented to them the moment they alight from the elephant. They have also the satisfaction of knowing that in the event of their death the pay will be continued to their widows, and that their sons will be appointed to the same situation. The mischief with which this amusement is attended does not always terminate with the death of the rider: it often happens that some of the spectators are knocked down and trampled upon by the elephants, or by the crowd; for the rush is terrible when, to avoid the infuriated combatants, men and horses in confusion take to flight. The second time I witnessed this exhibition I owed my safety entirely to the goodness of my horse and the exertions of my two servants.

FRANCIS BERNIER (1620-88)
Travels in the Moghul Empire (1656-68)
translated by A. CONSTABLE

Lion Hunting

But of all the diversions of the field the hunting of the lion is not only the most perilous, but is peculiarly royal; for, except by special permission, the King and Princes are the only persons who engage in the sport. As a preliminary step, an ass is tied near the spot where the gamekeepers have ascertained the lion retires. The wretched animal is soon devoured, and after so ample a meal the lion never seeks for other prey, but without molesting either oxen, sheep, or shepherds, goes in quest of water, and after quenching his thirst, returns to his former place of retirement. He sleeps until the next morning, when he finds and devours another ass, which the gamekeepers have brought to the same spot. In this way they contrive, during several days, to allure the lion and to attach him to one place; and when information is received of the King's approach, they fasten at the spot an ass where so many others have been sacrificed, down whose throat a large quantity of opium has been forced. This last meal is of course intended to produce a soporific effect upon the lion. The next operation is to spread, by means of the peasantry of the adjacent villages, large nets, made on purpose, which are gradually drawn closer, in the manner practised in hunting the *nil-ghau*. Everything being in this state of preparation, the King appears on an elephant protected in places with thin plates of iron, and attended by the Grand Master of the Hunt, some *Omrahs* mounted on elephants, and a great number both of *gourze-berdars* on horseback and of gamekeepers on foot, armed with *half-pikes*. He immediately approaches the net on the outside, and fires at the lion with a large *musketoon*. The wounded animal make a spring at the elephant, according to the invariable practice of lions, but is arrested by the net; and the King continues to discharge his *musketoon*, until the lion is at length killed

FRANCIS BERNIER (1620-88)
Travels in the Moghul Empire (1656-68)
translated by A. CONSTABLE

The Chess Players

It was the age of Wajid Ali Shah*. Lucknow was sunk in pleasurable pursuits. Small and big, rich and poor, were alike dedicated to sensual joys. One would be devoted to song

---

* The last ruler of Oudh

and dance; another would be enjoying the fumes of opium. In every sphere of life pleasure reigned supreme. Luxury dominated everywhere, in the affairs of the administration, in literature, social organisation, in arts and crafts, industry and commerce and in the conduct and behaviour of people. Government servants were absorbed in the satisfaction of sensual pleasures; poets in themes of love and separation; artisans in gold and linen embroidery; and merchants in the trade of wares like mascara, perfumes, colouring for the teeth and pastes for anointing body. There was the intoxication of sensual joys in all eyes. Nobody knew what was happening in the world. There were cock-fights; preparations were being made for fights among partridges. Elsewhere the dice were being thrown; there were shouts and excitement. At another place, furious battles raged in the game of chess. Rulers and ruled were alike with such pleasures. Even beggars on receiving a little charity would not buy bread; instead, they squandered it on opium or some such intoxicant. A game of chess or cards sharpened the wits, developed intellectual power, accustomed one to deal with complicated issues! Such arguments were forcefully expressed and there is no dearth of such people in the world even today!

If, therefore, Mirza Sajjad Ali and Mir Roshan Ali spent most of their time in sharpening their wits, then what thoughtful person could raise an objection against this? Both had hereditary properties. They had no worries about livelihood. They had bouts the whole time. What else were they to do? Early morning the two friends breakfasted and spread out the chess-cloth; the chessmen were arranged and great battles developed. Then they never knew when it was midday or afternoon or evening! Reminders were sent repeatedly from home that food was ready. They always replied that they were coming and the table was to be laid. At last the cook would bring the food right into their room out of sheer despair. And both friends carried on the two occupations together! Mirza Sajjad

Ali had no elder in the household; therefore, his sitting-room became the centre of these battles. But it was not as though the other members of his family were pleased with this conduct of Mirza Sahib. Not only members of the family, but people in the locality and even servants offered hostile comments. They would say: "It is an ill-omened game. It destroys the family. Heaven forbid that anybody should ever develop a liking for it. One is no good for anything useful after such an affliction. It is a terrible disease!" The Mirza's wife was so hostile to this game that she was constantly seeking opportunities for scolding her husband. But she hardly ever found such openings. The battles began, while she was yet asleep. And at night the Mirza only appeared inside when she was already asleep! But the servants would get it in the neck. "He has asked for betel* leaves? Tell him to come and take them! He has no time for his food? Dump it there, let him feed the dogs if he so desires!" But she was not so displeased with her own husband as with Mir Sahib. She had nicknamed him Mir the Corruptor! Perhaps the Mirza cast the whole blame on Mir Sahib to get himself absolved.

One day the Begum Sahiba developed a headache. She asked her maid to call the Mirza Sahib so that he could get some medicine. She asked the maid to make haste. The Mirza Sahib said to the maid: "You go along. I am coming." The Begum Sahiba was in a bad temper. How could she tolerate that her husband should play chess, while she was down with a headache? Her face turned red. She said to the maid: "Go and ask him to come at once. Otherwise tell him that I shall myself go to the Hakim Sahib**!"

Mirzaji was immersed in a most interesting game. Another move or two and Mir Sahib would be beaten! He exclaimed

---

* Chewing these leaves is as common in India as smoking cigarettes elsewhere

** Native physician

with annoyance: "She is certainly not breathing her last! Can't she have a little patience?"

Mir Sahib: "Why not go and hear her? Women have delicate tempers."

Mirza: "Certainly, you would wish me to go. Another check and you would be beaten!"

Mir: "Don't you have such illusions! I have thought of a wonderful move. You will be beaten with all your pieces intact! But you had better go in and hear what she says. Why hurt her for nothing?"

Mirza: "I shall go after beating you."

Mir: "I shall not continue. You should hear her first!"

Mirza: "I shall have to go to the Hakim's. She has no headache nor nothing! It is just a device to tease me."

Mir: "Whatever it may be, you can't turn down such a request."

Mirza: "All right. But just one more move."

Mir: "Certainly not. Until you have gone and heard her. I am not going to touch the pieces."

Mirza Sahib had perforce to go in. Then the Begum Sahiba with a great frown but many groans said to him: "You love your miserable chess so much! One may die, but you won't get up! It would be difficult to find another like you!"

Mirza: "What could I do? The Mir was intractable. I have shaken him off after much trouble."

Begum: "He perhaps thinks everyone to be as useless a creature as he himself is! He too has a family, or has he wiped it off?"

Mirza: "He is a fiend for chess. I have to join unwillingly when he comes."

Begum: "Why don't you show him off?"

Mirza: "He is my equal in age and a little higher in status. I have to show him some consideration."

Begum: "Then I shall tick him off! If he gets angry, let him! He is no use to us whatsoever! We shall be well rid of him, if he only would take offence! ... Hiria, go and pick up the chessmen from outside. Tell Mir Sahib that *Mian Sahib* will play no more today and he is to go!"

Mirza: "No, no. Please don't do such a thing! Do you wish to disgrace me? Wait, Hiria! Don't go!"

Begum: "Why don't you let her go? May I perish, if you stop her! All right, you will stop her! But I shall see how you stop me!"

Saying this the Begum Sahiba started towards the sitting-room. Mirza Sahib turned white. He began to pray and implore: "I implore you in God's name! In the name of Prophet Hussain! May I die, if you move that side!" But the Begum was implacable. She reached the entrance to the sitting-room, but could not somehow proceed farther and show herself to a stranger. She peeped inside. As it happened, the room was unoccupied. Mir Sahib had tampered with the pieces and was strolling outside to prove his bona fides. The Begum thereupon became bolder; she entered the room and upset the pieces. She threw some of the chessmen under the seat and some outside; having done this, she bolted the door from inside. Mir Sahib was at the door itself; he saw the chessmen being hurled outside and heard the clink of bangles. Then the door was shut. He realised that Begum Sahiba was angry, and quietly withdrew homewards.

The Mirza exclaimed, "What have you done?"

Begum: "If the Mir Sahib comes again this way, then I shall have him turned out. If you had shown such devotion to God, you would have become a prophet! You are to play chess all the time and I am to perish of worry about the household! Are you going to Hakim Sahib's or is there still some hesitation?"

The Mirza left home, but instead of going to Hakim Sahib's, he made for the Mir's house and informed him about all that had happened. Mir Sahib said, "When I found the chessmen raining, I understood the whole thing at once and promptly retreated. She has a temper! But you should not let her go on like this! This is improper! What you do outside is no concern of hers! She has only to make the arrangements, that is all!"

Mirza: "Very well. But tell me this, where are we to play?"

Mir: "That is nothing. There is all this big house. Let us settle down here!"

Mirza: "But how should I placate Begum Sahiba? When I was at my own place, she found so much annoyance in it! Now that we are to play here, I think she might want to kill me!"

Mir: "Let her talk. After a couple of days, she will reconcile herself to it! But you should show a little strength yourself too!"

PREM CHAND (1881-1936)
translated by P.C. GUPTA

The Dancing Foot

Of course, our ancient Indian method of explaining these things is a poetic one. The art of dancing arose when the god Vishnu killed the demons, Madhu and Kailatioa. Lakshmi, the consort of Vishnu, noticed the graceful movements of her lord and asked to know what was indicated by them. Vishnu told her that they constituted the art of dancing. So that other people may enjoy the benefit of his skill, at Lakshmi's instance, Vishnu disclosed the secrets of the art of dancing to Brahma, who imparted it to Rudra [Shiva], enabling him thereby to acquire the title of Nateswara, the Master Dancer. Shiva, it is said, entertains his consort Parvati, every evening in his mountain abode in Kailasa, in the presence of all the gods and goddesses, who often join in the community dancing and singing to enhance the splendour of the evening dance known as the *Sandhya Tandava*.

One hundred and eighty different styles of dancing with different names are enumerated, and one hundred and one are described in the fragmentary work of the sage, Bharata. In the decorations of the outer gate of the Gopuram of the Shivaite temple at Chidambaram in Madras, there are ninety-seven stone panels, with the names and descriptions of the various poses, around the bas-relief figure of a dancing girl dancing with the appropriate, graceful disposition of limbs, indicative of the actual movements required in each stance.

Of the classical dances there are four well-known surviving forms, the subtle *Bharata-Natya* and *Kathakali* which are current in South India, the lighter *Kathak* and *Manipuri* which are popular in the North and North-East.

The *Bharata-Natya* style, which is the oldest and most perfect of all, is associated with the ritual of the Shiva cult as practised in the temples of the Southern peninsula. It was generally danced by *Devadassis*, slaves of the gods, trained from early childhood. Therefore it has come to be known as *Lasya* (soft), or feminine, as against the Tandava, masculine style. It is mostly performed solo and very rarely in groups. The elaborate and complicated symbolism makes this the most difficult form to master and comprehend, even as its interpretation by a self-conscious dancer like Rukmini Arundale, with her cadences of restraint, makes it highly esoteric and poetical in expression. The architecture of the Shivaite temples dominates it, impressing on it a richness of detail and intricate variety of expression not to be found in the other dances.

The *Kathakali* is a classic dance pattern of the Malabar coast. As against the *Bharata-Natya*, which is mainly *Lasya*, feminine or soft, the Kathakali is *Tandava*, masculine and vigorous. It is impressive for the fact that the whole body is involved in its rhythm. The dancers of the poet Vallathol's Academy are the most consistent exponents of it. But connoisseurs will remember Ram Gopal's interpretation of the peacock dance which is a well-known item of the repertory of Malabar.

The *Manipuri*, the dance of Eastern India, is like the Kirtan music of Bengal, a vivid but fleeting aerial phenomenon, lyrical like a tune and lacking in the contrasts of tempo, speed and movement which distinguish the other dances. The dancer alights upon the stage like a shooting star from the firmament, snatching the quick of human emotion and rising again in a sudden leap, to fall again and rise again.

Apart from these main forms there are the numerous folk-dances, the living receptacle of influences from the classical tradition, but more richly human and spontaneous in their expression than the dances of the canon, in so far as they took in all social, heroic and ritualistic impulses of the peasantry. The erotic Santal dance in Bengal is matched by the simple socialised *Saraikali* dance which interprets stories from the *Ramayana* in Bihar and Orissa, and by the *Banjara* dance of the Deccan, in which women clad in gorgeous scarlet robes dance in a circle in unvaried steps yodelling a monotonous tune the while.

MULK RAJ ANAND
Lines Written to an Indian Air

Going to the Cinema

They walked to the cinema. Chandran stopped at a shop to buy some betel leaves and a packet of cigarettes. Attending a night show was not an ordinary affair. Chandran

was none of your business-like automatons who go to a
cinema, sit there, and return home. It was an aesthetic
experience to be approached with due preparation. You must
chew the betel leaves and nut, chew gently, until the heart
was stimulated and threw out delicate beads of perspiration
and caused a fine tingling sensation behind the ears; on top
of that you must light a cigarette, inhale the fumes, and with
the night breeze blowing on your perspiring forehead, go to
the cinema, smoke more cigarettes there, see the picture, and
from there go to a hotel nearby for hot coffee at midnight,
take some more betel leaves and cigarettes, and go home and
sleep. This was the ideal way to set about a night show.
Chandran squeezed the maximum aesthetic delight out of the
experience, and Ramu's company was most important to him.
It was his presence that gave a sense of completion to things.
He too smoked, chewed, drank coffee, laughed (he was the
greatest laugher in the world), admired Chandran, ragged
him, quarrelled with him, breathed delicious scandal over the
names of his professors and friends and unknown people.

The show seemed to have already started, because there
was no crowd outside the Select Picture House. It was the
only theatre that the town possessed, a long hall roofed with
corrugated iron sheets. At the small ticket-window Chandran
inquired, "Has the show begun?"

"Yes, just," said the ticket man, giving the stock reply.

You might be three-quarters of an hour late, yet the man
at the ticket-window would always say, "Yes, just."

"Hurry up, Ramu," Chandran cried as Ramu slackened
his pace to admire a giant poster in the narrow passage leading
to the four-annas entrance.

The hall was dark; the ticket collector at the entrance took
their tickets and held apart the curtains. Ramu and Chandran
looked in, seeking by the glare of the picture on the screen
for vacant seats. There were two seats at the farthest end.

They pushed their way across the knees of the people already seated. "Head down!" somebody shouted from a back seat, as two heads obstructed the screen. Ramu and Chandran stooped into their seats.

It was the last five minutes of a comic in which Jas Jim was featured. That fat genius, wearing a ridiculous cap, was just struggling out of a paint barrel.

Chandran clicked his tongue in despair: "What a pity. I didn't know there was a Jas two-reeler with the picture. We ought to have come earlier."

Ramu sat rapt. He exploded with laughter. "What a genius he is!" Chandran murmured as Jas got on his feet, wearing the barrel around his waist like a kilt. He walked away from Chandran, but turned once to throw a wink at the spectators, and, taking a step back, stumbled and fell, and rolled off, and the picture ended. A central light was switched on. Chandran and Ramu raised themselves in their seats, craned their necks, and surveyed the hall.

The light went out again, the projector whirred. Scores of voices read aloud in a chorus, "Godfrey T. Memel presents Vivian Troilet and Georgie Lomb in 'Lightguns of Lauro ...'" and then came much unwanted information about the people who wrote the story, adapted it, designed the dresses, cut the film to its proper length, and so on. Then the lyrical opening: "*Nestling in the heart of the Mid-West, Lauro city owed its tranquility to the eagle-eyed sheriff —*"; then a scene showing a country girl (Vivian Troilet) wearing a check shirt, going up a country lane. Thus started, though with a deceptive quietness, it moved at a breathless pace, supplying love, valour, villainy, intrigue, and battle in enormous quantities for a whole hour. The notice "Interval" on the screen, and the lights going up, brought Chandran and Ramu down to the ordinary plane. The air was thick with tobacco smoke. Ramu yawned, stood up, and gazed at the people occupying the more expensive seats behind them. "Chandar, Brown is here with some girl in the First Class."

"May be his wife," Chandran commented without turning.

"It is not his wife."

"Must be some other, then. The white fellows are born to enjoy life. Our people really don't know how to live. If a person is seen with a girl by his side, a hundred eyes stare at him and a hundred tongues comment, whereas no European ever goes out without taking a girl with him."

"This is a wretched country," Ramu said with feeling.

At this point Chandran had a fit of politeness. He pulled Ramu down, saying that it was very bad manners to stand up and stare at the people in the back seats.

Lights out again. Some slide advertisements, each lasting a second.

"Good fellow, he gets through these inflictions quickly," said Chandran.

"For each advertisement he gets twenty rupees a month."

"No, it is only fifteen."

"But somebody said that it was twenty."

"It is fifteen rupees. You can take it from me," Chandran said.

"Even then, What a fraud! Not one stays long enough. I hardly take in the full name of that baby's nourishing food, when they tell me what I ought to smoke. Idiots. I hate advertisements."

The advertisements ended and the story started again from where it had been left off. The hero smelt the ambush ten yards ahead. He took a short cut, climbed a rock, and scared the ruffians from behind. And so on and on it went, through fire and water, and in the end the good man Lomb always came out triumphant; he was an upright man, a courageous man, a handsome man, and a strong man, and he had to win in the end. Who could not foresee it? And yet every day at every show the happy end was awaited with breathless suspense. Even the old sheriff (all along opposed to the union of Vivian with Georgie) was suddenly transformed, and with tears in his eyes he placed her hands on his. There was a happy moment before the end, when the lovers' heads were shown on an immense scale, their lips welded in a kiss. Good night.

Lights on. People poured out of the exits, sleepy, yawning, rubbing their smarting eyes. This was the worst part of the evening, this trudge back home, all the way from the Select Picture House to Lawley Extension. Two or three cars sounded their horns and started from the theatre.

"Lucky rascals. They will be in their beds in five minutes. When I start earning I shall buy a car first of all. Nothing like it. You can just see the picture and go straight to bed."

"Coffee?" Chandran asked, when they passed a brightly lit coffee hotel.

"I don't much care."

"Nor do I."

They walked in silence for the most part, occasionally exchanging some very dull, languid jokes.

As soon as his house was reached, Ramu muttered, "Good night. See you tomorrow," and slipped through his gate.

R.K. NARAYAN
The Bachelor of Arts

Elephant Riding

It was a superb and particularly lofty specimen, with goldmounted tusks; ate two hundred weight of food a day and must have cost at least six hundred a year to keep. An expensive pet. But for a man in the *thakur's* position, we gathered, indispensable, a necessity. Pachyderms in Rajputana are what glass coaches were in Europe a century and a half ago — essential luxuries.

The *thakur* was a charming and cultured man, hospitably kind as only Indians can be. But at the risk of seeming ungrateful, I must confess, that, of all the animals I have ever ridden, the elephant is the most uncomfortable mount. On the level, it is true, the motion is not too bad. One seems to be riding on a small chronic earthquake; that is all. The earthquake becomes more disquieting when the beast begins to climb. But when it goes downhill, it is like the end of the world. The animal descends very slowly and with infinite caution, planting one huge foot deliberately before the other, and giving you time between each calculated step to anticipate the next convulsive spasm of movement — a spasm that seems to loosen from its place every organ in the rider's body, that twists the spine, that wrenches all the separate muscles of the loins and thorax. The hills round Jaipur are not very high. Fortunately; for by the end of the three or four hundred feet of our climbing and descending, we had almost reached the limits of our endurance. I returned full of admiration for Hannibal. He crossed the Alps on an elephant.

ALDOUS HUXLEY (1894-1963)
Jesting Pilate

Raksha Bandhan

On Raksha Bandhan day, following an ancient Rajput custom, Hindu women tie bracelets of gold-trimmed silk on the wrists of their brothers and those they adopt as their brothers.

Beloved I offer to you
In tender allegiance anew,
A bracelet of floss. Let me twist
Its tassels, vermilion and blue
And violet, to girdle your wrist.

Accept this bright gage from my hand,
Let your heart its sweet speech understand,
The ancient high symbol and end
Inwrought on each gold-threaded strand,
The fealty of friend unto friend.

A garland how frail of design,
Our spirits to clasp and entwine
In devotion unstained and unbroken,
How slender a circle and sign
Of secret, deep pledges unspoken!

SAROJINI NAIDU
The Father of the Dawn

Holi, the Festival of Spring

Whatever else we do not know of the ancient countries, of one thing we may be sure, that in every case they must have had a yearly feast of Eros. We may gather, moreover, from the climatic and geographical associations of each land, the very moon of the festival in every case. It must always have taken place in the spring-time. The memory of this left behind, here a carnival, there a battle of flowers, and somewhere else a May Day frolic, to tell a future age the path it went. Here in India, where all ages persist, like geological strata piled one upon another, it is kept today as it may have been in Assyria or Egypt, in early Greece or in the empire of the Hittites.

On full-moon of the beautiful month of *Phalgun* — that month when the *asoka* tree and the mango are in bloom, when the foliage buds of the leaf-almond are long and slender against the blue, and when the scarlet plumes of the *palash* stand out on its naked branches — occurs the *Holi* festival, or *Dol-jatra* of some long pre-Hindu people. Pre-Hindu they certainly were although Hinduism has done its best to absorb and assimilate the poetry they brought to it. For the *Asoka* tree, they say, only blooms when the footfall is heard by it of a beautiful woman, and fragrance of mango-blossoms is one of the five arrows of Madan's bow — two morsels of the folk-lore that clearly belong to the spring and nature festival. Madan, the Indian Love, is always depicted as a young man, not as a child, who once upon a time went clad in flowers — nay, his very weapon was made of them. And as he wore it loose and unstrung beside his quiver, the eager bees hanging above it gave it its proper form of the bow. So at least we are told in Kalidas's immortal fragment. Wherever Madan is mentioned amongst the educated, Kalidasa must needs be remembered, for his was the brain that gave the beautiful young archer his life-myth, and to his poem must all go who would learn of the impious faring forth together of Love and his comrade Spring to shoot at the heart of the Great God, and of the fate that befell their enterprise in the sacred grove of meditation. All the love of the Indian soil and Indian nature that must have spoken in the wild poetic souls of the earliest aborigines is here poured, together with his own thought and learning, into the crucible of a great Hindu poet, to form the poem of the birth of Kartik the War-Lord. But long before Kalidasa took up his lute, the Indian feast of Eros had been Indianised, being interpreted as an incident in the idyll of the sporting of the child Krishna in the meadows of Brindaban.

Nothing is so exquisite as this — the tale of the divine childhood as a cow-herd amongst the herd-boys and herd-girls beside the Jumna. At the age of eleven Krishna passes off the peasant stage for ever, but years after, when his forest-friends visit him in his palace, they refuse to recognise their old playmate whom they now see in kingly robes, and will not be satisfied till he has donned once more for them his childhood's crown of a peacock's feather, with flute and simple village garments, thus revealing himself again to their adoring love as the same Gopala they knew of old.

Everyone who knows anything of the village customs of the North-West has seen the place that swinging holds in the Indian peasant's conception of a festival. Boys and girls, young men and young women, like English rustics at a fair, swing and shout, applaud and deride each other, with never a suggestion of that dignity which we commonly associate with Oriental humanity. It is wonderful how easily, with a rope and a few bamboos and a wooden seat, a swing can be made for a frolic. But in the Himalayas, near every temple, we find swing-posts of deodar and stout iron chains. Clearly there was a time when the festival was celebrated everywhere, and since Brindaban must so obviously have known the giddy delight, it followed that a swinging ceremony became part of the religious ritual of the altar on the day of the Spring Feast. In other words, Hinduism, by means of the Krishna legend, had absorbed into itself, and in doing so, lent a greater dignity of interpretation to, the Festival of Love of the country folk.

Hinduism absorbed, Hinduism reinterpreted, but she never criticised or discountenanced the gaiety of the child races. And still the lower castes maintained the old practices. And of the season. There are perhaps two essential elements characteristic of the festivals of Madan. One is the free mixing of men and women. With probably a certain element of rough buffoonery, something like the old St. Valentine's Day of

Europe; and the other the drawing together of all the classes, ignoring social differences of higher civilisations of later ages. These two characteristics have persisted to the present day in the *Holi Puja* observances of the Hindu lower classes and Hindu gentlefolk of mature age will tell how in their childhood their mothers would bend the head to receive the red-powder *tilaka* at the hands of their Hindustani servants.

Out in the streets meanwhile the boys are at war with passing pedestrians, all of whom are bound on this privileged day to submit to being pelted with red powder. Yellow powders are sometimes used, but this, say the best judges, is a mistake. The red alone is correct, symbolising the sand of the Jamna, all stained with the blood of the demons, whom Krishna slew. The wild and boisterous impatient of the priest's slow blessing, buy the powder straight from the shops and throw it. But gentler spirits wait, playing only that which is duly offered and sanctified in worship. And great is the reward of their patience, for such is the virtue of the blest powder that it confers immunity, it is said, from all diseases of the season!

Here then in India to this day is played out every year the old-time drama of the peasant in the spring; played, too, in a fashion of which, however it may annoy the Philistine, neither the scholar nor the poet could bear to sacrifice a single point. The joy of simple peoples in the bridal of nature, and the festival of the great democracy of caste and sex — these are two impulses that have given birth to all carnivals and *Holi Pujas* that the world has ever known. And behind, watching over them, suggesting a thought of poetry here, a touch of sanctity there, and working to moderate possible excess only by her own benign presence and her kindly tolerance, stands the ancient Mother-Church of Hinduism. There was a wonderful dramatic fitness in the fact that in the fulness of time it was on the full-moon of *Phalgun* the day of the *Holi* festival, that Chaitanya, apostle of rapture, lover of the poor and lowly, the national saint and the preacher of democracy, was born here in Bengal.

SISTER NIVEDITA
Studies from an Eastern Home

The Meaning of Dasehra

We have come to think of Dasehra only in terms of holidays, vacations and reduced railway fares; but what is the elemental significance of Dasehra? What is the meaning of this religious observance? We have only to look into the Ramayana to see that Dasehra is at once a sermon and an entrancing story of adventure, self-sacrifice and love.

A million years ago, there reigned over the Kingdom of Uttra Kosul the great Chattri king, Dasarath. His capital was at Ajodhia, a city which reared its head in grandeur overlooking the Sarju River near the present city of Fyzabad. The glories of this kingdom have been sung by Hindu bards and minstrels for centuries past and some of the lore has come down to us of the present day. I heard an ignorant cultivator describe the limits of that kingdom in the following lines:-

Purab marey Pur Patan tak,
Pacchim marey Bind pahar,
Dakhin marey garh Kabul tak.
Utter — sath Khand Naipal.

His geography was all wrong of course, but the limitations given suggest a vast kingdom.

Dasarath had three queens. His eldest son was Ram, who was born of the senior queen. His second son was Lachhman, born of the second queen, and his third and fourth sons,

Bharat and Shattrugun, were born of Kaikei, the third queen.

One day, as Dasarath stood before a mirror in the palace, he observed that his hair was turning grey and he decided that the time had come when he should go into retirement from worldly affairs. He resolved to abdicate in favour of his eldest son, Ram, who was particularly precious to him. All arrangements were made and an auspicious day was fixed for the coronation.

When the news reached Queen Kaikei, however, she was extremely envious because one of her sons should not be given the throne.

Now, Dasarath had promised Queen Kaikei long years before that he would be prepared to grant her any two requests she would make of him at any time. Queen Kaikei had remembered the promise and now felt the time had come to use the privilege to advantage. She reminded King Dasarath of his pledge and demanded that her son, Bharat, should be given the throne and that Ram should be banished to the outermost forests of the kingdom.

Torn between his pledged word on the one side, and his love for Ram on the other, Dasarath was distraught. To a Chattri of those days, however, the breaking of one's word of honour was a most contemptible and unpardonable act. After a tremendous mental struggle, he decided to keep his promise and issued orders in accordance with Queen Kaikei's request. With breaking heart, he told Ram he must go into the forest for a period of 14 years, knowing that he himself could never withstand the separation. Ram obeyed meekly but resolutely, taking leave of his parents. Along with Ram went Sita, his beautiful wife, and Lachhman, his devoted step-brother.

At the time, Bharat was away on the North-West Frontier visiting his mother's ancestral home and all unaware of the arrangements his mother was making for him at Ajodhia.

Dasarath could not survive the consuming sorrow of parting with his beloved Ram and very soon after, pined away and died. The funeral ceremonies had to be performed by one of his sons. Ram and Lachhman were untraceable in the distant forests, so Bharat was sent for. He performed the funeral rites and was then asked by his mother to ascend the throne.

Now, Bharat was an extremely right-thinking young man and when he heard of the manner in which his mother had paved his way to the throne, he was greatly annoyed. Denouncing the action of his mother and deploring the banishment of Ram, he proceeded into the forests to find the exiles and bring them home.

Deeper and deeper into the forest he went in his search till at last, on the hills of Chittra Kot, he caught a glimpse of three wandering figures. He bowed down in obeisance as he approached Ram and begged him to return to Ajodhia. Ram, however, was absolutely firm on the point that he would not disobey his father's orders and not until 14 years was complete would he place foot in Ajodhia.

Unable to pursuade him, Bharat took from Ram's foot his sandal and going back to Ajodhia, he placed this on the throne and ruled the State on Ram's behalf, awaiting his return.

Ram now proceeded farther and farther south till he was somewhere in the vicinity of Rameswaram. One day, he found his wife, Sita, missing. Lachhman and he started a vigorous search, but failed to find her. At last, they met the monkey-god, Hanuman, who helped them to trace Sita's whereabouts. She had been forcibly abducted by Rawan, King of Lanka (Ceylon) and imprisoned because she refused to marry him. On hearing this, Ram collected a great army of South Indian aborigines called "Banars," and marched towards Lanka. Before he could reach his objective, he was met by Rawan and a sanguinary battle ensued, Rawan being killed in the fray.

Thus, was Sita restored to Ram, and it is this battle which is commemorated at Ram Lila festivities when towering paper effigies of Rawan are burnt.

That is the story of Dasehra, but what a lesson it has, not only for the Hindu mind but for the world! Do we merely see the victory of Ram over Rawan or do we see through it and behind it, the triumph of virtue over evil, of truth over falsehood, of soulful submission over worldly desire? We see, personified, the obedience of a son, the faithfulness of wife, the loyalty and self-sacrifice of brothers and the love of a noble father — all wrapped together in one grand conception. Is it any wonder then, that the Hindu mind is stirred by these historical facts and that the Hindu heart is softened with the beauty of the character of these heroes?

It is thus, at Dasehra time, when the colossal image of Rawan bursts into flames and crashes to the ground two hundred million Hindu voices cry, *"Jai Sita Ram!"* Victory to Sita and Ram! Victory to Honour over Dishonour! Victory to Right over Wrong!

This is Dasehra.

L.H. NIBLETT
India in Fable, Verse and Story

Diwali: The Festival of Light

Diwali is the Festival of Light. It is celebrated on the darkest night following Dasehra, midway in time between newmoon and full-moon, and commemorates the return of Ram to ascend the throne of Ajodhia after his 14 years of exile in the forests of his kingdom. His arrival was awaited by a vast concourse of subjects who gathered round

the throne waiting in anxious expectation for the advent of
their king.

Then, through the brushwood and the forest, emerged the
mendicant King, saffron-clothed, bare-footed and bare-headed,
with a sheaf of arrows across his back and a giant bow in his
hand; all Ajodhia went mad with transports of joy.

The Capital and the Kingdom alike, welcomed their King
with jubilant acclamation. Ram ascended the throne which
had lain vacant for him through that long period of time.
Timbrel and cymbal, *dholak* and *sarangi*, vied with each other
to fill the air with music worthy of the occasion.

Thus passed the hours of "Raj Gaddi" day, the day of
enthronement.

Night came. A thousand flares went up in old Ajodhia.
A myriad lights scintillated in the darkening sky and made
day of night, while the warrior king sat in Royal State, in the
splendour of his simple regalia. There sat a victor over mighty
Rawan; a victor over himself. Had he not met temptation and
conquered it! Had there not been placed before him, with
entrancing imagery, the vision of the throne of Ajodhia should
he but decide to mount it, forgetful of his father's command
that for 14 years he should remain a wanderer on the face
of the earth with the trees of the forest for his canopy and
the cold, bare ground for his bed.

There sat Ram, listening to the temple-bells which rang
out into the night-air, listening to a chorus of hautboys and
conches that bellowed forth their message of welcome,
listening to the murmuring refrain of the multitude who had
gathered outside the Palace gates and massed themselves
together in every street and every public resort within the
city walls.

Those glimmering lights that shone out in serried lines,
had a dual significance. They constituted the outward sign of
jubilation and welcome; but they also operated as a means

of driving away the powers of darkness which, in unseen and intangible shapes, hover around scenes of grandeur on the most auspicious occasions. That belief held sway in Ajodhia as it held sway in Ancient Rome. It is that belief which the great Plutarch recorded and which Shakespeare put into the mouth of Horatio, the Danish courtier, with ominous significance, as he stood on his night-watch just the ghost of Hamlet's father reappeared.

> In the most high and palmy state of Rome
> A little ere the mightiest Julius fell,
> The graves stood tenantless and the sheeted dead
> Did squeak and gibber in the Roman streets.

It was these precursors of future ill fortune, these

> ... harbingers preceding still the fates
> and prologue to the omen coming on

that the people of Ajodhia wished to keep away from their beloved sovereign and King.

In the course of the centuries which have passed, other observances have come to be recognised in connection with Diwali. To some, it is a festival which connotes cleanliness, and the occasion is observed by whitewashing, dung-coating and repairing the home. All the collected rubbish is then conveyed to the village dung-hill where it is thrown and, in token that this has been done, a little cruse, with lighted wick, is placed upon the rubbish heap. Then, the home is lighted up. Scores of dips, in little earthen platters, are lit along the walls of the courtyard and the home. Presumably, the significance of this procedure is that as the righteous Ram purged Ajodhia of all its dross, so should the individual cleanse his home of all the litter and rubbish which has collected during the year.

Another legend has sprung up through the ages, in connection with Diwali. Long, long ago there lived a mighty king, the Raja Nal. As he reclined upon his sofa, he called to a courtier and commanded that he should play him in a game of chance. The bashful courtier made excuse that there were no dice to be had.

Raja Nal burst into a passion at so poor a plea and, unsheathing his sword, severed his own thigh-bone, flinging it to the courtier with the command "No dice in all my kingdom! Take this, and from the bones make me the dice I want." The dice were made and the game was played. Half the kingdom of Raja Nal was the stake.

The courtier won. The shock of defeat, even more than the amputation of his leg, resulted in the death of Raja Nal, whose body was thrown into the river. The bones of that body have made all the shells and cowries which are yielded up by sea and river alike and thus, these substitutes for dice are used to the present day.

Since then, the receptacle for the stakes, the pool, is known in Hindi as the '*nal*' and the subject, like the courtier, gambles on Diwali night to enrich himself and to propitiate the ancient Raja Nal.

Perhaps, it is with the crystallisation of this belief that the festival has come to be associated with Lakshmi, the Goddess of Wealth. It is in the hope that Lakshmi will smile upon her devotee and grant him a free ticket to the get- rich-quick state, that gambling is universally indulged in by the Hindu at Diwali time, almost as a religious rite. Thus, also, the festival is sometimes called Dip Malika, the latter word having a possessory significance.

Philologically, the word Diwali is of more than usual interest. The most common interpretation is that the word is Dipvali. Where *dip* means exactly the same in Hindi as in English, viz. a wick dipped in wax or oil, and *vali* is a contortion of *mala*, a ring or wreath. Thus, Diwali would mean "Wreath of Light"; but the correspondence of the English and Hindi word *dip*, together with the unsatisfactory connection between *vali* and *mala* almost indicate that the western root *valere* in French, suggesting "value", would be more appropriate. Reasoning a *posteriori* from the fact that the Goddess of Wealth is worshipped at this time, we are almost led to the conclusion that this is a more acceptable theory.

However that may be, what of it? Diwali is the festival of light and joy, of good cheer and of abandon, of gambling and of wealth, of *lawa* and of *batashas*, of toys of clay and toys of sugar, of feasts and of fairs. India is happier for it. Little else matters.

L.H. NIBLETT
India in Fable, Verse and Story

Muharram

I must first endeavour to represent the principal causes for the observance of Muharram: and, for the information of those who have witnessed its celebration, as well as for the benefit of others who have not had the same opportunity, describe the manner of celebrating the event, which occurred more than twelve hundred years ago.

Hasan and Hosein were the two sons of Fatima and Ali, from whom the whole Syaad race have generated; Hasan was poisoned by an emissary of the usurping Calipha's; and Hussein, the last sad victim of the family to the King Yuzeed's fury, suffered a cruel death, after the most severe trials, on the plains of Kraabaallah, on the tenth day of the Arabian

month Muharram; the anniversary of which catastrophe is
solemnised with the most devoted zeal.

*

This annual solemn display of the regret and veneration they
consider due to the memory for departed excellence,
commences on the first day of the Moon (Muharram). The
Mussulmaun year has twelve moons; every third year one
moon is added, which regulation, I fancy, renders their years,
in a chronological point of view, very nearly equal with those
of Europe. Their day commences and ends when the stars are
first visible after sunset.

The first day of Muharram invariably brings to my
recollection the strongly impressed ideas of "The Deserted
Village." The profound quiet and solemn stillness of an
extensively populated native city, contrasted with the incessant
bustle usual at all other times, are too striking to Europeans
to pass by unheeded. This cessation of the animated scene,
however, is not of long duration; the second day presents to
the view vast multitudes of people parading backwards and
forwards, on horseback, in *palkies*, and on foot, through the
broad streets and roadways, arrayed in their several mourning
garbs, speeding their way to the Emaumbaarahs of the great
men, and the houses of friends, to pay the visit of respect
(*zeearut*), wherever a Tazia is set up to the remembrance of
Hasan and Hosein.

The word Tazia signifies grief. The term is applied to a
representation of the mausoleum at Kraabaallah, erected by
their friends and followers, over the remains of Hasan and
Hosein. It is formed of every variety of material, according,
from the purest silver down to bamboo and paper, strict
attention being always paid to preserve the model of
Kraabaallah, in the exact pattern with the original building.
Some people have them of ivory, ebony, sandalwood, cedar,

etc., and I have seen some beautifully wrought in silver filigree.

*

The more common Tazias are conveyed in the procession on the tenth day, and finally deposited with funeral rites in the public burial-grounds, of which there are several outside the town. These cemeteries are denominated Kraabaallah, and the population of a large city may be presumed on by the number of these dispersed in the suburbs. They do not bury their dead in the vicinity of a mosque, which is held too sacred to be allowed the pollution.

*

Mourning assemblies are held in the Emaumbaarahs twice every day during Muharram; those of the evening, however, are the most attractive and have the fullest attendance of visitors. The master of the house, at the appointed hour, takes his seat on the floor near the pulpit, surrounded by the males of family and intimate friends, and the crowd of strangers themselves — wherever there is sitting-room — without impeding the view of the Tazia.

*

In commemorating this remarkable event in Mussulmaun history, the expressions of grief, manifested by the ladies, are far greater and appear to me more lasting than with the other sex; indeed, I never could have given credit to the extent of their bewailings without witnessing, as I have done for many years, the season for tears and profound grief return with the month of Muharram. In sorrowing for the martyred Emaums, they seem to forget their private griefs; the bereavement of a beloved object even is almost overlooked in the dutiful remembrance of Hasan and Hosein at this period; and I have had opportunities of observing this triumph of religious feeling in women, who are remarkable for their affectionate attachment to their children, husbands, and parents; — they tell me, "We must not indulge selfish sorrows of our own, whilst the Prophet's family alone have a right to our tears."

The religious zeal of these people is evinced, likewise, in a stern, systematic, line of privations, during the period of Muharram; no one is obliged by any law or command; it is voluntary abstinence on the part of each individual — they impose it on themselves, out of pure pity and respect for their Emaums' well-remembered sufferings. Everything which constitutes comfort, luxury, or even convenience at other times, on these occasions is rigidly laid aside.

*

I have conversed with many sensible men of the Mussulmaun persuasion on the subject of celebrating Muharram, and from all I can learn, the pompous display is grown into a habit, by a long residence amongst people, who make a merit of showy parades at all their festivals. Foreign Mussulmauns are equally surprised as Europeans, when they visit Hindoostaun, and first see the Tazia conveyed about in procession, which would be counted sacrilegious in Persia or Arabia; but here, the ceremony is not complete without a mixture of pageantry with the deeply expressed and public exposure of their grief.

*

The most imposing spectacle in the celebration of Muharram, is reserved for the last day; and, judging from the activity of all classes, the zealous exertions of the multitude, the deep interest marked on every face, male and female; a mere spectator might well imagine this morning to be of more importance than any other in the Mussulmaun's catalogue of days.

At the earliest hour of the dawning day, the preparations for the march being complete — which had occupied the hours usually devoted to sleep — the streets and roads present a very animated picture. From the bustle and outpouring of the multitude, on this one absorbing engagement, a stranger might be led back in imagination to the flight from Egypt; the object, however, is very different from that of the children of Israel. The order of the day being to commemorate the death of Hosein, a grand military funeral is portrayed in each person's cavalcade, all pressing forward to their chosen Kraabaallah — the poor man, with his humble Tazia and flags, falling in the rear of the more affluent person's display, as well for protection as for speed. There is so much of similarity in these processions, that the description of one will be sufficient to convey the ideal of the whole, as they pass on in succession to the chosen place of burial.

*

The whole line of march is guarded in each procession by burkhandhars (matchlock men), who fire singly, at intervals on the way. Several bands of music are dispersed in the cavalcade, performing solemn dirge-like airs, peculiar to the style of composition in Hindoostaun and well-suited to the occasion — muffled drums and shrill trumpets, imitating the reiteration of "Hasan, Hosein," when Mortem is performed.

*

The procession having reached Kraabaallah, the whole ceremony of a funeral is gone through. The Tazia is committed to the grave with equal solemnity to that which is observed when their dead are deposited in the tomb; this occupies some time. I never witnessed the movements at Kraabaallah — the season of the year, the confusion, and the anticipated feuds between Sheahs and Soonies, ever deterred me from gratifying my curiosity. It is always expected that the bad feelings between the two sects, amongst the lower orders of the people, may produce a real battle on the imitative ground of Kraabaallah; and I have heard of many such terminations of the Muharram at Lucknow, where the enthusiastic Sheahs and Soonies — having reserved their long hatred for a favourable opportunity of giving it vent — have found an early grave on the very ground to which their Tazia has been consigned. Private quarrels are often reserved for decision on the field of Kraabaallah.

MRS. B. MIR HASSAN ALI
Observations on the Mussulmauns of India (1832)

The Fast of Rumzaun

I have, however, reason to think that the Mussulmauns generally, in fulfilling the commanded fast of Ramzaun, have an unexceptionable motive. They are taught by their Lawgiver, that the due performance of this rigid fast is an acceptable service to God the Creator, from man the creature: they believe this, and therefore they fast.

Amongst the well-informed it is persevered in as a duty delightful to be permitted to perform; the ignorant take some merit to themselves in having faithfully observed the command; yet all the fasting population are actuated more or less by the same motive — the desire to please God by fulfilling His commands, delivered to them by their acknowledged Prophet.

The severity of a Mussulmaun's fast can alone be understood by those who have made the trial, as I frequently have, of the strict rules of abstinence which they observe; and with the additional privations to be endured at the period of the hottest months and the longest days in the same climate, as will sometimes be the case with all their movable fasts.

The Mussulmaun fast commences when the first streak of light borders the Eastern horizon, and continues until the stars are clearly discerned in the heavens. During this period not the slightest particle of food, not one single drop of water, or any other liquid, passes the lips; the hooka, even, is disallowed during the continuance of the fast, which of itself forms not only a luxury of great value but an excellent antidote to hunger.

Amongst the really religious Mussulmauns the day is passed in occasional prayer, besides the usual Namaaz, reading the Khoraun, or the Lives of the Prophets. I have witnessed some, in their happy employment of these fatiguing days, who evinced even greater animation in their conversation than at other times; towards the decline of a day, when the thermometer has stood at eighty-nine in the shade of a closed house, they have looked a little anxious for the stars appearing, but — to their credit be it told — without the slightest symptom of impatience or fretfulness at the tardy approach of evening.

*

The fast is first broken by a cooling draught called tundhie; the same draught is usually resorted to in attacks of fever. The tundhie is composed of the seeds of lettuce, cucumber, and melon, with coriander, all well pounded and diluted with cold water, and then strained through muslin, to which is added rose-water, sugar, syrup of pomegranate, and kurah (a pleasant-flavoured distilled water from the blossom of species of aloe). This cooling draught is drank by basins' full amongst the Rozedhaars (fasters), and it is generally prepared in the zeenahnah apartments for the whole establishment, male and female. Some of the aged and more delicate people break their fast with the juice of spinach only, others choose a cup

of boiling water to sip from. My aged friend, Meer Hadjee
Shah, has acquired a taste for tea, by partaking of it so often
with me; and with this he has broken his fast for several years,
as he says, with the most comforting sensations to himself.
I have seen some people take a small quantity of salt in the
first instance, preparatory to a draught of any kind of liquid.
Without some such prelude to a meal, after the day's fast, the
most serious consequences are to be apprehended.

*

When anyone is prevented fulfilling the fast of Rumzaun in
his own person he is instructed to consider himself bound to
provide food for opening the fast of a certain number of poor
men who are Rozedhaars. The general food of the peasantry
and lower orders of the people — bread and dhall — is
deemed sufficient, if unable to afford anything better.

*

There are some few who are exempt from the actual necessity
of fasting during Rumzaun; the sick, the aged, women giving
nourishment to infants, and those in expectation of adding
to the members of the family, and very young children, these
are all commanded not to fast. There is a latitude granted to
travellers also; but many a weary pilgrim whose heart is bent
heavenward will be found taking his rank amongst the
Rozedhaars of the time, without deeming he has any merit
in refraining from the privileges his code has conferred upon
him; such men will fast whilst their strength permits them to
pursue their way.

*

The conclusion of the month Rumzaun is celebrated as Eade
(festival) and, if not more splendid than any other in the
Mussulmaun calender, it is one of the greatest heart rejoicing

days. It is a sort of thanksgiving day amongst the devout
people who have been permitted to accomplish the task; and
with the vulgar and ignorant, it is hailed with delight as the
season of merriment and good living — a sort of reward for
their month's severe abstinence.

The namaaz of the morning, and the prayer for Eade,
commence with the dawn; after which the early meal of Eade
is looked forward to with great exactness (for they adhere
to custom as to a law): plain boiled rice, with dahie (sour
curd) and sugar, forms the first morning repast of this; dried
dates are eaten with it (in remembrance of the Prophet's
family, whose greatest luxury was supposed to be the dates
of Arabia). A preparation of flour (similar to our vermicelli)
eaten with cold milk and sugar, is amongst the good things
of this day, and triffling as it may appear, the indulgence is
so great to the native population, that they would consider
themselves unfortunate Rozedhaars, if they were not gratified,
on this occasion, with these emblems of long-used custom.
The very same articles are in request in Mussulmaun society,
by this custom, from the King to the meanest of his subjects.

The ladies' assemblies, on this Eade, are marked by all the
amusements and indulgences they can possibly invent or enjoy,
in their secluded state. Some receiving, others paying visits in
covered conveyances; all doing honour to the day by wearing
their best jewellery and splendid dresses. The zeenahnah sings
with the festive songs and loud music, the cheerful meeting of
friends, the distribution of presents to dependants, and
remembrances to the poor; all is life and joy, cheerful bustle
and amusement, on this happy day of Eade, when the good
lady of the mansion sits in state to receive nuzzas from inferiors,
and granting proofs of her favour to others.

MRS. B. MIR HASSAN ALI
Observations on the Mussulmauns of India (1832)

Buckrah Eade

Buckrah Eade, for instance, is a festival about as interesting to the Natives, as Christmas Day is to the good people of England; and the day is celebrated amongst all classes and denominations of Mussulmauns with remarkable zeal and energy.

The particular event which gives rise to Buckrah Eade is the well-known circumstance of Abraham offering his son in sacrifice to God. The Mussulmauns, however, insist that the son so offered was Ishmael, and not Issac, as our Scriptures declare.

*

On this day all classes of people, professing "the faith," sacrifice animals, according to their circumstances; some offer up camels, others sheep and goats, lambs or kids. It is a day of religious veneration, and therefore by the pious prayers are added to sacrifice — it is also a day of joyful remembrances, consequently one of festivity amongst all ranks of the Mussulmaun population.

Kings, Princes, or Nuwaubs, with the whole strength of their establishments, celebrate the event, by going in great state to an appointed place, which is designated "The Eade-Gaarh," where the animals designated for immediate sacrifice are previously conveyed. On the arrival of the cavalcade at the Eade-Gaarh, the head Moolah reads the form of prayer appointed for the occasion, and then presents the knife to the royal personage, who with his own hand sheds the blood of the camel he offers in sacrifice, repeating an impressive prayer as he presents the steel to the throat of the animal. The exact moment of the King's sacrifice is announced by signal, when a grand salute from the artillery and infantry commences the days' rejoicing.

MRS. B. MIR HASSAN ALI
Observations on the Mussulmauns of India (1832)

Poems, Songs and Tales

In war we need a hero's courage,
And for counsel a wise man's calm;
For pleasure we seek out boon companions,
Judgment alone we seek in plight.

Mahasara Jataka

Such is the Sage

When one, O Prithâ's Son! —
Abandoning desires which shake the mind —
Finds in his soul full comfort for his soul,
He hath attained the Yôg — that man is such!
In sorrows not dejected, and in joys
Not overjoyed; dwelling outside the stress
Of passion, fear, and anger; fixed in calms
Of lofty contemplation; — such a one
Is Muni, is the Sage, the true Recluse!
He who to none and nowhere overbound
By ties of flesh, takes evil things and good
Neither desponding nor exulting such
Bears wisdom's plainest mark! He who shall draw
As the wise tortoise draws its four feet safe
Under its shield, his five frail senses back
Under the spirit's buckler from the world
Which else assails them, such a one, my Prince!
Hath wisdom's mark! Things that solicit sense
Hold off from the self-governed; nay, it comes,
The appetites of him who lives beyond
Depart, — aroused no more. Yet may it chance,
O Son of Kunti! that a governed mind
Shall some time feel the sense-storms sweep, and wrest
Strong self-control by the roots. Let him regain
His kingdom! let him conquer this, and sit

On Me intent. That man alone is wise
Who keeps the mastery of himself! If one
Ponders on objects of the sense, there springs
Attraction; from attraction grows desire;
Desire flames to fierce passion, passion breeds
Recklessness; then the memory — all betrayed —
Lets noble purpose go, and saps the mind,
Till purpose, mind, and man are all undone.
But, if one deals with objects of the sense
Not loving and not hating, making them
Serve his free soul, which rests serenely lord,
Lo! such a man comes to tranquility;
And out of that tranquility shall rise
The end and healing of his earthly pains,
Since the will governed sets the soul at peace.
The soul of the ungoverned is not his,
Nor hath he knowledge of himself; which lacked,
How grows serenity? and, wanting that,
Whence shall he hope for happiness?

Bhagavad Gita (100 B.C. — A.D. 100)
translated by SIR EDWIN ARNOLD

Easy and Hard Life

Easy is life to live for a shameless man,
Impudent as a crow, and backbiting,
Aggressive, bold, depraved.

Hard is life for a modest man,
Ever in quest of what is pure,
Disinterested, retiring, clean-lived, clear-sighted.

He who destroyeth life and speaketh lies,

Who taketh in the world what is not given,
And goeth to another's wife; —

And the man who is addicted to strong drink,
E'en in this world doth his own root dig up.

Easy to see the fault of others,
But hard one's own to see:
His neighbour's faults as chaff one winnoweth,
But hideth his own, as a cheating gambler his die.

In one who looketh for another's faults,
Conscious always of annoyance,
His passions grow,
From passional destruction he is far.

> *Dhammapada* (70 B.C.)
> (*Hymns of the Faith*)
> translated from the Pali by A.J. EDMUNDS

To Taste or Not

As my heart ponders whether I could ever
Have wed this woman that has come to me
In tortured loveliness, as I endeavour
To bring it back to mind, then like a bee
That hovers round a jasmine flower at dawn,
While frosty dews of morning still o'erweave it,
And hesitates to sip ere they be gone
I cannot taste the sweet, and cannot leave it.

> KALIDASA (*c.* A.D. 400-500)
> *Shakuntala*
> translated by A.W. RYDER

A Lover's Separation

XLI

I see thy limbs in graceful-creeping vines,
Thy glances in the eyes of gentle deer,
Thine eyebrows in the ripple's dancing lines,
Thy locks in plumes, thy face in moonlight clear —
Ah, jealous! But the whole sweet image is not here.

XLII

And when I paint that loving jealousy
With chalk upon the rock, and my caress
As at thy feet I lie, I cannot see
Through tears that to mine eyes unbidden press —
So stern a fate denies a painted happiness.

XLIII

And when I toss mine arms to clasp thee tight,
Mine own though but in visions of a dream —
They who behold the oft-repeated sight,
The kind divinities of wood and stream,
Let fall great pearly tears that on the blossoms gleam.

XLIV

Himalaya's breeze blows gently from the north,
Unsheathing twigs upon the deodar
And sweet with sap that it entices forth —
I embrace it lovingly; it came so far,
Perhaps it touched thee first, my life's unchanging star!

XLV

Oh, might the long, long night seem short to me!
Oh, might the day his hourly tortures hide!

Such longings for the things that cannot be
Consume my helpless heart, sweet-glancing bride,
In burning agonies of absence from thy side.

XLVI

Yet much reflection, dearest, makes me strong,
Strong with an inner strength; nor shouldst thou feel
Despair at what has come to us of wrong;
Who has unending woe or lasting weal?
Our fates move up and down upon a circling wheel.

> KALIDASA (c. A.D. 400-500)
> *The Cloud-Messenger*
> translated by A.W. RYDER

Virgin Beauty

She seems a flower whose fragrance none has tasted.
A gem uncut by workman's tool,
A branch no describing hands have wasted,
Fresh honey, beautifully cool.

No man on earth deserves to taste her beauty,
Her blameless loveliness and worth,
Unless he has fulfilled man's perfect duty —
And is there such a one on earth?

> KALIDASA (c. A.D. 400-500)
> *Shakuntala*
> translated by A.W. RYDER

Love

It is my body leaves my love, not I;
My body moves away, but not my wind;
For back to her my struggling fancies fly
Like silken banners borne against the wind.

In face of sweet presentment
Or harmonies of sound,
Man e'er forgets contentment,
By wistful longings bound.

There must be recollections
Of things not seen on earth,
Deep nature's predilections,
Love earlier than birth.

KALIDASA (*c.* A.D. 400-500)
Shakuntala
translated by A.W. RYDER

The Maiden Dressed in Bark

Beneath the barken dress
Upon the shoulder tied,
In maiden loveliness
Her young breast seems a hide.
As when a flower amid
The leaves by autumn tossed —
Pale, withered leaves — lies hid,
And half its grace is lost.

The meanest vesture glows
On beauty that enchants:
The lotus lovelier shows
Amid dull water-plants;

The moon in added splendour
Shines for its spot of dark;
Yet more the maiden slender
Charms in her dress of bark.

Her shoulders droop; her palms are reddened yet;
Quick breaths are struggling in her bosom fair;
The blossom o'er her ear hangs limply wet;
One hand restrains the loose, dishevelled hair.

Although she does not speak to me,
She listens while I speak;
Her eyes turn not to see my face,
But nothing else they seek.

KALIDASA (c. A.D. 400-500)
Shakuntala
translated by A.W. RYDER

A Maiden of Heavenly Beauty

He saw a maiden of heavenly beauty whose lips, in close proximity to her moon-like face, resembled buds glowing in the evening light. Her eyes were long and delicate like pine-blossoms. They were like windows for Love who lived in the chamber of her heart. The corners of those eyes were red, as if angry because the ears hindered their extension. Her nose was like a bridge between the two oceans of her eyes, and her delicate brows were like clusters of black-bees hovering around blue lotuses. Her waist seemed full of sorrow, unable to see her face which was hidden by two well-rounded obstructions. These were themselves accumulations of loveliness — like two lilies emerging from the pool of the heart. Her girdle was the golden rampart of the treasure house of the city of delight.

She seemed to be made of planets — of the Sun because of her splendour, of the Moon because she had a beautiful round face, of Venus because she had a lotus-like eyes, of Saturn because she had dark, heavy hair and her gait was languid. She was like a picture nailed on the wall of life; the meeting place of all the elegance of the three worlds; the perfect elixir for Siva in his youth; the repository of delight. She was like Cupid's flag of conquest; a potion to tame the senses; the sole sanctuary of good fortune. She was like the glacier from which the river of loveliness originates. She was like a sleight-of-hand of Love, the great juggler.

SUBANDHU (late 6th cent. A.D.)
Vasavadatta

My Straining Eyes

My straining eyes are as though dug out by
The force of the piercing darkness;
Though open wide, the lid of the dark is upon them;
The dark clings to the body, the sky rains darkness upon
    me,
And the sight is as useless now as the service of one
    unworthy.

In the darkness of night you cannot be seen,
Like lightning lost in the depths of the raincloud,

But you can be traced by the fragrance of your garlands
And the twinkle of the little bells on your ankles.

SHUDRAKA (4th cent. A.D.)
The Little Clay Cart
translated by A.L. BASHAM

Some Good Counsels

Death

Weep not! Life the hired nurse is, holding us a little space;
Death, the mother who doth take us back into our proper
    place.

Gone, with all their gauds and glories: gone, like peasants,
    are the Kings,
Whereunto the world is witness, whereof all her record
    rings.

For the body, daily wasting, is not seen to waste away,
Until wasted, as in water set a jar of unbaked clay.

And day after day man goeth near and nearer to his fate,
As step after step the victim thither where its slayers wait.

Like as a plank of drift-wood
Tossed on the watery main,
Another plank encountered,
Meets — touches — parts again;

So tossed, and drifting ever,
On life's unresting sea,
Men meet, and greet, and sever,
Parting eternally.

Halt, traveller! rest i' the shade: then up and leave it!
Stay, Soul! take fill of life; nor losing, grieve it!

Each beloved object born
Sets within the heart a thorn,
Bleeding, when they be uptorn.

When thine own house, this rotting frame, doth wither,
Thinking another's lasting — goest thou thither?

Meeting makes a parting sure,
Life's is nothing but death's door.

As the downward-running rivers never turn and never stay,
So the days and nights stream deathward, bearing human
  lives away.

Bethinking him of darkness grim, and death's unshunnëd
  pain,
A man strong-souled relaxes hold, like leather soaked in
  rain.

*

Death, that must come, comes nobly when we give
Our wealth, and life, and all, to make men live.

Courage

By the valorous and unskilful great achievements are not
  wrought;
Courage, led by careful Prudence, unto highest ends is
  brought.

*

Pitiful, who fearing failure, therefore no beginning makes,
Why forswear a daily dinner for the chance of stomach-
  aches?

Solitude

Seek not the wild, sad heart! thy passions haunt it;
Play hermit in thine house with heart undaunted;
A governed heart, thinking no thought but good,
Makes crowded houses holy solitude.

Fate and Fortune

Ah! it is the Cowards' babble, 'Fortune taketh, Fortune
    gave';
Fortune! rate her like a master, and she serves thee like
    a slave.

Two-fold is the life we live in — Fate and Will together
    run;
Two wheels bear life's chariot onward — will it move on
    only one?

Look! the clay dries into iron, but the potter moulds the
    clay:
Destiny today is master — Man was master yesterday.

Worthy ends come not by wishing. Wouldst thou? Up, and
    win it, then!
While the hungry lion slumbers, not a deer comes to his
    den.

                              *

Wouldst thou know whose happy dwelling
Fortune entereth unknown?
His, who careless of her favour, standeth fearless in his
    own;
His, who for the vague tomorrow barters not the sure
    today —

Master of himself, and sternly steadfast to the rightful
    way;
Very mindful of past service, valiant, faithful, true of
    heart —
Unto such come Lakshmi smiling — comes, and will not
    lightly part.

*

'Tis the fool who, meeting trouble, straightway destiny
    reviles;
Knowing not his own misdoing brought his own mischance
    the whiles.

*

By their own deeds men go downward, by them men
    mount upward all,
Like the diggers of a well, and like the builders of a wall.

Wealth

Enough is never what we have —
Looking down on lives below them, men of little store
    are great;
Looking up to higher fortunes, hard to each man seems
    his fate.

*

Give, and it shall swell thy getting; give, and thou shalt
    safer keep:
Pierce the tank-wall; or it yieldeth, when the water waxes
    deep.
When the miser hides his treasure in the earth, he doeth
    well;
For he opens up a passage that his soul may sink to hell.

Wisdom

Silly glass, in splendid settings, something of the gold may
gain;
And in company of wise ones, fools to wisdom may attain.
On the eastern mountains lying, common things shine in
the sun,
And, by learned minds enlightened, lower minds may
show as one.

*

Grief kills gladness, winter summer, midnight-gloom the
light of day,
Kindnesses ingratitude, and pleasant friends drive pain
away;
Each ends each, but none of other surer conquerers can
be
Than Impolicy of Fortune — of Misfortune Policy.
Wisdom answers all who ask her, but a fool she cannot
aid;
Blind men in the faithful mirror see not their reflection
made.

Passion

Passion will be Slave or Mistress: follow her, she brings
to woe;
Lead her, 'tis the way to Fortune. Choose the path that
thou wilt go.

NARAYANA
Hitopadesa (12th cent. A.D.)
(*The Book of Good Counsels*)
translated by SIR EDWIN ARNOLD

Women

What is the best of sights? The face of a satisfied girl.
The best of odours? Her breath. Of sounds? Her voice.
The best of tastes? Her lips. Of contacts? Her body.
The best of thoughts? Her beauty. She entrances every
　　sense.

Is there a heart that girls cannot subdue
When they walk like swans,
Their bangles jingling, their girdles tinkling, their anklets
　　jangling,
And their eyes like those of deer glance frank but timid?

BHARTRIHARI (*c.* 600 A.D.)
Sringar-Satakam
(Verses on Sex)
translated by A.L. BASHAM

Some Love Songs of Vidyapati

Vidyapati was born sometime in the second half of the 14th
century in the eastern side of north Bihar and he composed
his famous love songs in Maithili in the period between 1380
and 1406.

Twin Hills

Her hair dense as darkness,
Her face rich as the full moon:
Unbelievable contrasts
Couched in a seat of love.
Her eyes rival lotuses.
Seeing that girl today,
My eager heart
Is driven by desire.

Innocence and beauty
Adorn her fair skin.
Her gold necklace
Is lightning
On the twin hills,
Her breasts ...

The End of Youth

I hide my shabby cheeks
With locks of hair,
And my grey hairs
In folds of flowers.
I paint my eyes
With black mascara.
The more I try
The more absurd I look.
My breasts loosely dangle.

My curving lines are gone.
My youth is ended
And love roams wild
In all my skin and bones.
O sadness, my sadness,
Where is my youth?

Ecstasy

Her hair, dishevelled,
Veils the beauty of her face
As evil shadows eat the glowing moon.
Strings of blossom in her hair
Wantonly play
As flooded rivers
Twine about their twins.

Exquisite today,
This sport of love,
As Radha rides on Krishna.
Beads of sweat glisten on her face
Like pearls on the moon,
A present to her
From the god of love.

With all her force
She kisses her lover's lips,
Like the moon swooping
To drink a lotus bloom.
Her necklace dangles
Below her hanging breasts,
Like streams of milk

Trickling from golden jars.
The jingling bells around her waist
Sang glory to the god of love.

Waxing Moon

Do not abandon
Her delicate limbs
For fear of crushing.
Who has ever seen
A blossom smothered
By the weight of a bee?
Madhava, mark my words:
Do not hold back
If she cries "No, no",
Or futile comes the dawn.
With your ardent kissing
Give her lips
The hue of dusk
And slowly bring her
To the height of joy.
The play of love,
Its keen delights,
Should grow and grow
Like the white brilliance
Of a waxing moon.

Ocean of Nectar

Sweet girl,
So strange you seem today
And your eyes and your face
Look different.
As you speak,
You lose the thread of your thoughts.
Your lips turn pale.
Beloved in passion,
Who shared the joys of love with you?
Your secret is out, why are you so shy?
His forces of love
The god has roused in you.
Your thighs tremble.
The golden skin of your breasts
Is scarlet from his nails
Yet still you try to hide them.

Radha, you are an ocean of nectar
And Krishna is afloat in it
Like a furious elephant.

Love Songs of Vidyapati
translated by D. BHATTACHARYA

What Will Be, Will Be

Long not for a dwelling in heaven, and fear not to dwell
   in hell;
What will be, will be; O my soul, hope not at all.

Sing the praises of God from whom the supreme reward
is obtained.
What is devotion, what penance and austerities, what
fasting and ablutions,
Unless thou know the way to love and serve God?
Be not glad at the sight of prosperity and grieve not at
the sight of adversity;
As is prosperity so is adversity; what God proposeth shall
be accomplished.
Saith Kabir, through the saints I now know in my heart
That the worshipper in whose heart God dwelleth,
performeth the best worship.

KABIR (1440-1518)
translated by M.A. MACAULIFFE

God Alone is True

The limbs *anointed with* ground aloe-wood, sandal, and
fragrant soap,
Shall be burnt with wood.
What is there to be proud of in this body and in wealth?
Both shall remain on earth and not go *with the soul* to
the other world.
They who sleep at night and work by day,
Who utter not God's name for a moment,
Who eat betel, and stretch out their hands for *more*,
Shall at the hour of death be firmly bound as thieves.
If under the guru's instruction thou joyfully sing the
praises of God,
And utter the name of Him who filleth all creation, thou
shalt be happy.

He in whose heart God mercifully establisheth His name,
Giveth the odour and perfume of God a place in *his heart*.
Saith Kabir, think, O blind man,
God is true, all worldly occupations are false.

KABIR (1440-1518)
translated by M.A. MACAULIFFE

The Fearless Love

I have the god Girdhar and no other;
He is my spouse on whose head is a crown of peacock
    feathers,
Who carrieth a shell, discus, mace, and lotus, and who
    weareth a necklace.
I have forfeited the respect of the world by ever sitting
    near holy men.
The matter is now public; everybody knoweth it.
Having felt supreme devotion I die as I behold the world.
I have no mother, father, son, or relation with me.
I laugh when I behold my beloved; people think I weep.
I have planted the vine of love, and irrigated it again and
    again with the water of tears.
I have cast away fear of the world; what can anyone do
    to me?
Mira's love for her god is fixed, come what may.

MIRA BAI
translated by M.A. MACAULIFFE

Poems from Ghalib

I wonder how, O Puritan,
I can agree to follow thee without hypocrisy?
Thou lurest me with glories of a Paradise beyond.
That virtue be the slave of gain has no appeal for me.

*

Man owes his zest for life to his mortality.
Had we both world and time,
Love would have lost its urgency
And desire stretched itself lazily
Nor called for urgent fulfilment.
How many hopes and desires jostle in man's breast,
And crowd within the brief span of his life!

*

Ask me not why I am sad,
What grief doth clutch my hearth.
My heart hath built me a prison-cell
And raised grim walls of narrow truths,
Of camping loves and hates.
It shuts in the horizons of my thought
And clips my fancy's wings.

*

Desire inspires the coward heart with valiant aspiration;
Desire drives the little drop of water towards the ocean;
Desire nerves the humble man to shoot high at a star;
Desire blows a speck of dust to desert sands afar.

*

Non-attachment is not indifference
Of shrinking from the world of men;
Nor does renunciation justify
Estrangement from our fellow-men.

If thou dost dread life's fever-fret,
Or if to thee life seems to be
A waste and wilderness,
Then shun thine ego; It is the source
Of thine unhappiness.
Shun not thy fellow-men.

*

How can man free himself
From the struggle and strife of life?
Do what he will, he cannot cut
Its strangling tentacles.
The river seeks freedom in its flow,
But look! how, in its onward rush,
It frets and fumes, and bubbles and boils,
In its own eddies churned and chained,
On its way all along.

*

I would not mind thine angry looks,
And could forgive thy teasing ways,
Thy wilful negligence;
For we could hope to make it up,
If thou wert angry for a while.
But what I dread as poison is
Thy look of indifference.
It tells me of thine unconcern
And that I matter nought to thee.

*

Leave me, oh! leave me alone,
And let me weep.
Why shall I not weep?
Why shall I gulp down my tears?
I am not stock nor stone;

I am not wood.
I have a tender heart,
Moved by compassion and pain.

*

If thou canst not see the Ocean in the water drop,
Nor visualise the Whole from each specific part,
Thou has not the seeing eye, the seer's vision blest;
Thou art but a child who cannot see beyond
The toys and trinkets and puppet-show of things.

*

Were there no ugliness, beauty could not shine.
Bitter and sweet, beauty and ugliness
Are foils and necessary opposites,
By contrast setting off each other's worth;
Beauty with ugliness; with evil, good;
With bitter, sweet; and with impure, the pure.
The garden verdure is spring's verdigris,
A foil to the mirror of its balmy breeze,
Which set off and reflects its loveliness.

*

Since sorrow follows joy
As autumn doth the spring,
Man must transcend the joys
Of earth, which sorrows bring.

MIRZA GHALIB (1797-1869)
translated by J.L. KAUL

Anxious Love

Why did the lamp go out?
I shaded it with my cloak to save it

from the wind, that is why the lamp went out.

Why did the flower fade?
I pressed it to my heart with anxious
love, that is why the flower faded.

Why did the stream dry up?
I put a dam across it to have it for
my use, that is why the stream dried up.
Why did the harp-string break?
I tried to force a note that was
beyond its power, that is why the harpstring is broken.

RABINDRANATH TAGORE (1861-1941)
The Gardener

God is not in thy Temple

Leave this chanting and singing and
telling of beads! Whom dost thou
worship in this lonely dark corner of a
temple with doors all shut? Open
thine eyes and see thy God is not before thee!
He is there where the tiller is tilling
the hard ground and where the path maker
is breaking stones. He is with
them in sun and in shower, and his
garment is covered with dust. Put off
thy holy mantle and even like him come
down on the dusty soil!
Deliverance? Where is this deliverance
to be found? Our master himself
has joyfully taken upon him the bonds
of creation; he is bound with us all for ever.

Come out of thy meditations and
leave aside thy flowers and incense!
What harm is there if thy clothes
become tattered and stained? Meet
him and stand by him in toil and in
sweat of thy brow.

RABINDRANATH TAGORE (1861-1941)
Gitanjali

The Bondage of Finery

The child who is decked with prince's
robes and who has jewelled chains
round his neck loses all pleasure in his
play; his dress hampers him at every step.
In fear that it may be frayed, or
stained with dust he keeps himself from
the world, and is afraid even to move.
Mother, it is no gain, thy bondage of
finery, if it keep one shut off from the
healthful dust of the earth, if it rob
one of the right of entrance to the
great fair of common human life.

RABINDRANATH TAGORE (1861-1941)
Gitanjali

Modern Man

"Love fled, mind stung him like a snake"; he could not

Force it to vision's will;
He Sought the orbits of the stars, yet could not
Travel his own thoughts' world;
Entangled in the labyrinth of his learning,
Lost count of good and ill;
Enchained the sunbeams, yet his hand no dawn
On life's dark night unfurled.

IQBAL (1873-1938)
Poems from Iqbal
translated by V.G. KIERNAN

Life is Preserved by Purpose

Life is preserved by purpose:
Because of the goal its caravan-bell tinkles.
Life is latent in seeking,
Its origin is hidden in desire.
Keep desire alive in thy heart,
Lest thy little dust become a tomb.
Desire is the soul of this world of hue and scent,
The nature of every thing is faithful to desire.
'Tis desire that enriches Life,
And the intellect is a child of its womb.
What are social organisation, customs, and laws?
What is the secret of the novelties of science?
A desire which broke through by its own strength
And burst forth from the heart and took shape
Nose, hand, brain, eye, and ear,
Thought, imagination, feeling, memory, and
     understanding —
All these are weapons devised for self-preservation
By him that rides into the battle of Life.

The object of the garden is not the bud and the flower.
Science is an instrument for the preservation of Life,
Science is a means of establishing the Self.
Science and art are servants of Life,
Slaves born and bred in its house.

IQBAL (1873-1938)
The Secrets of the Self

Nature

What pang in this lone vigil lies?
Are not the stars your brethren? See;
That silent heaven in majesty,
Drowsed earth, that wilderness, those hills —
Creation one white rosebed fills.
Sweet are the teardrops that have pearled
Like gleaming gems, like stars, your eyes;
What thing is it you crave? All Nature,
Oh my heart, is your fellow-creature.

IQBAL (1873-1938)
Poems from Iqbal
translated by V.G. KIERNAN

Learn to Love

The luminous point whose name is the Self
Is the life-spark beneath our dust.
By Love it is made more lasting,

More living, more burning, more glowing.
From Love proceeds the radiance of its being
And the development of its unknown possibilities.
Its nature gathers fire from Love,
Love instructs it to illumine the world.
Love fears neither sword nor dagger,
Love is not born of water and air and earth.
Love makes peace and war in the world,
The Fountain of Life is Love's flashing sword.
The hardest rocks are shivered by Love's glance:
Love of God at last becomes wholly God.
Learn thou to love, and seek to be loved:
Seek an eye like Noah's, heart like Job's!

IQBAL (1873-1938)
The Secrets of the Self

She was Breaking Stones

She was breaking stones;
I saw her on the pathway of Allahabad —
She was breaking stones.
The trees under which she sat resigned,
They gave no shade;
The body dark, the full and swelling breasts confined,
Eyes down-cast, and the mind in work absorbed,
The heavy hammer in her hand,
She gave repeated blows;
In front of her a storied house
Fenced with a row of trees.
The sun was rising high,
Those were the summer days,
The red-hot glowing face of day,

The scorching wind arose,
The earth like cotton burned,
The sparks of dust hung overhead,
It was about midday,
And she was breaking stones.
She looked at me,
And then she looked at that tall building once
With broken heart;
She looked at me with eyes that had not wept
Beneath the blows of fate;
The chords of her heart thrilled
With such a quivering sound
As I had never heard.
A moment after, she
Trembled beauteously,
And drops of perspiration from her brow
Fell rolling down and thus she said,
"Well, I am breaking stones upon the road!"

NIRALA
translated by B.L. SAHNEY

The Test of Goodness

The stories of the Jatakas go back to the days of the Buddha himself, but in their present form they were written about 500 A.D.

Once upon a time the Bodhisattva was born as Brahmadatta, the prince of Banaras. He grew up into a fine lad and at the age of sixteen went to the University at Takshashila where he mastered all the branches of learning. On his father's death he mounted the throne and became the king of Banaras. He ruled with rectitude and wisdom. He was upright and just. And he never allowed his whims to influence the administration.

As the master, so the assistants. Following the King's example the ministers also acted justly. After a while everything at Banaras was justly done. No one brought a false suit in the court. The palace was free from the bustle of complainants. The ministers sat all day long with nothing to do and went back without seeing a single suitor. All the courts were deserted.

At last a day came when the Bodhisattva felt disturbed and thought: "How quiet is everything! No one comes to try any issue in the court. My government is accepted as perfectly just. And yet there must be *some* faults in me, even if injustice is not one of them. I must find out what my faults are, so that I may overcome them and lead a better life."

And so Brahmadatta tried to find someone who would tell him his defects. But, although he talked to every single person at the court, he could hear nothing but praise of himself. Suspecting that people spoke to people outside the palace. But he got the same answer. Then he spoke to the citizens at large, but was still unable to hear of his faults. He wandered as far as the four city gates and talked to people in the suburbs. But even in the suburbs, no one had anything but praise for the king.

Finally, determined to find a man who would reveal his faults, the Bodhisattva entrusted his government to the care of ministers and left the city in disguise taking only his driver with him. He traversed the countryside far and wide right up to the frontier. Then he turned homewards by the high road.

Now, by a unique coincidence, Mallika, the king of Kosala, was at that time wandering about for exactly the same purpose. He, too, was a just sovereign, and wanted to know his own faults. Hearing nothing but praise, he too had wandered far and wide in search of a person who would point out his limitations.

The two kings chanced to meet at a place where the road was narrow and there was no room for one carriage to overtake the other. Clearly, it was necessary that one party should give right of way to the other.

Mallika's driver addressed the driver of the king of Banaras and asked him to remove his carriage. But the Bodhisattva's driver would not agree to this. "No, no, my friend", said he, "it is you who must make way for us. You must know that in this carriage sits Brahmadatta, the great monarch of Banaras."

"And you must know, driver", replied the other, "that in my carriage sits the great King Mallika, lord of the realm of Kosala. Please take your carriage to one side and give us passage."

The driver of the king of Banaras was now perplexed. He did not know how to determine the priority between the two kings. It occurred to him that the younger should make way for the elder. But when he inquired of King Mallika's age it was discovered that the two kings had been born on the same day. The driver then made inquiries about Mallika's power, resources, fame, and also concerning his caste, clan and family. To his utter surprise he found that on every one of these points the two kings were equals. At last Brahmadatta's driver came to the right of passage — he who was the nobler man of the two should have priority. So he requested the other driver to describe his master's virtues. King Mallika's driver proudly recited this verse:

Great King Mallika is rough to the rough,
But to the gentle he returns gentleness.
The good he conquers by greater goodness,
And badness bestows on those that are bad.
Such are the ways of the King of Kosala,
Give place, oh driver, give place.

Hearing this, the driver of the king of Banaras exclaimed: "Is that all you have to say about you King's nobility? If these are his virtues, what may his faults be!" The other man said, "Call them faults, or call them anything else. But let us now hear the virtues of *your* king." "Certainly," rejoined the first, and he recited a stanza:

> By mildness alone he conquers anger,
> By goodness he repays the bad.
> By lavish gifts he vanquishes misers,
> And falsehood he overcomes with truth.
> Such are the virtues of the king of Banaras,
> Make way, oh driver, make way.

King Mallika and his driver were deeply impressed by these words. They realised that he who returns mildness for harshness is superior to him who is rough to the rough and mild to the mild; that to repay evil by good and falsehood by truth proclaims true nobility. And so they descended from their carriage, loosed the horses, and moved them out of the way so as to make room for the king of Banaras.

The Bodhisattva gave good advice to King Mallika and instructed him in the ways of righteousness. Then he returned to Banaras and spent his life in deeds of kindness and charity until at last he joined the hosts of heaven.

King Mallika took the lesson to heart. After traversing the length and breadth of the land, he returned to his own city.

And he too gave alms throughout his life, and did many other things that were good, until he attained heaven.

Rajovada Jataka
translated by V.S. Naravane

The Obtuse Monkeys

Once upon a time a tribe of monkeys lived happily in the pleasure-garden of the king of Banaras. The King's gardener looked upon them as his friends and they, in their turn, were devoted to him.

Now one day a great festival was to take place in city. The festive drum sounded early in the morning, and the townsfolk turned out in thousands to keep holiday. The king's gardener felt a craving to join the festivities. He thought: "Why should I not have a holiday once in a while? After all, there is very little to do in the park. Only a few young saplings have to be watered. Surely my friends, the monkeys, can do that much for me."

So he went to the leader of the monkeys and said, "My friend, you know that this park has to be well looked after. His Majesty and his subjects enjoy many benefits from it. Today there is holiday-making in the city and I desire to take the day off. At the same time I cannot neglect the park. As you know, young plants have got to be watered every day. Couldn't you do the job for me, just for today?" The leader of the monkeys said, "Oh yes, brother. We shall look after your plants. Go and make merry to your heart's content."

"Thank you," said the gardener, "but see that you do not let me down." And then, after supplying the monkeys with waterskins and wooden buckets, he went off to the city.

The monkeys immediately started their work of watering the young plants. Their leader instructed them in this way: "Friend, remember that we have only a limited amount of water. We must not waste it, because if it is finished before the work is done we shall find it difficult to get more. We should water the trees according to their requirements. So it would be better if you pull out each young plant and examine the size of its roots. Then you can give plenty of water to those which have big and long roots. On the contrary, a small quantity of water will do for plants with tiny roots."

"You are quite right, Sir," said the other monkeys, and did as their leader told them. They pulled out all the young plants in the garden and watered them according to the size of their roots.

Thus, with every desire to do good, the faithful monkeys did great harm to their friend, the gardener, to the king, and to all those who enjoyed the benefits of the pleasure-garden.

And that is what the ignorant and the foolish always do — they harm those whom they want to help.

Aramadusaka Jataka
translated by V.S. NARAVANE

The Blue Jackal

Once a Jackal named Chandarava lived near the suburbs of a city. One day hunger goaded him inside the city where he roamed the streets, looking for food. The city dogs barked at him and snapped at his limbs with their sharp teeth, until the poor jackal was terrified. He fled blindly, trying to escape from the dogs, and strayed into a dyer's house. There he fell into an indigo tub and lay concealed for many hours.

At dawn he managed to crawl out of the tub and somehow reached the forest, his body dyed a deep blue. All the animals of the forest gaped at him in amazement. They thought that an exotic creature had mysteriously appeared, and, scared for their lives, kept at a distance.

Taking advantage of their dismay, Chandarava called to

them, "Now, now, you foolish creatures! Don't be afraid. Indra has taken mercy on you. Since you had no monarch Indra has appointed me as your king. My name is Chandarava. You may live peacefully under my protection."

At this all the animals of the forest — lions, tigers, monkeys, leopards, elephants, rabbits, and the rest — bowed before him and swore loyalty. "Oh, Master," they said, "tell us our duties, and we shall carry them out." So Chandarava appointed a lion as his chief minister, a tiger as his personal valet and a leopard as the custodian of his betel-box. An elephant was made the doorkeeper and a monkey was placed in charge of the royal umbrella. But when jackals came near him he insulted them and drove them away, although they were his own kith and kin.

In this way Chandarava lived in kingly glory. Lions and tigers killed animals for him and he ate the most delicious morsels. And then he distributed the remainder of the food in a grand, royal manner.

One day, while he was sitting in his court, he heard the noise made by a pack of jackals nearby. At this his body quivered with pleasure and tears of joy filled his eyes. He jumped up and gave vent to a piercing howl. For a moment the animals surrounding him were stunned. But soon they understood the situation and felt ashamed at the discovery that they had been imposed upon by a mere jackal. They pounced on him. Chandarava tried to escape but a tiger pursued him and tore him to bits.

The Panchatantra (*c.* 400 A.D.)
translated by V.S. NARAVANE

The Rabbit who Outwitted a Lion

There was once a lion named Bhasuraka. He was proud of his strength and killed the animals of the forest without mercy. So one day all the animals met in a conference and decided to approach the lion with a proposal. "Oh King," they said, "please do not kill us indiscriminately. Think of the other world. It is sinful to take life in excess of your needs. We propose that you remain at home and one animal be sent to you every day to satisfy your hunger. In this way your sustenance will continue and our families, too, will not be rooted out. A cow must not be milked every hour, but only in the morning. Remember that the loss of his subjects is also the king's loss. Have mercy, then, and accept our suggestion."

The lion said, "Gentlemen, your words are quite convincing. I accept the arrangement. But remember, if an animal does not come to me every day I shall destroy you all at a single stroke." And so the animals began to roam the woods without fear, choosing one among them to serve as the King's meal every day. The different species sent their members by turns, selecting an individual who had become old, or indifferent to life through religious feelings.

One day it was the turn of the rabbits. The rabbit selected happened to be a pluck and clever fellow. Instead of going to his death meekly he made up his mind to try his wits and lead the lion to destruction. So he lingered on the way and deliberately arrived in the lion's presence several hours after the appointed time. The King was in a rage, vowing to exterminate all the animals the first thing next morning.

The rabbit approached at a leisurely pace, bowed low, and stood before the lion. Bhasuraka thundered, "So you are supposed to be my dinner! Measly thing, you are no more than a single morsel to me. And you dare to keep me waiting for hours! Is that how the animals keep their agreement? I shall kill every single one of them."

The rabbit said with great show of respect, "Master, the fault is not mine, nor are the other animals to blame. Something unexpected happened."

"What happened? Tell me quickly, while you are still outside my jaws."

"Master, as you see I am too small to satisfy your appetite. That is why five other rabbits were sent along with me. We were all coming here at the appointed time, but a lion emerged from a big hole under the ground and stopped us. 'Where are you going?' he asked. On our replying he said, 'Pray to your family deity. I want to eat you.' We replied, 'You have no right to eat us. We are the dinner of Bhasuraka, our mighty king.' At this he jeered at us and said, 'This forest belongs to me. Bhasuraka is a thief. Bring him here at once and I shall show you who is the master.' And so he detained my comrades, sending me to you with his challenge. That is why, Oh King, I could not come in time."

"Who is this rascal?" said Bhasuraka, "Lead me to him at once. I shall have no peace of mind until I drive him away."

The rabbit said, "Quite so. A true warrior brooks no insult. But you must be cautious. This fellow lives in a fortress. And a single fortress is equal in might to a thousand elephants."

"I don't care where he hides. I shall kill all the same. An enemy must be destroyed at once. He must never be permitted to grow."

"Very well. But it was my duty to warn you of your enemy's strength. You must not underestimate him."

"What business is it of yours, you imp? Show me his fortress."

Thereupon the rabbit led Bhasuraka to a deep well and said, "Master, your very approach has terrified the thief. He has crawled into his hole. You can see him if you peep into it."

The lion peeped into the well and saw his own reflection in the water. Fool that he was, he mistook the reflection for a real lion and roared loudly. The sound re-issued from the well with redoubled loudness. At this Bhasuraka was mad with anger, hurled himself upon his imaginary rival, and met his death. The rabbit carried the happy news to the animals, who thereafter lived contentedly in the forest.

The Panchatantra (*c.* 400 A.D.)
translated by V.S. NARAVANE

Religions and Beliefs

We have to learn yet that all religions, under whatever name they may be called, either Hindu, Buddhist, Mohammedan or Christian, have the same God, and he who derides any one of these derides his own God.

SWAMI VIVEKANANDA

The Evolution of Hinduism

The Religion of the Indus People
c. 2500-1550 B.C.

We have seen that certain figures at Mohenjo-daro and Harappa resemble the Sumerian Eabani or Enkidu, the half-human, half-bovine Satyr, who became the companion of Gilgamesh; and Gilgamesh himself may be represented by the leaf-clad hunter on a copper table with a bow in his hand and horns on his head. That a close connection exists between these figures and the Mesopotamian heroes is hardly likely to be disputed. The resemblance is too marked to be the result of chance or of independent evolution, nor can it be explained on the hypothesis that they were sprung from a common prototype foreign to both countries. Either the Indus Valley type must have been borrowed from the Mesopotamian or the Mesopotamian from the Indian, and seeing how intimately the Gilgamesh-Eabani legend is bound up with Sumer, it is reasonable to conclude that the borrowing was done by India. At the same time, the possibility must not be overlooked that the types of these horned or half-bovine figures may have been created in the Indus Valley and subsequently adapted to Sumerian legend.

We have seen, too, that the use of bull's or bison's horns as a symbol of divinity and the officiant beasts on one of the Harappa seals are indicative of religious contact between the Indus Valley and Western Asia, but apart from these few elements and the sacral trefoil patterning on the robe of the image, all the material of a religious nature recovered at Mohenjo-daro and Harappa appears to be characteristically Indian. Although relatively meagre in proportion to the extent and importance of the sites, this material is sufficient at any rate to make it clear that iconic and aniconic cults existed side by side, and were just as compatible five thousand years ago as they are in the Hinduism of today. It exhibits to our eyes, on the one hand, the worship of the Mother Goddess, who still occupies a foremost place among the teeming village population of India; and side by side with her god, whom we have seen good reason to recognise as the ancestor of the historic Siva, the principal male deity of the Hindu pantheon. On the other hand, it shows us the worship of animals and trees and inanimate stones or other objects in much the same form as it meets us in historic times. Animals appear deified or venerated sometimes in their natural, at other times in semi-human, at others in syncretic and fabulous shape. Trees, too, are worshipped in their natural state, but their indwelling spirits are already completely anthropomorphised. The *linga* and *yoni* both have their places in the religious scheme, as they have in Saivism, and along with these emblems are other stones, apparently of a baetylic nature. Chrematheism is exemplified in the worship of the sacred "incense-burners"; amulets and charms are common attesting the existence of that demonophobia with which Hinduism has always been incurably afflicted. And there is evidence that *yoga* was already playing its part as a religious practice.

SIR JOHN MARSHALL
Mohenjo Daro and the Indus Civilisation

The Vedas

Of the four Vedas, *Rigveda* is oldest, composed in the period between 1200 B.C. and 900 B.C.

What can be more tedious than the Veda, and yet what can be more interesting, if once we know that it is the first word spoken by the Aryan man?

The Veda has a two-fold interest: it belongs to the history of the world and to the history of India ... As long as man continues to take an interest in the history of his race, and as long as we collect in libraries and museums the relics of former ages, the first place in that long row of books which contains the records of the Aryan branch of mankind, will belong for ever to the Rigveda.

F. MAX MUELLER

Who Created This World?

Then was not non-existent nor existent: there was no realm of air, no sky beyond it.

What covered in, and where? And what gave shelter?

Was water there, unfathomed depth of water?

Death was not then, nor was there aught immortal: no sign was there, the day's and night's divider.

That One Thing, breathless, breathed by its own nature: apart from it was nothing whatsoever.

Darkness there was: at first concealed in darkness this All was indiscriminated chaos.

All that existed then was void and formless: by the great power of Warmth was born that Unit.

Thereafter rose Desire in the beginning, Desire, the primal
    seed and germ of Spirit.
Sages who searched with their heart's thought discovered
    the existent's kinship in the non-existent.
Transversely was their severing line extended: what was
    above it then, and what below it?
There were begetter, there were mighty forces, free action
    here and energy up yonder.
Who verily knows and who can here declare it, whence
    it was born and whence comes this creation?
The gods are later than this world's production. Who
    knows then whence it first came into being?
He, the first origin of this creation, whether he formed
    it all or did not form if,
Whose eye controls this world in highest heaven, he verily
    knows it, or perhaps he knows not.

The Rigveda (1200-900 B.C.) X. *Hymn* 129
translated by R.T.H. GRIFFITH

God Varuna

Let me not yet, King Varuna, enter into the house of clay:
Have mercy, spare me, mighty lord.
When, thunderer! I move along tremulous like a wind-
    blown skin,
Have mercy, spare me, mighty lord.
O bright and powerful god, through want of strength I
    erred and went astray:
Have mercy, spare me, mighty lord.
Thirst found thy worshipper though he stood in the midst
    of water-floods:
Have mercy spare me, mighty lord.

O Varuna, whatever the offence may be which we as men
   commit against the heavenly host,
When through our want of thought we violate thy laws,
   punish us not, O god, for that iniquity.

The Rigveda (1200-900 B.C.) Hymns 88 and 89
translated by R.T.H. GRIFFITH

Soul, The Finest Essence

"Place this salt in the water. In the morning come unto
   me."
Then he did so.
Then he said to him: "That salt you placed in the water
   last evening — please, bring it hither."
Then he grasped for it, but did not find it, as it was
   completely dissolved.
"Please, take a sip of it from this end," said he. "How
   is it?"
"Salt."
"Take a sip from the middle," said he. "How is it?"
"Salt."
"Take a sip from that end," said he. "How is it?"
"Salt."
"Set it aside. Then come unto me."
He did so, saying, "It is always the same."
Then he said to him: "Verily, indeed, my dear, you do not
   perceive Being here. Verily, indeed, it is here.
That which is the finest essence — this whole world has
   that as its soul. That is Reality. That is Atman (Soul).
That art thou, Svetaketu."

Chandogya Upanishad (600-500 B.C.)
translated by R.E. HUME

He is God

The one who, himself without colour, by the manifold
    application of his power (*sakti-yoga*)
Distributes many colours in his hidden purpose,
And into whom its end and its beginning, the whole world
    dissolves — He is God (deva)!
May he endow us with clear intellect!

Svetasvatara Upanishad 4.1. (300-200 B.C.)
translated by R.E. HUME

Religion is Not His

But for earthly needs
Religion is not his who too much fasts
Or too much feasts, nor his who sleeps away
An idle mind; nor his who wears to waste
His strength in vigils. Nay, Arjuna! call
That the true piety which most removes
Earth-aches and ills, Where one is moderate
In eating and resting, and in sport;
Measured in wish and act; sleeping betimes.
Waking betimes for duty.

Bhagavad Gita (200 B.C. — A.D. 200)
translated by SIR EDWIN ARNOLD

That Man I Love

Who hateth nought
Of all which lives, living himself benign,
Compassionate, from arrogance exempt,
Exempt from love of self, unchangeable
By good or ill; patient, contented, firm
In faith, measuring himself, true to his word,
Seeking Me, heart and soul; vowed unto Me, —
That man I love! Who troubleth not his kind,
And is not troubled by them; clear of wrath,
Living too high for gladness, grief, or fear,
That man I love! Who dwelling quiet-eyed,
Stainless, serene, well-balanced, unperplexed,
Working with me, yet from all works detached,
That man I love! Who, fixed in faith on Me,
Dotes upon none, scorns none; rejoices not,
And grieves not, letting good or evil hap
Light When it will, and when it will depart,
That man I love! Who, friend and foe
Keeping an equal heart, with equal mind
Bears shame and glory; with an equal peace
Takes heat and cold, pleasure and pain; abides
Quit of desires, hears praise or calumny
In passionless restraint, unmoved by each;
Linked by no ties to earth, steadfast in Me,
That man I love! But most of all I love
Those happy ones to whom 'tis life to live
In single fervid faith and love unseeing,
Drinking the blessed Amrit of my Being!

Bhagavad Gita (200 B.C. — A.D. 200)
translated by SIR EDWIN ARNOLD

Passion Leads him to his Ill

Arjuna: Yet tell me, Teacher! by what force doth man
            Go to his ill, unwilling; as if one
            Pushed him that evil path?
Krishna: Kama it is!
            Passion it is! born of the Darknesses,
            Which pusheth him. Mighty of appetite,
            Sinful, and strong is this! — man's enemy!
            As smoke blots the white fire, as clinging rust
            Mars the bright mirror, as the womb surrounds
            The babe unborn, so is the world of things
            Foiled, soiled, enclosed in this desire of flesh.
            The wise fall, caught in it; the unresting foe
            It is of wisdom, wearing countless forms,
            Fair but deceitful, subtle as a flame.
            Sense, mind, and reason — these, O Kunti's Son!
            Are booty for it; in its play with these
            It maddens man, beguiling, blinding him.
            Therefore, thou noblest child of Bharata!
            Govern thy heart! Constrain th' entangled sense!
            Resist the false, soft sinfulness which saps
            Knowledge and judgment!

Bhagavad Gita (200 B.C. — A.D. 200)
translated by SIR EDWIN ARNOLD

Let Right Deeds Be Thy Motive

But thou, want not! Ask not! Find full reward
Of doing right in right! Let right deeds be

Thy motive, not the fruit which comes from them.
And live in action! Labour! Make thine acts
Thy piety, casting all self aside,
Contemning gain and merit; equable
In good or evil: equability
Is Yôg, is piety!

*

Abstaining from attachment to the work,
Abstaining from rewardment in the work,
While yet one doeth it full faithfully,
Saying, "'Tis right to do!" that is "true" act
And abstinence! Who doeth duties so,
Unvexed if his work fail, if it succeed,
Unflattered, in his own heart justified,
Quit of debates and doubts, his is "true" act:
For, being in the body, none may stand
Wholly aloof from act; Yet, who abstains
From profit of his acts is abstinent.

Bhagavad Gita (200 B.C. — A.D. 200)
translated by SIR EDWIN ARNOLD

Transmigration

Action, which springs from the mind, from speech, and from the body, produces either good or evil results; by action are caused the various conditions of men, the highest, the middling, and the lowest.

Know that the mind is the instigator here below, even to that action which is connected with body, and which is of three kinds, has three locations, and falls under ten heads.

Coveting the property of other, thinking in one's heart of what is undesirable, and adherence to false doctrines, are the three kinds of sinful mental action.

Abusing others, speaking untruth, detracting from the merits of all men, and talking idly, shall be the four kinds of evil verbal action.

Taking what has not been given, injuring creatures without the sanction of the law, and holding criminal intercourse with another man's wife, are declared to be the three kinds of wicked bodily action.

A man obtains result of a good or evil mental act in his mind, that of a verbal act in his speech, that of a bodily act in his body.

*

I will briefly declare in due order what transmigrations in this whole world a man obtains through each of these qualities.

Those endowed with Goodness reach the state of gods, those endowed with Activity the state of men, and those endowed with Darkness ever sink to the condition of beasts; that is the threefold course of transmigrations.

But know this threefold course of transmigrations that depends on the three qualities to be again threefold, low, middling, and high, according to the particular nature of the acts and of the knowledge of each men.

The Laws of Manu (A.D. 100-200)
XII. 3-8, 39-41
translated by G. BUEHLER

The Origin and Function of Castes

But in order to protect this universe He, the most resplendent one, assigned separate duties and occupations to those who sprang from his mouth, arms, thighs, and feet.

To Brâhmanas he assigned teaching and studying the Veda, sacrificing for their own benefit and for others, giving and accepting of alms.

The Kshatriya he commanded to protect the people, to bestow gifts, to offer sacrifices, to study the Veda, and to abstain from attaching himself to sensual pleasures.

The Vaisya to tend cattle, to bestow gifts, to offer sacrifices, to study the Veda, to trade, to lend money, and cultivate land.

One occupation only the lord prescribed to the Sûdra, to serve meekly even these other three castes.

Man is stated to be purer above the navel than below; hence the Self-existent has declared the purest part of him to be his mouth.

As the Brâhmana sprang from Brahma's mouth, as he was the first-born, and as he possesses the Veda, he is by right the lord of this whole creation.

*

The seniority of Brâhmanas is from sacred knowledge, that of Kshatriya from valour, that of Vaisyas from wealth in grain and other goods, but that of Sûdras alone from age.

*

A Brâhmana should always fear homage as if it were poison; and constantly desire to suffer scorn as he would long for nectar.

*

Having dwelt with a teacher during the one-fourth part of a man's life, a Brâhmana shall live during the second quarter of his existence in his house, after he has wedded a wife.

A Brâhmana must seek a means of subsistence which either causes no, or least little pain to others, and live by that except in times of distress.

For the purpose of gaining bare subsistence, let him accumulate property by following those irreproachable occupations which are prescribed for his caste, without unduly fatiguing his body.

*

Let him never, for the sake of subsistence, follow the ways of the world; let him live the pure, straightforward, honest life of a Brâhmana.

*

Teaching, studying, sacrificing for himself, sacrificing for others, making gifts and receiving them are the six acts prescribed for a Brâhmana.

But among the six acts ordained for him three are his means of subsistence, viz. sacrificing for others, teaching, and accepting gifts from pure men.

Passing from the Brâhmana to the Kshatriya, three acts incumbent on the former are forbidden, viz. teaching, sacrificing for others, and thirdly, the acceptance of gifts.

The same are likewise forbidden to a Vaisya, that is a settled rule; for Manu, the lord of creatures, has not prescribed them for men of those two castes.

To carry arms for striking and for throwing is prescribed for Kshatriyas as a means of subsistence; to trade, to rear cattle, and agriculture for Vaisyas; but their duties are liberality, the study of the Veda, and the performance of sacrifices.

The Laws of Manu (A.D. 100-200)
I. 87-93; II. 155, 162;
IV. 1-7, 11, 15; X.75-79
translated by G. BUEHLER

Position of Women

By a girl, by a young woman, or even by an aged one, nothing must be done independently, even in her own house.

In childhood a female must be subject to her father, in youth to her husband, when her lord is dead to her sons; a woman must never be independent.

*

Though destitute of virtue, or seeking pleasure elsewhere, or devoid of good qualities, yet a husband must be constantly worshipped as a god by a faithful wife.

A virtuous wife who after the death of her husband constantly remains chaste, reaches heaven, though she may have no son, just like those chaste men.

But a woman who from a desire to have offspring violates her duty towards her deceased husband brings on herself disgrace in this world, and loses her place with her husband in heaven.

*

No man can completely guard women by force; but they can be guarded by the employment of the following expedients:

Let the husband employ his wife in the collection and expenditure of his wealth, in keeping everything clean, in the fulfilment of religious duties, in the preparation of his food, and in looking after the household utensils.

Women, confined in the house under trustworthy and obedient servants, are not well guarded; but those who of their own accord keep guard over themselves, are well guarded.

*

By sacred tradition the woman is declared to be the soil, the man is declared to be the seed; the production of all corporeal beings takes place through the union of the soil with the seed.

In some cases the seed is more distinguished, and in some the womb of the female; but when both are equal, the offspring is most highly esteemed.

On comparing the seed and the receptacle of the seed, the seed is declared to be more important; for the offspring of all created beings is marked by the characteristics of the seed.

Whatever kind of seed is sown in a field, prepared in due season, a plant of that same kind, marked with the peculiar qualities of the seed, springs up in it.

*

Once is the partition of the inheritance made, once is a maiden given in marriage, and once does a man say, "I will give"; each of those three acts is done once only.

*

A barren wife may be superseded in the eighth year, she whose children all die in the tenth, she who bears only

daughters in the eleventh, but she who is quarrlesome without
delay.

The Laws of Manu (A.D. 100-200)
V. 147-48, 154, 160-61;
IX. 3, 8-12, 33-36, 47, 81
translated by G. BUEHLER

Yoga

The investigations of the Psychical Research Society
into what are called "spiritualistic" phenomena have
begun to shake the hardiest faith in the truths hitherto accepted
in the name of science, that intelligence and memory are
functions dependent on the integrity of the cerebral mechanism,
which will disappear when that mechanism decays. Some
thinkers are now beginning to believe that the brain is by no
means indispensable for conscious activities. Psychologists tell
us that the human mind has other perceptive faculties than
those served by the five senses, and philosophers are slowly
accepting the view that we have mental powers other than
those of ratiocination and a memory conditioned by the brain.
The ancient thinkers of India had a good working knowledge
of what may be called the science of metaphysics, and were
quite familiar with cryptesthesia and other kindred powers.
They tell us that we can acquire the power of seeing and
knowing without the help of the outer senses, and can become
independent of the activity which we exercise through the
physical senses and the brain. They assume that there is a
wider world about us than we are normally able to apprehend.
When some day our eyes open to it, we may have an extension
of our perception as stupendous as a blind man has when he

first acquires sight. There are laws governing the acquisition of this larger vision and manifestation of latent powers. By following the principles of the Yoga, such as heightening the power of concentration, arresting the vagaries of mind by fixing one's attention on the deepest sources of strength, one can master one's soul even as an athlete masters his body. The Yoga helps us to reach a higher level of consciousness, through a transformation of the psychic organism, which enables it to get beyond the limits set to ordinary human experience. We discern in the Yoga those cardinal conceptions of Hindu thought, such as the supremacy of the psychic over the physical, the exultation of silence and solitude, meditation and ecstasy, and the indifference to outer conditions, which make the traditional Hindu attitude to life appear so strange and fantastic to the modern mind. It is, however, conceded, by many who are acquainted with it, that it is a necessary corrective to our present mentality, overburdened with external things and estranged from the true life of spirit by humdrum toil, material greed and sensual excitement.

The word Yoga is used in a variety of senses. It may simply mean "method." It is often used in the sense of yoking. In the Upanishads and the *Bhagavadgita,* the soul in its worldly and sinful condition is said to live separate and estranged from the supreme soul. The root of all sin and suffering is separation, disunion, estrangement. To be rid of sorrow and sin, we must attain spiritual unification, the consciousness of two in one, or Yoga. In Patanjali, Yoga does not mean union, but only effort, or, as Bhoja says, separation (viyoga) between purusa and prakrti. It is the search for what Novalis called "Our transcendental me," the divine and eternal part of our being. It also signifies exertion, strenuous endeavour, and so come to be used for the system of the restraint of the senses and the mind. Though it is sometimes used as a synonym for the end of samadhi, it is more often employed to indicate the way of reaching it. Passages are not wanting where it signifies the supreme power possessed by God. Yoga, according to Patanjali, is a methodical effort to attain perfection, through the control of the different elements of human nature, physical and psychical. The physical body, the active will and the understanding mind are to be brought under control. Patanjali insists on certain practices which are intended to cure the body of its restlessness and free it from impurities. When we secure through these practices increased vitality, prolonged youth and longevity, these are to be employed in the interests of spiritual freedom. The other methods are employed to purify and tranquillise citta. The main interest of Patanjali is not metaphysical theorising, but the practical motive of indicating how salvation can be attained by disciplined activity.

*

The reality of the self is to be found not by means of an objective use of the mind, but by a suppression of its activities and penetration beneath the mental strata with which our ordinary life and activity conceal our diviner nature. Though the seed of spirit is present in each one of us, it is not realised by our consciousness, which is too busily engaged with other things. We must undergo a severe discipline before we can achieve the redirection of our consciousness. The Yoga philosophy urges that the necessary inhibition of mental states is brought about by practice and conquest of desire. While the latter is the result of a life of virtue the former refers to the effort towards steadiness, of thought, which is gained by purificatory action, continence, knowledge and faith. Vairagya or passionlessness, is the consciousness of mastery possessed by one who has rid himself of thirst for either seen or revealed objects. Such a one is supremely indifferent to the pleasures of heaven or of earth. In the highest form of vairagya, where the discernment of the self arises, there is no danger of any subjection to the desire for objects or their qualities. This leads to ultimate freedom, while the lower form of vairaygya, which has a trace of rajas (and so pravrtti) in it, results in the condition of absorption in prakrti (Prakrtilaya).

In the human organism we find the physical body, the vital dynamism, the psychic principles, in addition to the purusa. The purusa, is hidden behind veils of corruptible flesh and restless mind, all of which offer hindrances to the method of Yoga. The close connection of body and mind is insisted on, for "pain, despondency, unsteadiness of the body, and inspiration and expiration are the accompanishments of distractions." Though physical health is not the end of human life, it is still one of its essential conditions. We cannot look upon man as a physical machine to which spiritual life is attached from outside. The body is the instrument for the expression of spiritual problem. To overcome the hindrances, the Yoga gives us the eightfold method, consisting of yama (abstention), niyama (observance), asana (posture), pranayama (regulation of breath), pratyahara (withdrawal of the senses), dhyana (fixed attention), dharana (contemplation), and samadhi (concentration). The last three are direct or internal (antaranga) aids, while the first five are indirect or external (bahiranga).

S. RADHAKRISHNAN
A Source Book in Indian Philosophy

Lord Siva

Among the various sects of Hinduism the Tamil Sivaite School has produced the richest devotional literature. Of its many great poets the greatest is Mânikkavâchakar.

The darkness today Thou dravest away, didst
Dawn in my heart as the sun.
In thought beyond thought my spirit hath sought
Thy being: save Thee there is none.
Thou art One, art the Energy stirred for aye,
Self-subliming to endless degree;
Thou art other than aught; save Thee
There is naught — Oh, who may have knowledge of Thee?
Outspreading in single expanse of light, Thy
Blossom the earth and the spheres,
Fire water-laden, pure dweller for aye in being
Which thought not nears,
O Sweetness welling within the heart by the flood
Of Thy mercy made bright,
Here who is my kindred, and who is not? Oh, Bliss-giving
　　heavenly Light!

Thou gavest Thyself, and me didst take; wert
Thou the more cunning, or I?
I got of Thee bliss everlasting, O Thou whose Home is
　　in Perun-durai;
From me what hast Thou won, my Sovran? For
Thou hast made of my spirit Thy fane,
And hast set Thine abode in my body today —
All mine the unrecompensed gain!

MÂNIKKAVÂCHAKAR
Tiru-vachakam (9th cent. A.D.)
translated by F. KINGSBURY and G.E. PHILLIPS

His Form is Universal

He whose form is universal; who is eternal; who Himself witnesses all that passes in every heart, who exists immutably throughout the universe, and is free from all shadow, is called God. Neither in earth nor metal, wood or stone, painted walls or images, does that great Spirit dwell so as to be percieved.

We take a skin, and form it into a pretty puppet; we make it play, and then throw it away. But who can see Him who plays with us?

Those who roam [to other lands in pilgrimage] to find the God that dwells within them are like a shepherd who searches in his flock for the sheep that he has under his arm.

"Benares! Benares!" they cry, and delight to travel thither. Yet is not the same God here as there? If thy heart be aright, He is there and here also.

Kine are of diverse colours, but all milk is alike; the kinds of flowers vary, yet all worship is one; systems of faith are different, but the Deity is one.

If thy heart become calm as the breezeless firmament and the unruffled waveless deep, changeless and unmoving — this is called Salvation.

What Thou sayest I will say; where Thou dwellest I will remain enrapt; my thoughts shall be like to Thine; and when Thou smilest, I will also smile.

*

Will the application of white ashes do away with the smell of a wine-pot? Will a cord over your neck make you twice-born?

What are you the better for smearing your body with ashes? Your thoughts should be set on God alone; for the rest, an ass can wallow in dirt as well as you.

The books that are called the Vedas are like courtesans, deluding men, and wholly unfathomable; but the hidden knowledge of God is like an honourable wife.

O ye asses! why do you make balls of food and give them to the crows in the name of your ancestors! How can a dung-eating crow be an ancestor of yours?

He that fasts shall become [in his next birth] a village pig; he that embraces poverty shall become a beggar; and he that bows to a stone shall become like a lifeless image.

VEMANA
Padyamulu
translated by C.P. BROWN

Seeking

From Vedic student first the truth I sought,
And found them full of "Thou shalt," "Thou shalt not."
Never shall they posses tranquillity,
For mighty in them is the power of "me".

From Scripture scholars sought I once again
The form divine, but found them rent in twain.
Not one agrees with what the others say,
But pride and error lead them all astray.

Next in Purans I sought that form so fair,
But still, alas, no place of rest was there.
The preachers preach of Brahm but set their mind
On lust, and so true peace they never find.

Ask of the Haridas the way devout;
You'll find in him no faith at all but doubt.

He tells in words the Name's high excellence,
While all the time engrossed with things of sense.

Weary with seeking, here at last am I.
Low at thy feet, O Pandurang I lie.
My worldly life is full of fears, but thou
('Tis Nama cries), O save me, save me now.

> NAMDEV (14th cent. A.D.)
> *Psalms of The Maratha Saint*
> translated by NICOL MACNICOL

He is not of Stone

What are thine idols but lumps of stone?
What but stone the temples that are thine?
Venerable Brahman, why alone
Offerings to these to make Divine?

Hold the breaths that in thy body rise,
Meditating on the One alone;
So thou be of understanding wise
And thou know Him to be not of stone.

*

Thou art the Heavens, and Thou the Earth:
Thou alone art day and night and air:
Thou Thyself art all things that have birth,
Even the offerings of flowers fair.

Thou art, too, the sacrificial meal:
Thou the water that is poured on Thee:
Thou art unction of the things that heal.
Dost then need an offering from me?

How came I hither? And by what road?
Whither shall I go? And by What way?
There art Thou and I in one abode:
Here an empty breath I pass my day.

*

Slay first the thieves — desire, lust and pride;
Learn thou then to be the slave of all.
Robbers only for a while abide;
Ever liveth the devoted Call.

All a man's gain here is nothing worth,
Save when his service shall be his sword;
Ash from the fire is the sun of birth:
Gain thou then the Knowledge of the Lord.

LALLA (14th cent. A.D.)
A Kashmiri preacher of Saiva Hinduism
translated by Sir R.C. TEMPLE

God Dwells in All

God dwells in all, and yet we find,
To him the faithless man is blind.

Water or stones or what you will, —
What is it that he does not fill?

Lo, God is present everywhere,
Yet faithless eyes see nothing there.

If Ekanath unfaithful be,
Then God he also shall not see.

EKANATH (1548-99)
translated by NICOL MACNICOL

Neither in Temple nor in Mosque

O servant, where dost thou seek Me?
Lo! I am beside thee.
I am neither in temple nor in mosque:
I am neither in Kaaba nor in Kailash:
Neither am I in rites and ceremonies,
Nor in Yoga and renunciation
If thou art a true seeker, thou shalt at
Once see Me: thou shalt meet Me in a moment of time.
Kabir says, "O Sadhu! God is the breath of all breath."

*

There is nothing but water at the holy bathing places; and
    I know
That they are useless, for I have bathed in them.
The images are all lifeless, they cannot speak; I know,
For I have cried aloud to them.
The Purana and the Koran are mere words;
Lifting up the curtain, I have seen.
Kabir gives utterance to the words of experience; and he
Knows very well that all other things are untrue.

*

I laugh when I hear that the fish in the water is thirsty:
You do not see that the Real is in your home,
And you wander from forest to forest listlessly!
Here is the truth! Go where you will, to Benares or to
    Mathura;
If you do not find your soul, the world is unreal to you.

*

The Yogi dyes his garments, instead of dyeing

His mind in the colours of love:

He sits within the temple of the Lord, leaving Brahma to
worship a stone.

He pierces holes in his ears, he has a great beard

And matted locks, he looks like a goat:

He goes forth into the wilderness, killing all his desires,

And turns himself into a eunuch:

He shaves his head and dyes his garments; he reads the
Gita

And becomes a mighty talker.

Kabir says: "You are going to the doors of death, bound
hand and foot!"

*

If God be within the mosque, then to whom does this
world belong?

If Ram be within the image which you find upon your
pilgrimage, then

Who is there to know what happens without?

All the men and women of the world are His living forms.

Kabir is the child of Allah and of Ram: He is my Guru,
He is my Pir.

KABIR (1440-1518)
translated by RABINDRANATH TAGORE

The Soul Departeth Alone

When the body is burnt, it becometh ashes; when it is not
burnt, a host of worms eat it up.

A soft clay vessel will break when water is put into it —
such is the nature of the body.

Why, O brother, goest thou about puffing and blowing
    thyself out?
How hast thou forgotten the ten months thou didst remain
    inverted in the womb?
As the bee collecteth honey with great zest, so the fool
    collecteth wealth.
When a man is dead, they say "Take him away! Take him
    away!"
"Why allow a ghost to remain?"
His wedded wife accompanieth him to the door, and after
    that his male friends.
All the *other* members of his family go as far as the
    cremation-ground; the soul departeth alone.
Saith Kabir, hear, O mortals, they who have entangled
    themselves with the deceitful world,
Are seized by Death, and fall into the pit like the parrot
    deceived by the trap.

KABIR (1440-1518)
translated by M. A. MACAULIFFE

Some Psalms of Tukaram
(1608-49)

The Restless Heart

As on the bank the poor fish lies
And gasps and writhes in pain,
Or as a man with anxious eyes
Seeks hidden gold in vain, —

So is my heart distressed and cries
To come to thee again.

Thou knowest, Lord, the agony
Of the lost infant's wail,
Yearning his mother's face to see.
(How oft I tell this tale!)
O at thy feet the mystery
Of the dark world unveil!

The fire of this harassing thought
Upon my bosom preys.
Why is it I am thus forgot?
(O, who can know thy ways?)
Nay, Lord, thou seest my hapless lot;
Have mercy, Tuka says.

Keep me from Vanity

Keep me from vanity
Keep me from pride,
For sure I perish if
I quit thy side.

From this deceiving world
How hard to flee!
Ah, thou, Vaikuntha's Lord,
Deliver me!

If once thy gracious face
I look upon,
The world's enticement then
Is past and gone.

Love Finds Out God

Thy nature is beyond the grasp
Of human speech or thought.
So love I've made the measure-rod,
By which I can be taught.

Thus with the measure-rod of love
I mete the Infinite.
In sooth, to measure him there is
None other means so fit.

Not Yoga's power, nor sacrifice,
Nor fierce austerity,
Nor yet the strength of thought profound
Hath ever found out thee.

And so, says Tuka, graciously,
Oh Kesav, take, we pray
Love's service that with simple hearts
Before thy feet we lay.

God's Counterfeit

Is there a man who says of all,
Whether upon them sorrow fall,
Or whether joy — "These, these are mine"?
That is the saint: mark well the sign
God dwells in him. The good man's breast
Is of all men's the tenderest.
Is any helpless or undone?
Be he a slave, be he a son:—

On all alike he mercy shows,
On all an equal love bestows.

How oft must I this tale ·repeat!
That man is God's own counterfeit.

translated by NICOL MACNICOL

A Defence of Hinduism

For a period of upwards of fifty years, this country (Bengal) has been in exclusive possession of the English nation; during the first thirty years of which, from their word and deed, it was universally believed that they would not interfere with the religion of their subjects, and that they truly wished every man to act in such matters according to the dictates of his own conscience. Their possessions in Hindoostan and their political strength, through the grace of God, gradually increased. But during the last twenty years, a body of English gentlemen, who are called missionaries, have been publicly endeavouring, in several ways to convert Hindoos and Mussulmans of this country into Christianity. The first way is that of publishing and distributing among the natives various books, large and small, reviling both religions, and abusing and ridiculing the gods and saints of the former: the second way is that of standing in front of the doors of the natives or in the public roads to preach the excellency of their own religion and the debasedness of that others: the third way is that if any natives of low origin become Christians from the desire of gain or from any other motives, these gentlemen employ and maintain them as a necessary encouragement to others to follow their example.

It is true that the apostles of Jesus Christ used to preach the superiority of the Christian religion to the natives of different countries. But we must recollect that they were not of the rulers of those countries where they preached. Were the missionaries likewise to preach the Gospel and distribute books in countries not conquered by the English, such as Turkey, Persia, etc., which are much nearer England, they would be esteemed a body of men truly zealous in propagating religion and in following the example of the founders of Christianity. In Bengal, where the English are the sole rulers, and where the mere name of Englishman is sufficient to frighten people, an encroachment upon the rights of her poor timid and humble inhabitants and upon their religion, cannot be viewed in the eyes of God or the public as a justifiable act. For wise and good men always fell disinclined to hurt those that are of much less strength than themselves, and if such weak creatures be dependent on them and subject to their authority, they can never attempt, even in thought, to mortify their feelings.

We have been subjected to such insults for about nine centuries, and the cause of such degradation has been our excess in civilisation and abstinence from the slaughter even of animals; as well as our division into castes, which has been the source of want of unity among us.

It seems almost natural that when one nation succeeds in conquering another, the former, though their religion may be quite ridiculous, laugh at and despise the religion and manners of those that are fallen into their power.

For example, Mussulmans, upon their conquest of India, proved highly inimical to the religious exercises of Hindoos. When the generals of Chungezkhan, who denied God and were like wild beasts in their manners, invaded the western part of Hindoostan, they universally mocked at the profession of God and of futurity expressed to them by the natives of

India. The savages of Arracan, on their invasion of the eastern part of Bengal, always attempted to degrade the religion of Hindoos. In ancient days, the Greeks and the Romans, who were gross idolaters and immoral in their lives, used to laugh at the religion and conduct of their Jewish subjects, a sect who were devoted to the belief of one God. It is therefore not uncommon if the English missionaries, who are of the conquerors of this country, revile and mock at the religion of its native. But as the English are celebrated for the manifestation of humanity and for administering justice, and as a great many gentlemen among them are noticed to have had an aversion to violate equity, it would tend to destroy their acknowledged character if they follow the example of the former savage conquerors in disturbing the established religion of the country; because to introduce a religion by means of abuse and insult, or by affording the hope of worldly gain, is inconsistent with reason and justice. If by the force of argument they can prove the truth of their own religion and the falsity of that of Hindoos, many would of course embrace their doctrines, and in case they fail to prove this, they should not undergo such useless trouble, nor tease Hindoos any longer by their attempts at conversion. In consideration of the small huts in which Brahmans of learning generally reside, and the simple food, such as vegetables, etc., which they are accustomed to eat, and the poverty which obliges them to live upon charity, the missionary gentlemen may not, I hope, abstain from controversy from contempt of them, for truth and true religion do not always belong to wealth and power, high names, or lofty palaces.

RAJA RAM MOHAN ROY (1772-1833)

The Sayings of Ramakrishna
(1834-86)

Man is like a pillow-case. The colour of one may be red, another blue, another black, but all contain the same cotton. So it is with man — one is beautiful, one is black, another is holy, a fourth wicked; but the Divine dwells in them all.

*

The Master said: "Everything that exists is God." The pupil understood it literally, but not in the true spirit. While he was passing through a street, he met with an elephant. The driver (mâhut) shouted aloud from his high place, "Move away, move away!" The pupil argued in his mind, "Why should I move away? I am God, so is the elephant also God. What fear has God of Himself?" Thinking thus he did not move. At last the elephant took him up by his trunk, and dashed him aside. He was severely hurt, and going back to his Master, he related the whole adventure. The master said, "All right, you are God. The elephant is God also, but God in the shape of the elephant-driver was warning you also from above. Why did you not pay heed to his warnings?"

*

There is a fabled species of birds called "Homâ," which live so high up in the heavens, and so dearly love those regions, that they never condescend to come down to the earth. Even their eggs, which, when laid in the sky, begin to fall down to the earth attracted by gravity, are said to get hatched in the middle of their downward course and give birth to the young ones. The fledgelings at once find out that they are falling down, and immediately change their course and begin to fly up towards their home, drawn, thither by instinct. Men such as Suka Deva, Nârada, Jesus, Samkarâchârya and others, are like those birds, who even in their boyhood give up all attachments to the things of this world and betake themselves to the highest regions of true Knowledge and Divine Light. These men are called Nitya Siddhas.

*

Once a holy man, while passing through a crowded street, accidently trod upon the toe of a wicked person. The wicked man, furious with rage, beat the Sâdhu mercilessly, till he fell to ground in a faint. His disciples took great pains and adopted various measures to bring him back to consciousness, and when they saw that he had recovered a little one of them asked, "Sir, do you recognise who is attending upon you?" The Sâdhu replied, "He who beat me." A true Sâdhu finds no distinction between a friend and a foe.

*

So long as a man calls aloud, "Allah Ho! Allah Ho!" (O God! O God!), be sure that he has not found God, for he who has found him becomes still.

So long as the bee is outside the petals of the lotus, and has not tasted its honey, it hovers round the flower, emitting its buzzing sound; but when it is inside the flower, it drinks its nectar noiselessly. So long as a man quarrels and disputes about doctrines and dogmas, he has not tasted the nectar of true faith; when he has tasted it he becomes still.

*

When a man is in the plains he sees the lowly grass and the mighty pine-tree and says, "How big is the tree and how small is the grass!" But when he ascends the mountain and looks from its high peak to the plain below, the mighty pine-tree and the lowly grass blend into one indistinct mass of green verdure. So in the sight of worldly men there are differences of rank and position, but when the Divine sight is opened there remains no distinction of high and low.

*

Why does the God-lover find such pleasure in addressing the Deity as Mother? Because the child is more free with its mother, and consequently she is dearer to the child than anyone else.

*

A sage was lying in a deep trance (Samâdhi) by a roadside; a thief passing by, saw him, and thought within himself, "This fellow, lying here, is a thief. He has been breaking into some house by night, and now sleeps exhausted. The police will very soon be here to catch him. So let me escape in time." Thus thinking, he ran away. Soon after a drunkard came upon the sage, and said, "Hallo! Thou hast fallen into the ditch by taking a drop too much. I am steadier than thou, and am not going to tumble." Last of all came a sage, and understanding that a great sage was in a trance (Samâdhi), he sat down, and touched him, and began to rub gently his holy feet.

*

Sugar and sand may be mixed together, but the ant rejects the sand and goes off with the sugar-grain; so pious men sift the good from the bad.

*

Worldly persons perform many pious and charitable acts with a hope of worldly rewards, but when misfortune, sorrow, and poverty approach them, they forget them all. They are like the parrot that repeats the Divine name "Râdhâ-Krishna, Râdha Krishna" the livelong day, but cries "Kaw, Kaw" when caught by a cat, forgetting the Divine name.

*

This world is like a stage, where men perform many parts under various disguises. They do not like to take off the mask, unless they have played for some time. Let them play for a while, and then they will eave off the mask of their own accord.

*

What you wish others to do, do yourself.

*

Once upon a time conceit entered the heart of the Divine Sage Nârada, and he thought there was no greater devotee than himself. Reading his heart, the Lord Sri Vishnu said, "Nârada, go to such and such a place, there is a great Bhakta of mine there, and cultivate his acquaintance." Nârada went there and found an agriculturist, who rose early in the morning, pronounced the name of Hari only once, and taking his plough went out to till the ground all day long. At night he went to bed after pronouncing the name of Hari once more. Nârada said within himself, "How can this rustic be called a lover of God? I see him busily engaged in worldly duties, and he has no signs of a pious man in him." Nârad then went back to the Lord and said all he thought of his new acquaintance. The Lord said, "Nârada, take this cup full of oil, go round this city and come back with it, but beware lest a drop of it fall to the ground." Nârada did as he was told, and on his return he was asked, "Well, Nârada, how often did you remember me in your walk?" "Not once, my Lord," replied Nârada, "and how could I when I had to watch this cup brimming over with oil?" The Lord then said, "This one

cup of oil did so divert your attention that even you did forget
me altogether, but look to that rustic who, carrying the heavy
load of a family, still remembers me twice every day."

There are three kinds of love, selfish, mutual, and unselfish.
The selfish love is the lowest. It only looks towards its own
happiness, no matter whether the beloved suffers weal or
woe. In mutual love the lover not only wants the happiness
of his or her beloved, but has an eye towards his or her own
happiness also. The unselfish love is of the highest kind. The
lover only minds the welfare of the beloved.

*

The sunlight is one and the same wherever it falls; but bright
surfaces like water, mirror and polished metals, etc. can reflect
it fully. So is the Light Divine. It falls equally and impartially
on all hearts, but the pure and clean hearts of the good and
holy Sâdhus only can fully reflect it.

Translated by F. MAX MUELLER in
Ramakrishna, His Life and Sayings

The Ideal of a Universal Religion

Unity in variety is the plan of the universe. We are all
men, and yet we are all distinct from one another. As
a part of humanity, I am one with you, and as Mr. So-and-
so I am different from you. As a man you are separate from
the woman; as a human being you are one with the woman.
As a man you are separate from the animal, but as living
beings, man, woman, animal, and plant, are all one; and as
existence, you are one with the whole universe. That universal
existence is God, the ultimate Unity in the universe. In Him

we are all one. At the same time, in manifestation, these differences must always remain. In our work, in our energies, as they are being manifested outside, these differences must always remain. We find then that if by the idea of a universal religion it is meant that one set of doctrines should be believed in by all mankind, it is wholly impossible. It can never be, there can never be a time when all faces will be the same. Again, if we expect that there will be one universal mythology, that is also impossible; it cannot be. Neither can there be one universal ritual. Such a state of things can never come into existence, if it ever did, the world would be destroyed, because variety is the first principle of life. What makes us formed beings? Differentiation. Perfect balance would be our destruction. Suppose the amount of heat in this room, the tendency of which is towards equal and perfect diffusion, gets that kind of diffusion, then for all practical purposes that heat will cease to be. What makes motion possible in this universe? Lost balance. The unity of sameness can come only when this universe is destroyed, otherwise such a thing is impossible. Not only so, it would be dangerous to have it. We must not wish that all of us should think alike. There would then be no thought to think. We should be all alike, as the Egyptian mummies in a museum, looking at each other without a thought to think. It is this difference, this differentiation, this losing of the balance between us, which is the very soul of our progress, the soul of all our thought. This must always be.

What then do I mean by the ideal of a universal religion? I do not mean any one universal philosophy, or any one universal mythology, or any one universal ritual, held alike by all; for I know that his world must go on working, wheel within wheel, this intricate mass of machinery, most complex, most wonderful. What can we do then? We can make it run smoothly, we can lessen the friction, we can grease the wheels, as it were. How? By recognising the natural necessity of variation. Just as we have recognised unity by our very natures, so must we also recognise variation. We must learn that truth may be expressed in a hundred thousand ways, and that each of these ways is true as far as it goes. We must learn that the same thing can be viewed from a hundred different standpoints, and yet be the same thing. Take for instance the sun. Suppose a man standing on the earth looks at the sun when it rises in the morning; he sees a big ball. Suppose he starts on a journey towards the sun and takes a camera with him, taking photographs at every stage of his journey, until he reaches the sun. The photographs of each stage will be seen to be different from those of the other stages; in fact, when he gets back, he brings with him so many photographs of so many different suns, as it would appear; and yet we know that the same sun was photographed by the man at the different stages of his progress. Even so it is with the Lord. Through high philosophy or low, through the most exalted mythology or the grossest, through the most refined ritualism or arrant fetishism, every sect, every soul, every nation, every religion, consciously or unconsciously, is struggling upward, towards God; every vision of truth that man has, is a vision of Him and of none else. Suppose we all go with vessels in our hands to fetch water from a lake. One has a cup, another a jar, another a bucket and so forth, and we all fill our vessels. The water in each case naturally takes the form of the vessel carried by each of us. He who brought the cup, has the water in the form of a cup; he who brought the jar — his water is in the shape of a jar, and so forth; but, in every case, water, and nothing but water, is in the vessel. So it is in the case of religion; our minds are like these vessels, and each one of us is trying to arrive at the realisation of God. God is like that water filling these different vessels, and in each vessel, the vision of God comes in the form of the vessel. Yet He is One. He is God in every case. This is the only recognition of universality that we can get.

SWAMI VIVEKANANDA (1863-1902)

The Beliefs of Arya Samaj

Arya Samaj — the Society of the Aryans — was founded by Dayanand in 1875.

I believe in a religion based on universal and all-embracing principles which have always been accepted as true by mankind, and will continue to command the allegiance of mankind in the ages to come. Hence it is that the religion in question is called the *'primeval eternal religion'*, which means that it is above the hostility of all human creeds whatsoever. Whatever is believed in by those who are steeped in ignorance or have been led astray by sectaries is not worthy of being accepted by the wise. That faith alone is really true and worthy of acceptance which is followed by *Aptas,* i.e. those who are true in word, deed and thought, promote public good and are impartial and learned; but all that is discarded by such men must be considered as unworthy of belief and false.

My conception of God and all other objects in the universe is founded on the teachings of the *Vedas* and other true *Shástras,* and is in conformity with the beliefs of all the sages, from *Brahmá* down to Jaimini. I offer a statement of these beliefs for the acceptance of all good men. That alone I hold to be acceptable which is worthy of being believed by all men in all ages. I do not entertain the least idea of founding a new religion or sect. My sole aim is to believe in truth and help others to believe in it, to reject falsehood and help others to do the same. Had I been biased, I would have championed any one of the religions prevailing in India. But I have not done so. On the contrary, I do not approve of what is objectionable and false in the institutions of this or any other country, nor do I reject what is good and in harmony with the dictates of true religion, nor have I any desire to do so, since a contrary conduct is wholly unworthy of man. He alone is entitled to be called a man who possesses a thoughtful nature and feels for others in the same way as he does for his own self, does not fear the unjust however powerful but fears the truly virtuous, however weak. Moreover, he should always exert himself to his utmost to protect the righteous, and advance their good, and conduct himself worthily, towards them even though they be extremely poor and weak and destitute of material resources. On the other hand, he should constantly strive to destroy, humble, and oppose the wicked, sovereign rulers of the whole earth and men of great influence and power though they be. In other words, a man should, as far as it lies in his power, constantly endeavour to undermine the power of the unjust and to strengthen that of the just, he may have to bear any amount of terrible suffering, he may even have to quaff the bitter cup of death in the performance of this duty, which devolves on him on account of being a man, but he should not shirk it.

*

I hold that the four *Vedas* — the repository of Knowledge and Religious Truths — are the Word of God. They comprise what is known as the *Sanhita-Mantra* portion only. They are absolutely free from error, and are an authority unto themselves. In other words, they do not stand in need of any other book to uphold their authority. Just as the sun (or a lamp) by his light, reveals his own nature as well as that of other objects of the universe, such as the earth — even so are the *Vedas*.

*

In other words I believe what is worthy of belief in the eyes of all, such as veracity in speech; while I do not believe what is considered wrong by all, such as untruthfulness. I do not approve of the mutual wrangling of the sectaries, since they have by propagating their creeds led the people astray and turned them into each other's enemy. The sole aim of my life, which I have also endeavoured to achieve, is to help to put an end to this mutual wrangling, preach universal truths, bring all men into the fold of one religion whereby they may cease to hate each other and, instead, may firmly love one another, live in peace and work for their common weal. May this doctrine, through the grace and help of God, with the support of all truthful, honest and learned men who are devoted to the cause of humanity (*Aptas*) reach every nook and corner of this earth so that all may acquire righteousness, wealth, gratify legitimate desires and attain salvation and thereby elevate themselves and live in happiness. This alone is the chief object (of my life).

SWAMI DAYANAND (1824-83)

From Violence to Non-Violence

If we turn our eyes to the time of which history has any record down to our own time, we shall find that man has been steadily progressing towards *ahimsa*. Our remote ancestors were cannibals. Then came a time when they were fed up with cannibalism and they began to live on chase. Next came a stage when man was ashamed of leading the life of a wandering hunter. He therefore took to agriculture and depended principally on mother earth for his food. Thus from being a nomad he settled down to civilised stable life, founded villages and towns, and from member of a family he became member of a community and a nation. All these are signs of progressive *ahimsa* and diminishing *himsa*. Had it been otherwise, the human species should have been extinct by now, even as many of the lower species have disappeared.

Prophets and *avatars* have also taught the lesson of *ahimsa* more or less. Not one of them has professed to teach *himsa*. And how should it be otherwise? *Himsa* does not need to be taught. Man as animal is violent, but as spirit is non-violent. The moment he awakes to the spirit within he cannot remain violent. Either he progresses towards *ahimsa* or rushes to his doom. That is why the prophets and *avatars* have taught the lessons of truth, harmony, brotherhood, justice, etc. — all attributes of *ahimsa*.

And yet violence seems to persist, even to the extent of thinking people like the correspondent regarding it as the final weapon. But, as I have shown, history and experience are against him.

If we believe that mankind has steadily progressed towards *ahimsa*, it follows that it has to progress towards it still further. Nothing in this world is static, everything is kinetic. If there is no progression, then there is inevitable retrogression. No one can remain without the eternal cycle, unless it be God Himself.

MAHATMA GANDHI (1869-1948)
Harijan, 11 August 1940

My Hinduism is not Sectarian

My Hinduism is not sectarian. It includes all that I know to be best in Islam, Christianity, Buddhism, and Zoroastrianism. I approach politics as everything else in a religious spirit. Truth is my religion and *ahimsa* is the only way of its realisation. I have rejected once and for all the doctrine of the sword. The secret stabbings of innocent persons, and the speeches I read in the papers, are hardly the thing leading to peace or an honourable settlement.

Again I am not approaching the forthcoming interview in any representative capacity. I have purposely divested myself of any such. If there are to be any formal negotiations, they will be between the President of the Congress and the President of the Muslim league. I go as a lifelong worker in the cause of Hindu-Muslim unity. It has been my passion from early youth. I count some of the noblest of Muslims as my friends ...

I may not leave a single stone unturned to achieve Hindu-Muslim unity. God fulfils Himself in strange ways. He may, in a manner least known to us, both fulfil Himself through the interview and open a way to an honourable understanding between the two communities. It is in that hope that I am looking forward to the forthcoming talk. We are friends, not strangers. It does not matter to me that we see things from different angles of vision. I ask the public not to attach any exaggerated importance to the interview. But I ask all lovers of communal peace to pray that the God of truth and love may give us both the right spirit and the right word and use us for the good of the dumb millions of India.

MAHATMA GANDHI (1869-1948)
Communal Unity

Jainism

Mahavira (540-468 B.C.) the founder of Jainism was a contemporary of Buddha. Unlike Buddhism, Jainism never spread beyond India. It still has some two million adherents in India.

The Non-Violent way of Life

Earth, water, fire, wind; grass, trees, and corn; and the moveable beings, viz. the oviparous, viviparous, those generated from dirt, and those generated in fluids; these classes (of living beings) have been declared (by the Ginas); know and understand that they (all desire) happiness; by (hurting) these beings (men) do harm to their own souls, and will again and again be born as one of them.

Every being born high or low in the scale of the living creation, among moveable and immoveable beings, will meet with its death. Whatever sins the evildoer commits in every birth, for them he must die.

In this world or in the next (the sinners suffer themselves what they inflicted on other beings), a hundred times, or (suffer) other punishment. Living in the Samsára they ever acquire new Karman, and suffer for their misdeeds.

Some leave their mother and father to live as Sramanas, but they use fire; (the prophet) says: "People are wicked who kill being for the sake of their own pleasure."

He who lights a fire, kills living beings; he who extinguishes it, kills the fire. Therefore a wise man who well considers the Law, should light no fire.

Earth contains life, and water contains life; jumping (or

flying) insects fall in (the fire); dirtborn vermin (and beings) living in wood: all these beings are burned by lighting a fire.

Sprouts are beings possessed of natural development, their bodies (require) nourishment, and all have their individual life. Reckless men who cut them down out of regard for their own pleasure, destroy many living beings.

By destroying seeds, when young or grown up, a careless man does harm to his own soul. (The prophet) says: "People are wicked who destroy seeds for the sake of their own pleasure."

Jaina Sutras (Sutrakritanga) (c. 300 B.C.)
translated by H. JACOBI

What Causes the Bondage of Soul?

One should know what causes the bondage of Soul, and knowing (it) one should remove it.

Gambûsvâmin asked Sudharman: What causes the bondage of Soul according to Mahâvira? and what must one know in order to remove it?

Sudharman answered: He who owns even a small property in living or lifeless things, or consents to others holding it, will not be delivered from misery.

If a man kills living beings, or causes other men to kill them, or consents to their killing them, his iniquity will go on increasing.

A sinner who makes the interest of his kinsmen and companions his own, will suffer much; for the number of those whose interest he takes to heart constantly increases.

All this, his wealth and his nearest relations, cannot protect him (from future misery); knowing (this) and (the value of) life, he will get rid of Karman.

Jaina Sutras (Sutrakritanga) (c. 300 B.C.)
translated by H. JACOBI

Penance and Self-control

*M*an, cease from sins! For the life of men will come to an end. Men who are drowned in lust, as it were, and addicted to pleasure will, for want of control, be deluded.

Exert and control yourself! For it is not easy to walk on ways where there are minutely small animals. Follow the commandments which the Arhats have well proclaimed.

Heroes of faith who desist from sins and exert themselves aright, who subdue wrath, fear, etc., will never kill living beings; they desist from sins and are entirely happy.

It is not myself alone who suffers, all creatures in the world suffer; this a wise man should consider, and he should patiently bear such calamities as befall him, without giving way to his passions.

As a wall covered with a plastering of dried cow-dung is by a shock made thin, so a monk should make his body lean by fasting, etc. He should abstain from slaughter of living beings. This is the Law proclaimed by the Sage.

Jaina Sutras (Sutrakritanga) (c. 300 B.C.)
translated by H. JACOBI

The Final Liberation

Itvara consists in starving oneself to death. A religious death was permitted only to those who had undergone preparatory penance for twelve years.

A mendicant who is fitted out with one robe, and a bowl as second (article), will not think: I shall beg for a second robe. He should beg for such a robe only as is allowed to be begged for, and he should wear it in the same state as he receives it.

But when the hot season has come, one should leave off the used-up clothes; one should be clad with one or no garment — aspiring to freedom from bonds.

When the thought occurs to a mendicant: "I am myself, alone; I have nobody belonging to me, nor do I belong to anybody," then he should thoroughly know himself as standing alone — aspiring to freedom from bonds. Penance suits him. Knowing what the Revered One has declared, one should thoroughly and in all respects conform to it. A male or female mendicant eating food, etc. should not shift the morsel from the left jaw to the right jaw, nor from the right jaw to the left jaw, to get a fuller taste of it, not caring for the taste of it — aspiring to freedom from bonds. Penance suits him. Knowing what the Revered One has declared, one should thoroughly and in all respects conform to it.

If this thought occurs to a monk: "I am sick and not able, at this time, to regularly mortify the flesh," that monk should regularly reduce his food; regularly reducing his food, and diminishing his sins, "he should take proper care of his body, being immovable like a beam; exerting himself he dissolves his body."

Entering a village, or a scot-free town, or a town with an earth-wall, or a town with a small wall, or an isolated town, or a large town, or a sea-town, or a mine, or a hermitage, or the halting-places of processions, or caravans, or a capital — a monk should beg for straw; having begged for straw he should retire with it to a secluded spot. After having repeatedly examined and cleaned the ground, where there are no eggs, nor living being, nor seeds, nor sprouts, nor dew, nor water, nor ants, nor mildew, nor waterdrops, nor mud, nor cobwebs — he should spread the straw on it. Then he should there and then effect the religious death called *itvara*.

Jaina Sutras (Akaranga Sutra)
translated by H. JACOBI

Some Jain Beliefs

The following verses were compiled by Jain ascetics sometime in the 12th century A.D.

The lamb before the sacrificer

The lamb in the ruddy slaughter-house will crop the fragrant shoots that dangle from the garland in the slayer's hand; such transient gladness of the thoughtless, youthful hour is never found amid the wise.

Penitence puts sin to flight

As when a lamp enters darkness dies, so sin stands not before man's penitence. As, when in a lamp the oil wastes, darkness rushes in, so evil takes its stand where deeds of virtue cease.

Pleasure and pain

Though wretched men suffer afflictions many a day, yet one day's delight they eagerly desire. The men of calm and full wisdom, in pleasure's core see pain, and quit the pleasant household paths.

Rashness in speech hurts one's self

If a man open his mouth and speak unguarded words, his words will ceaselessly burn his soul. The wise who ceaselessly hear, and ponder well and calmly, even in their wrath, will never give utterance to words of fire.

Return not evil for evil

When men stand forth as our enemies, and would begin the conflict, to decline the strife is not, in the language of the wise, lack of power. Even when men have confronted and done us intolerable evils, it is good not to do them evil in return.

Never desire evil, nor eat with improper persons, nor lie

Though ruin seize you, plan not ruin to the just! Though body's flesh should waste, eat not from hands unfit! Though the whole earth o'er-arched by heaven accrue as gain, never speak word with falsehood mixed!

If a friend act doubtfully, forgive or quietly withdraw

When two with strict accord unite in friendship's bond, if one betray the other's confidence by unkind act, this latter should endure as best he may. And if he can't endure, he should not divulge it, but withdraw himself.

If a friend do evil to you, think it good, refrain from anger and blame yourself; but never forsake him

Lord of the woodlands! Separation is hard even to beasts; therefore if friends do things that are unpleasant, think them pleasant, bid yourself cease (from wrath), and blame yourself alone; but forsake not those that have been joined to you in the intimacy of friendship.

Forbearance cements friendship

Is not the reason why the close friendship of the great is sought, that they will bear even with faults hard to endure? Lord of the good land of high mountains with resounding waterfalls! — to good people are intimate friends rare?

Bad companion

Even things (soft and soothing) like *ghee,* when joined with the fierce heat of fire, will blaze and burn, and cause bitter anguish: so even upright men are perverted and give themselves up to deeps of utter evil, when they attach themselves to those whose deeds are evil.

Enmity of the wise better than friendship of the mean

In proportion to the degree of one's intimacy with men essentially mean and without good qualities sorrow accrues; but even the hostility of those who do not desire forbidden things even in jest will confer dignity.

Do charity for the sake of this world and the future; and beg not

Regarding the other world and this world, give to any suppliant, in fitting way, according to your ability. And if on account of poverty giving is not possible, yet refraining from begging is twice as meritorious as giving.

Give to him who cannot recompense thee

Denying to no out-stretched hand, to give to needy men as he hath power, is duty of a man. — Lord of the swelling sea's cool shore! — A gift to those that can return the gift is usury!

Deeds come home to the doer

Although you send for the tender calf amid many cows, it has unerring skill to seek out its own mother. Deeds of old days have even so the power to search him out to whom their fruit pertains.

Cows of many colours, milk always white. Virtue one — many sects

Though cows in form are diverse, the milk they yield is not diverse. The way of virtue, like that milk, is one in nature, though the schools that teach it here are like those cows, of many forms.

When a man should be deaf, blind, and dumb

Deaf to other's secrets, blind, to his neighbour's wife, dumb to evil backbiting — if, knowing what is befitting, a man thus abides, it is not necessary to teach him any virtuous precepts.

Humility, Self-restraint, Charity

The greatness of the great is the quality of littleness in their own sight, humility; the real acquisition of those who have acquired any one science is modest self-restraint. If you rightly understand things, those possessors of wealth only are really wealthy who relieve the wants of those that approach them as suppliants.

Learning, the best legacy

It cannot be taken from its place of deposit; it does not perish anywhere by fire; if kings of surpassing grandeur are angry they cannot take it away; and therefore what any man should provide for his children as a legacy is learning. Other things are not real wealth.

The benefits of association with the learned. The pot impregnated with odour

Though themselves unlearned, if men live in association with the learned they advance daily in excellent knowledge. The new vessel, by contact with the *Padri*-flower of old renown and lustrous hue, imparts fragrance to the cold water it contains.

Why the goddess Fortune avoids the learned

Men of vast and varied lore are seen in low estate, and suffer want. Would you know the reason? The anciently renowned "Lady of the tongue" abides with them. "The Lady of the flower" is jealous, and draws not near!

The noble have an instinctive sense of propriety

Rising from their seat at the approach of worshipful persons, going forth to meet them, departing when they dismiss, and such-like things, the well-born maintain as invariable decorum. The low understand not one of these things. [Or, these are not to be confounded with the low.]

The moon when half in the serpent's mouth still gives light

Like the moon which affords light to the fair and spacious earth with one side, while the dragon holds the other, the nobly born do not become remiss in works of seemly benevolence, though poverty inability stand fronting them.

Aim high! Better miss a lion, than hit a jackal

Whether success attend, or do not attend the work, the excellent will ever ponder blameless ends. — Is the shaft that missed the lion worse than the arrow sent forth, that with its impulse pierced the jackal's heart?

The good listen with patient courtesy to the orations of the ignorant

Even when one speaks who has an ungrammatical knowledge

of the letter, but not of the meaning, who is of a low empty school, and is unlearned, the good with kindly compassion will listen, though it is plain to them, being grieved that he should be put to shame in the presence of many.

"The way of true love near did run smooth."

Lord of the cool shore of the deep bay, where the gleaming ocean's restless billows beat!

"If there be no fond embrace, a sickly hue will spread itself over her face; and, if there be no lovers' quarrels, love will lack its zest."

To embrace and disagree is the one way of life.

What is good or bad caste?

When men speak of "good *caste*" and "bad *caste*" it is a mere form of speech, and has no real meaning. Not even by possessions, made splendid by ancient glories, but by self-denial, learning, and energy is *caste* determined.

Good friends like trees that afford both shade and fruit

To yield ready protection alike to all, as a tree affords shade to those that seek its shelter when the heat grows fierce; and to live toiling so that many may enjoy the gain, resembling thus a fruit-producing tree, is the duty of the manly man.

Four bad things

Better hate than friendship of the *ignorant*.
Better death than disease which comes on yielding to no remedy.
Sweeter is killing than contempt that breaks the spirit.
Better abuse than undeserved praise.

The evil qualities of a bad wife and their effects

Death is the wife that stands and dares her spouse to strike!

Disease is she who enters not the kitchen betimes! *Demon domestic* is she who cooks and gives no alms! These three are *sword* to slay their lords!

Different modes of life

The *best* thing is a life spent in penitential practices. The *middle* course is to live with dear ones around. The *worst* of all is, with the thought that we have not enough, through desire of wealth, subserviently to follow those who understand us not.

The Naladiyar (c. 1200 A.D.)
(Four hundred quatrains in Tamil)
translated by G.V. POPE

Buddhism

The Eightfold Path

Thus have I heard: Once the Exalted One was dwelling near Benares, at Isipatana, in the Deer-Park.

Then the Exalted One thus spake unto the company of five monks:

Monks, these two extremes should not be followed by one who has gone forth as a wanderer. What two?

Devotion to the pleasures of sense, a low practice of villagers, a practice unworthy, unprofitable, the way of the world on the one hand; and on the other devotion to self-mortification, which is painful, unworthy and unprofitable.

By avoiding these two extremes the Tathagata has gained knowledge of that middle path which giveth vision, which giveth knowledge, which causeth calm, special knowledge, enlightenment, Nibbana.

And what, monks is that middle path which giveth vision ... Nibbana?

Verily it is this Ariyan eightfold way, to wit: Right view, right aim, right speech, right action, right living, right effort, right mindfulness, right concentration. This, monks is that middle path which giveth vision, which giveth knowledge, which causeth calm, special knowledge enlightenment, Nibbana.

Now this, monks, is the Ariyan truth about Ill:

Birth is Ill, decay is Ill, sickness is Ill, death is Ill, likewise sorrow and grief, woe, lamentation and despair. To be conjoined with things which we dislike: to be separated from things which we like, — that also is Ill. Not to get what one wants, — that also is Ill. In a word, this fivefold mass which is based on grasping, — that is Ill.

Now this, monks, is the Ariyan truth about the arising of Ill:

It is that craving that leads back to birth, along with the lure and the lust that lingers longingly now here, now there: namely, the craving for existence to end. Such, monks, is the Ariyan truth about the arising of Ill.

And this, monks, is the Ariyan truth about the ceasing of Ill:

Verily it is the utter passionless cessation of, the giving up, the forsaking, the release from, the absence of longing for this carving.

Sanyutta-Nikaya (1st cent. B.C.)
(*The Book of the Kindred Sayings*)
translated from the Pali by F.L. WOODWARD

By Self Alone Everything is Done

By self alone is evil done,
By self is one disgraced;
By self is evil left undone,
By self alone is he purified;
Purity and impurity belong to self:
No one can purify another.

*

Easily done are things not good,
Unhealthful to oneself;
But what is healthful and good,
That indeed is hard in the highest to do.

Dhammapada (70 B.C.)
(*Hymns of the Faith*)
translated from the Pali by A.J. EDMUNDS

Deeds! Not Birth

I

Pity and need
Make all flesh kin. There is no caste in blood,
Which runneth of one hue, nor caste in blood,
Which trickle salt with all; neither comes man
To birth with tilak-mark stamped on the brow,
Nor sacred thread on neck. Who doth right deed
Is twice-born, and who doeth ill deeds vile.

SIR EDWIN ARNOLD (1832-1904)
The Light of Asia

II

I call him alone a Brahman, who knows his former abode, who sees both heaven and hell, and has reached the extinction of births.

What is called "Name," or "Tribe," in the world, arises from usage only. It is adopted here and there by common consent.

It comes from long and uninterrupted usage, and from the false belief of the ignorant. Hence the ignorant assert — "that a Brahman is such from birth."

One is not a Brahman nor a non-Brahman by birth: by his conduct alone is he a Brahman, and by his conduct alone he is a non-Brahman.

By his conduct he is a husbandman; by his conduct he is an artisan; by his conduct he is a merchant; by his conduct he is a servant.

By his conduct he is a thief; his conduct a warrior; by his conduct a sacrificer; by his conduct a king.

Thus, the wise, who see the case of things, and understand the result of action, know this (kamma) matter as it really is.

Sutta Nipáta (1st cent. B.C.)
(*Dialogues and Discourses of Buddha*)
translated by SIR. M. COOMARA SWAMI

Mind Shapes the Character

Creatures from mind their character derive,
Mind-marshalled are they, and mind-made;
If with a mind corrupt one speak or act,
Him doth pain follow,
As the wheel the beast of burden's foot.

Creatures from mind their character derive,
Mind-marshalled are they, and mind-made:
If with pure mind one speak or act,
Him doth happiness follow,
Even as a shadow that declineth not.

"He abused me, beat me,
Overcame me, robbed me!"
Those with such thoughts imbued
Have not their anger calmed.

"He abused me, beat me,
Overcame me, robbed me!"
Those not with such thoughts imbued
Have their anger calmed.

Not indeed by anger
Are angers here calmed ever:
By meekness are they calmed.
This is an ancient doctrine.

The many know not
That we here must end;
But those who know it
Have their quarrels calmed.

The man who dwelleth contemplating pleasure,
With faculties incontinent,

In food immoderate,
Slothful, weak of will,
Him surely Mâro overthrows,
As wind a weakling tree.

The man who dwelleth unregarding pleasure,
With faculties thoroughly continent,
In food moderate, having faith, of strenuous will
Him Mâro no more overthroweth
Than wind a stony mount.

Dhammapada (70 B.C.)
(*Hymns of the Faith*)
translated from the Pali by A. J. EDMUNDS

Conquest of Fear

Seek not ever for things pleasant or unpleasant:
Not seeing pleasant things is pain,
And seeing the unpleasant is.

Therefore make nothing dear:
The loss of the endeared is evil;
Bonds are unknown to those
For whom there is naught dear or otherwise.

From endearment sorrow is born.
From endearment fear is born:
For him who from endearment is delivered
Sorrow is not, much less fear.

Sorrow is born from love,
And fear from love is born:
For him who is emancipated from love,
Sorrow is not, nor fear.

From delight is sorrow born,
And fear from delight is born:
For one delivered from delight,
Sorrow is not, nor fear.

Sorrow is born from lust,
And fear from lust is born:
For one from lust delivered,
Sorrow is not, nor fear.

From Thirst is sorrow born,
And fear is born from Thirst:
For one from Thirst set free,
Sorrow is not, nor fear.

With virtue and insight endued,
Righteous, truth-telling,
Minding his own affairs,
Him do the common folk hold dear.

*

Anger renounce, relinquish pride,
Pass beyond every fetter:
Him who to Name and Form doth cling not,
Him who possesseth nothing,
Pains never overtake.

Overcome anger with kindness,
Overcome evil with good,
Overcome meanness with a gift,
Ay, and a liar with truth.

Dhammapada (70 B.C.)
(*Hymns of the Faith*)
translated from the Pali by A.J. EDMUNDS

Victory Breedeth Anger

Victory breedeth anger,
For in pain the vanquished lieth:
Lieth happy the man of peace,
Renouncing victory and defeat.

There is no fire like passion,
No evil luck like hate,
No pain compared to finite elements,
No happiness higher than peace.

Dhammapada (70 B.C.)
(*Hymns of the Faith*)
translated from the Pali by A.J. EDMUNDS

Walk Alone Like a Rhinoceros

1

Having abandoned the practising of violence towards all objects, not doing violence to any one of them, let one wish not for children. Why wish for a friend? Let one walk alone like a rhinoceros.

2

There are friendships to one who lives in society; this our present grief arises from having friendships; observing the evils resulting from friendship, let one walk alone like a rhinoceros.

3

He who is kind towards much-beloved friends, loses his own good from his mind becoming partial; observing such in friendship, let one walk alone like a rhinoceros.

4

As a spreading bush of bambu is entangled in various ways, so is the longing for children and wives: not clinging to these even like a bambu just sprouting forth, let one walk alone like a rhinoceros.

5

As a beast of the forest prowls, free, whithersoever he will for pasture, even so let a wise man, observing solitude, walk alone like a rhinoceros.

6

Whilst resting, standing, going, travelling, leave must be obtained by one living in the midst of friends; let one, observing solitude which is not pleasing to others, walk alone like a rhinoceros.

7

If one lives in the midst of company, love of amusement and desire arises; strong attachment for children arises; let therefore one who dislikes separation which must happen sooner or later from those beloved walk alone like a rhinoceros.

Sutta Nipáta (1st cent. B.C.)
(*Dialogues and Discourses of Buddha*)
translated by SIR M. COOMARA SWAMI

The Five Rules

Kill not — for Pity's sake — and lest ye slay
The meanest thing upon its upward way.

Give freely and receive, but take from none
By greed, or force, or fraud, what is his own.

Bear not false witness, slander not, nor lie;
Truth is the speech of inward purity.

Shun drugs and drinks which work the wit abuse;
Clear minds, clean bodies, need no Sôma juice.

Touch not thy neighbour's wife, neither commit
Sins of the flesh unlawful and unfit.

SIR EDWIN ARNOLD (1832-1904)
The Light of Asia

Why all Men are not Alike

The king said: "Are the five Ayatanas (eye, ear, nose, tongue, and body), Nâgasena, produced by various actions, or by one action?" that is, the result of various Karmas, or of one Karma.

"By various actions, not by one."

"Give me an illustration."

"Now, what do you think, O king? If I were to sow in one field five kinds of seed, would the produce of those various seeds be of different kinds?"

"Yes, certainly."

"Well, just so with respect to the production of Ayatanas."

"Very good, Nâgasena!"

The king said. "Why is it, Nâgasena, that all men are not alike, but some are short-lived and some long-lived, some sickly and some healthy, some ugly and some beautiful some without influence and some of great power, some poor and some wealthy, some low born and some high born, some stupid and some wise?"

The Elder replied: "Why is it that all vegetables are not alike, but some, sour, and some salt, and some pungent, and some acid, and some astringent, and some sweet?"

"I fancy, Sir, it is because they come from different kinds of seeds."

"And just so, great king, are the differences you have mentioned among men to be explained. For it has been said by the Blessed One: "Beings, O brahmin, have each their own Karma, are inheritors of Karma, belong to the tribe of their Karma, are relatives by Karma, have each their Karma as their protecting overlord. It is Karma that divides them up into low and high and the like divisions."

"Very good, Nâgasena!"

The Questions of King Milinda (c. 100 A.D.)
translated from the Pali by T.W. RHYS DAVIDS

Reasoning and Wisdom

The king said: "What is the characteristic mark of reasoning, and what of wisdom?"

"Reasoning has always comprehension as its mark; but wisdom has cutting off."

"But how is comprehension the characteristic of reasoning, and cutting off of wisdom? Give me an illustration."

"You remember the barley reapers?"

"Yes, certainly."

"How do they reap the barley?"

"With the left hand they grasp the barley into a bunch, and taking the sickle into the right hand, they cut it off with that."

"Just even so, O king, does the recluse by his thinking grasp his mind, and by his wisdom cut off his failings. In this way is it that comprehension is the characteristic of reasoning, but cutting off of wisdom."

"Well put, Nâgasena!"

The Questions of King Milinda (c. 100 A.D.)
translated from the Pali by T.W. RHYS DAVIDS

Nirvana

The king said: "Is cessation Nirvâna?"

"Yes, your Majesty."

"How is that, Nâgasena?"

"All foolish individuals, O king, take pleasure in the senses and in the objects of sense, find delight in them, continue to cleave to them. Hence are they carried down by that flood (of human passions), they are not set free from birth, old age, and death, from grief, lamentation, pain, sorrow, and despair — they are not set free, I say, from suffering. But the wise, O king, the disciple of the noble ones, neither takes pleasure in those things, nor finds delight in them, nor continues cleaving to them. And inasmuch as he does not, in him craving ceases, and by the cessation of craving grasping ceases, and when becoming has ceased birth ceases, and with its cessation birth, old age, and death, grief, lamentation, pain, sorrow, and despair cease to exist. Thus is the cessation brought about the end of all that aggregation of pain. Thus is it that cessation is Nirvâna."

"Very good, Nâgasena!"

The Questions of King Milinda (c. 100 A.D.)
translated from the Pali by T.W. RHYS DAVIDS

Religious Tolerance

King Priyadarsi [Asoka], Beloved of the Gods, wishes that all religious sects should live harmoniously in all parts of his dominions. In fact, all of them desire to achieve self-control and purity of thought. People, however, are of diverse inclinations and diverse passions. They will perform either the whole or only a part of their duty. However, even if a person practises great liberality but does not possess self-control, purity of thought, gratitude and firm devotion he is quite worthless.

*

King Priyadarsi, Beloved of the Gods, honours men of all religious communities with gifts and with honours of various kinds, irrespective of whether they are ascetics or householders. But the Beloved of the Gods does not value either the offering of gifts or the honouring of people so highly as the following, viz. that there should be a growth of the essentials of Dharma among men of all sects.

And the growth of the essentials of Dharma is possible in many ways. But its root lies in restraint in regard to speech, which means that there should be no extolment of one's own sect or disparagement of other sects on inappropriate occasions and that it should be moderate in every case even on appropriate occasions. On the contrary, other sects should be duly honoured in every way on all occasions.

If a person acts in this way, he not only promotes his own sect but also benefits other sects. But if a person acts otherwise, he not only injures his own sect but also harms other sects. Truly, if a person extols his own sect and disparages other sects with a view to glorifying his sect owing merely to his attachment to it, he injures his own sect very severely by acting in that way. Therefore restraint in regard to speech is commendable, because people should learn and respect the fundamentals of one another's Dharma.

This indeed is the desire of the Beloved of the Gods that persons of all sects become well-informed about the doctrines of different religions and acquire pure knowledge. And those who are attached to their respective sects should be informed as follows: "The Beloved of the Gods does not value either the offering of gifts or the honouring of people so highly as the following, viz. that there should be a growth of the essentials of Dharma among men of all sects."

Indeed many of my officers are engaged for the realisation of the said end, such as the Mahamatras in charge of the affairs relating to Dharma, the Mahamatras who are superintendents of matters relating to the ladies of the royal household, the officers in charge of my cattle and pasture lands, and other classes of officials. And the result of their activities, as expected by me, is the promotion of each one's sect and the glorification of Dharma.

Inscriptions of Asoka (269-232 B.C.)
Rock Edicts 7 and 12
translated by D.C. SIRCAR

Buddhism, the Fulfilment of Hinduism

I am not a Buddhist, as you have heard, and yet I am. If China, or Japan, or Ceylon follow the teachings of the Great Master, India worships him as God incarnate on earth. You have just now heard that I am going to criticise Buddhism, but by that I wish you to understand only this. Far be it from me to criticise him whom I worship as God incarnate on earth. But our views about Buddha are that he was not understood properly by his disciples. The relation between Hinduism (by Hinduism, I mean the religion of the Vedas) and what is called Buddhism at the present day, is nearly the same as between Judaism and Christianity. Jesus Christ was a Jew, Shâkyá Muni was a Hindu. The Jews rejected Jesus Christ, nay, crucified him, and the Hindus have accepted Shâkya Muni as God and worship him. But the real difference that we Hindus want to show between modern Buddhism and what we should understand as the teachings of Lord Buddha lies principally in this: Shâkya Muni came to preach nothing new. He also, like Jesus, came to fulfil and not to destroy. Only, in the case of Jesus, it was the old people, the Jews, who did not understand him, while in the case of Buddha, it was his own followers who did not realise the import of his teachings. As the Jews did not understand the fulfilment of the Old Testament, so that Buddhist did not understand the fulfilment of the truths of the Hindu religion. Again, I repeat, Shâkya Muni came not to destroy, but he was the fulfilment, the logical conclusion, the logical development of the religion of the Hindus.

SWAMI VIVEKANANDA (1863-1902)

Islam

The basic doctrines of Islam were developed in Arabia during the life of Muhammad the Prophet (c. 570-632 A.D.). The first invasions of India by the Arabs tooks place in A.D. 711, about a hundred years after the death of the Prophet. By then Islam had divided itself into two main sects — Shias and Sunnis; the majority of the Muslims in India belong to the latter sect. By the end of the twelfth century, Sufism (Muslim mysticism) had been incorporated into orthodox Islam. By representing a direct personal relationship between the individual and his god Sufism made a strong appeal to converted Hindus. The interaction of Islam and Hinduism led to the growth of syncretic religions in the 16th century.

The Love of God

Man's love towards God is a quality which manifests itself in the heart of the pious believer, in the form of veneration and magnification, so that he seeks to satisfy his Beloved and becomes impatient and restless in his desire for vision of Him, and cannot rest with anyone except Him, and grows familiar with the remembrance of Him, and adjures the remembrance of everything besides. Repose becomes unlawful to him and rest flees from him. He is cut off from all habits and associations, and renounces sensual passion and turns towards the court of love and submits to the law of love and knows God by His attributes of perfection. It is impossible that man's love of God should be similar in kind to the love of his creatures towards one another, for the former is desire to comprehend and attain the beloved object, while the latter is a property of bodies. The lovers of God are those who devote themselves to death in nearness to Him, not those who seek His nature because the seeker stands by himself, but he who devotes himself to death stands by his Beloved; and the truest lovers are they who would fain die thus, and are overpowered, because a phenomenal being has no means of approaching the Eternal save through the omnipotence of the Eternal. He who knows what is real love feels no more difficulties, and his doubts depart.

SHAIKH ALI HUJWIRI
Kashf ul-mahjub (11th cent. A.D.)
(*Discovery of the Beloved*)
translated in the *Sources of Indian Tradition*

The Creation

There is a difference between human souls and the pure soul of Muhammad the Prophet. As the prophets have said, he was the first thing God created. They called him a light and a spirit and he himself was the existence of existences, the fruit and the tree of created beings. As the tradition said, "But for you the heavens would not have been created"; for this, and no other, was the way in which creation began, like as a tree from whose seed spring the chief fruits of the tree. Then God Most High, when He wished to create created beings, first brought forth the light of Muhammad's soul from the ray of the light of His Unity as is reported in the Prophetic traditions. "I am from God and the believers are from me." In some traditions it is reported that God looked with a loving eye upon that light of Muhammad. Modesty overcame Him and the tears dropped from Him. From those drops He created the souls of the prophets. From those lights He created the souls of the saints, from their souls, the souls of believers, and from the souls of the believers He created the souls of the disobedient. From the souls of the disobedient He created the souls of hypocrites and infidels. From human souls He created the souls of the angels and from the rays of the souls of the angels He created the souls of jinns, and from their souls, devils. He created the different souls of animals according to their different kinds of ranks and states, all their descriptions of beings and souls — vegetation and minerals and compounds and elements He also brought forth.

UMAR MIHRABI
Hujjat ul-Hind (16th cent. A.D.)
(The Indian Proof)
translated in the *Sources of Indian Tradition*

Akbar's Religious Discourses

When the capital was illumined by the return of the Imperial presence, the old regulations came again into operation, and the house of wisdom shone resplendent on Friday nights with the light of holy minds. On the 20th Mihr, in that place of meeting, the lamp was kindled to brighten the solitude of seclusion in the banquet of society, and the merits of the philosophers of the colleges and monasteries were put to the test of the touchstone. *Sufis,* doctors, preachers, lawyers, *Sunnis, Shi'as,* Brahmans, Jains, Buddhists, *Chár-báks,* Christians, Jews, Zoroastrians, and learned men of every belief, were gathered together in the royal assembly, and were filled with delight. Each one fearlessly brought forward his assertions and arguments, and the disputations, and contentions were long and heated. Every sect, in its vanity and conceit attacked and endeavoured to refute the statements of their antagonists.

*

One night the *'ibádat-Khána* was brightened by the presence of Padre Radalf, who for intelligence and wisdom was unrivalled among Christian doctors. Several carping and bigoted men attacked him, and this afforded an opportunity for a display of the calm judgment and justice of the assembly! These men brought forward the old received assertions, and did not attempt to arrive at truth by reasoning. Their statements were torn to pieces, and they were nearly put to shame; and then they began to attack the contradictions in the Gospel, but they could not prove their assertions. With perfect calmness and earnest conviction of the truth, the Padre replied to their arguments, and then he went on to say, "If these men have such an opinion of our Book, and if they believe the Kurán to be the true word of God, then let a furnace be lighted, and let me with the Gospel in my hand, and *'ulamá* with their holy book in their hands, walk into that testing place of truth, and the right will be manifest." The black-hearted mean-spirited disputants shrank from this proposal, and answered only with angry words. This prejudice and violence greatly annoyed the impartial mind of the Emperor, and with great discrimination and enlightenment, he said: "Man's outward profession and the mere letter of Muhammdanism, without of heartfelt conviction, can avail nothing. I have forced many Brahmans, by fear of my power, to adopt the religion of my ancestors; but now that my mind has been enlightened with the beams of truth, I have become convinced that the dark clouds of conceit and the mist of self-opinion have gathered round you, and that not a step can be made in advance without the torch of proof. That course only can be beneficial which we select with clear judgment. To repeat the words of the Creed, to perform circumcision, or to lie prostrate on the ground from dread of kingly power, can avail nothing in the sight of God:

Obedience is not in prostration on the earth:

Practise sincerity, for righteousness is not borne upon the brow."

ABUL FAZL (1551-1602)
Akbar-Nama
translated by ELLIOT and DOWSON

Akbar's Divine Faith
(1582)

Akbar's Divine Faith was intended to find a common ground between Islam and Hinduism.

In the year A. H. 983 the buildings of the *'ibádat-khána*, were completed. The cause of their erection was this. In the course of the last few years the Emperor had gained in succession many great and remarkable victories, and his dominion had grown in extent from day to day. Not an enemy was left in the world. He had taken a liking for the society of ascetics and the disciples of the celebrated Mu'iniyyah (God rest his soul!). He spent much time in discussing the Word of God and the sayings of the Prophet; and he devoted his attention to questions of *sufism*, science, philosophy, law and other matters. He passed whole nights in meditation up on God and upon the modes of addressing him as *yá hu* and *yá hádi*. Reverence for the great Giver filled his heart. In order to show his gratitude for some of his blessings, he would sit many a morning alone in prayer and mortification upon the stone bench of an old cell which lay near the palace in a lonely spot. Thus engaged in meditation, he gathered the bliss of the early hours of dawn.

*

Having completed the building (of the 'ibadat-khána), he made a large hall in each of the four divisions of it. He also finished the construction of the tank called *anuptaláo*. He called the building 'ibádat-khána. On Fridays after prayers he would go from the new *khánkáh* of the Shaikhu-l Islám, and hold a meeting in this building. Shaikhs, learned and pious men, and a few of his own companions and attendants, were the only people who were invited. Discussions were carried on upon all kinds of instructive and useful topics.

*

Every Sabbath evening he invited *saiyids, shaikhs*, doctors and nobles. But ill-feeling arose in the company about the seats and order of precedence, so His Majesty ordered that the nobles should sit on the east side, the *saiyids* on the west, the *'ulamá* on the south, and *shaikhs* on the north. His Majesty would go from time to time to these various parties, and converse with them and ascertain their thoughts. Quantities of perfume were used, and large sums of money were distributed as rewards of merit and ability among the worthy people who obtained an entry through the favour of the Emperor's attendants. Many fine books which had belonged to 'Itimád Khán Gujaráti, and had been acquired in the conquest of Gujarát, were placed in the royal library, but were subsequently brought out and distributed by the Emperor among learned and pious men. Among the rest he gave me a book called *Anwáru-l mashkut*.

*

One night the vein of the neck of the *'ulamá* of the age swelled up, and a great outcry and tumult arose. This annoyed His Majesty, and he said to me (Badáuni), "In future report anyone of the assembled whom you find speaking improperly, and I will have him turned out." I said quietly to Asaf Khán, "According to this, a good many would be expelled." His Majesty asked what I had said. When I told him, he was much amused, and repeated my saying to those who were near him.

*

His Majesty used frequently to go to the *'ibádat-khána,* and converse with the *'ulamá* and the *shaikhs,* especially on Sabbath evenings, and would sometimes pass the whole night there. The discussions always turned upon religion, upon its principles, and upon its divarications. The learned doctors used to exercise the sword of their tongues upon each other, and showed great pugnacity and animosity, till the various sects at length took to calling each other infidels and perverts.

*

Innovators and schismatics artfully started their doubts and sophistries, making right appear to be wrong, and wrong to be right. And so His Majesty, who had an excellent understanding, and sought after the truth, but was surrounded by low irreligious persons, to whom he gave his confidence, was plunged into scepticism. Doubt accumulated upon doubt, and the object of his search was lost. The ramparts of the law and of the true faith were broken down; and, in the course of five or six years, not one trace of Islám was left in him. The state of affairs was changed.

There were many reasons for this. But as "small things are suggestive of great ones, and fear betrays the culprit," I will only mention a few. Learned men of various kinds and from every country, and professors of many different religions and creeds, assembled at his Court, and were admitted to converse with him. Night and day people did nothing but inquire and investigate. Profound points of science, the subtleties of revelation, the curiosities of history, the wonders of nature, of which large volumes could only give a summary abstract, were ever spoken of. His Majesty collected the opinions of everyone, especially of such as were not Muhammadans, retaining whatever he approved of, and rejecting everything which was against his disposition, and ran counter to his wishes. From his earliest childhood to his manhood, and from his manhood to old age, His Majesty has passed through the most diverse phases, and through all sorts of religious practices and sectarian beliefs, and has collected everything which people can find in books, with a talent of selection peculiar to him, and a spirit of inquiry opposed to every (Islámitic) principle. Thus a faith, based on some elementary principles, traced itself on the mirror of his heart, and, as the result of all the influences which were brought to bear on His Majesty, there grew, gradually as the outline on a stone, the conviction in his heart that there were sensible men in all religions, and abstemious thinkers, and men endowed with miraculous powers, among all nations. If some true knowledge was thus everywhere to be found, why should truth be confined to one religion, or to a creed like Islám, which was comparatively new, and scarcely a thousand years old? Why should one sect assert what another denies, and why should one claim a preference without having superiority conferred on itself?

Moreover, Samanis and Brahmans managed to get frequent private interviews with His Majesty. As they surpass other learned men in their treatises on morals, and on physical and religious sciences, and reach a high degree in their knowledge of the future, in spiritual power and human perfection, they brought proofs, based on reason and testimony, for the truth of their own, and the fallacies of other religions, and inculated their doctrines so firmly, and so skilfully represented things as quite self-evident which require consideration, that no man, by expressing his doubts, could now raise a doubt in His Majesty, even if mountains were to crumble to dust, or the heavens were to tear asunder.

Hence His Majesty cast aside the Islámitic revelations regarding resurrection, the Day of Judgment, and the details connected with it, as also all ordinances based on the tradition of our Prophet. He listened to every abuse which the courtiers heaped on our glorious and pure faith, which can be so easily followed; and eagerly seizing such opportunities, he showed, in words and gestures, his satisfaction at the treatment which his original religion received at their hands.

In AH 986 the missionaries of Europe, who are called Pádris, and whose chief Pontiff, called Pápá (Pope), promulgates his interpretations for the use of the people, and who issues mandates that even kings dare not disobey, brought their Gospel to the King's notice, advanced proofs of the Trinity, and affirmed the truth and spread abroad the knowledge of the religion of Jesus. The King ordered Prince Murád to learn a few lessons from the Gospel, and to treat it with all due respect, and Shaikh Abu-l Fazl was directed to translate it. Instead of the inceptive "Bismillah," the following ejaculation was enjoined: *"In nomine Jesu Christi,"* that is, "Oh! thou whose name is merciful and bountiful." Shaikh Faizi added to this, "Praise be to God! there is no one like thee — thou art he!" The attributes of the abhorred Anti-Christ were ascribed to our holy Prophet by these lying impostors.

The accursed Birbal tried to persuade the King, that since the sun gives light to all, and ripens all grain, fruits and products of the earth, and supports the life, of mankind, that luminary should be the object of worship and veneration; that the face should be turned towards the rising, not towards the setting, sun; that man should venerate fire, water, stones and trees, and all natural objects, even down to cows and their dung; that he should adopt the frontal mark and the Bráhminical cord. Several wise men at Court confirmed what he said, by representing that the sun was the chief light of the world, and the benefactor of its inhabitants, that it was friend to kings, and that kings established periods and eraṣ in conformity with its motions. This was the cause of the worship paid to the sun on the *Nau-roz Jaláh,* and of his being induced to adopt that festival for the celebration of his accession to the throne. Every day he used to put on clothes of that particular colour which accords with that of the regent-planet of the day. He began also, at midnight and at early dawn, to mutter the spells, which the Hindus taught him, for the purpose of subduing the sun to his wishes. He prohibited the slaughter of cows, and the eating of their flesh, because the Hindus devoutly worship them, and esteem their dung as pure. The reason was also assigned, that physicians have represented their flesh to be productive of sundry kinds of sickness, and to be difficult of digestion.

*

In this year (AH 989), in order to verify the circumstances of the case (of the man who heard without ears), an order was issued that several suckling infants should be kept in a secluded place far from habitations, where they should not hear a word spoken. Well-disciplined nurses were to be placed over them, who were to refrain from giving them any instruction in speaking, so as to test the accuracy of the tradition which says, "Every one that is born is born with an inclination to religion," by ascertaining what religion and sect these infants would incline to, and above all what creed they would repeat. To carry out this order, about twenty sucklings were taken from their mothers for a consideration in money, and were placed in an empty house, which got the name of

Dumb-house. After three or four years the children all came out dumb, excepting some who died there — thus justifying the name which had been given to the house.

*

Ten or twelve years after the commencement of these changes, matters came to such a pitch that wretches like Mirzá Jáni, chief of Tatta, and other apostates, wrote their declarations to the following effect: "I, so and so, son of so and so, have willingly and cheerfully renounced the false and pretended religion of Islám, which I have received from my ancestors, and have joined the Divine Faith (*Din-i Iláhi*) of Shah Akbar, and have assented to its fourfold rule of sincerity — (the readiness to) sacrifice wealth and life, honour and religion." These writings — there could be no more effectual letters of damnation — were handed into the *Mujtahid* of the new creed (Abu-l Fazl).

His Majesty gave his religious system the name of *Tauhid-i Iláhi,* Divine Monotheism.

BADAUNI (1542-1615)
Tarikh-i Badauni
(The author was hostile to Akbar)
translated by ELLIOT and DOWSON

The Reaction against
Pantheistic Mysticism

The sultan in relation to the world is like the soul in relation to the body. If the soul is healthy, the body is healthy, and if the soul is sick, the body is sick. The integrity of the ruler means the integrity of the world; his corruption, the corruption of the world. It is known what has befallen the people of Islam. Notwithstanding the presence of Islam in a foreign land, the infirmity of the Muslim community in previous generations did not go beyond the point where the Muslims followed their religion and the unbelievers followed theirs. As the Qur'an says, "For you, your way, for me, my way."

In the previous generation, in the very sight of men, unbelievers turned to the way of domination, the rites of unbelief prevailed in the abode of Islam, and Muslims were too weak to show forth the mandates of the faith. If they did, they were killed. Crying aloud their troubles to Muhammad, the beloved of God, those who believed in him lived in ignominy and disgrace; those who denied him enjoyed the prestige and respect due to Muslims, and with their feather brains condoled with Islam. The disobedient and those who denied Muhammad used to rub the salt of derision and scorn into the wounds of the faithful. The sun of guidance was hidden behind the veil of error and the light of truth was shut out and obscured behind the curtain of absurdity.

Today, when the good tidings of the downfall of what was prohibiting Islam [i.e. the death of Akbar] and the accession of the king of Islam [i.e. Jahangir] is reaching every corner, the community of the faithful have made it their duty to be the helpers and assistants of the ruler and to take as their guide the spreading of the Holy Law and the strengthening of the community. This assistance and support is becoming effective both by word and deed. In the very early days of Islam the most successful pens were those which clarified problems of Holy Law and which propagated theological opinions in accordance with the Qur'an, the Sunna, and the consensus of the community, so that such errors and innovations as did appear did not lead people astray and end in their corruption. This role is peculiar to the orthodox ulamá who should always look to the invisible world.

SHAIKH AHMAD SIRHINDI (1564-1624)
Maktubat (*Letters*)
translated in the *Sources of Indian Tradition*

Polygamy

It is lawful for a freeman to marry four wives, whether free or slaves; but it is not lawful for him to marry more than four, because God has commanded in the Qur'an saying: "Ye may marry whatsoever women are agreeable to you, two, three, or four," and the numbers being thus expressly mentioned, any beyond what is there specified would be unlawful. Shafi'i alleges a man cannot lawfully marry more than one woman of the description of slaves, from his tenet as above recited, that "the marriage of freemen with slaves is allowable only from necessity"; the text already quoted is, however, in proof against him, since the term "women" applies equally to free women and to slaves.

Hidaya (*Guidance*) (12th cent. A.D.)
translated in the *Sources of Indian Tradition*

Friday Prayers

A story was told that non-attendance at Friday prayers was being interpreted away [as not obligatory for a Muslim]. Shaikh Nizam ud-din said there is no such interpretation. Unless someone is a captive, on a journey, or ill, he who can go to Friday prayers and does not go has a very stubborn heart. Then he said, if a man does not go to one Friday congregational prayer, one black spot appears on his heart; if he misses two weeks' congregational prayer, then two black spots appear; and if he does not go three times in succession, his whole heart becomes black — which God forbid!

SHAIKH NIZAM UD-DIN AULIYA from AMIR HASAN SIJZI
Fawaid ul Fuwad
translated in the *Sources of Indian Tradition*

To me all Creation is an Interrogation

Poets begin their poetical works in the name of Allah
the Merciful and dispenser of Grace;
but I begin mine with a complaint to Thee.
For wherever I look, I see all creation,
animate and inanimate, sentient and insentient,
tree, flower and leaf,
bird, beast and man,
chained, though endowed with a passion to be free;
born to live yet ending in decay and death;
alive to rapture yet doomed to despair and grief;
rooted to earth yet aspiring to the Heavens above;

and set to solve a riddle which they cannot solve.
Would God, argues the curious man, be God
if He can't have his way? And can
His creatures cross his will? Or is it He
Who wants all things awry? — But why?
Fain would he know the why and wherefore of things:
A flame quivers within his day.
To me all creation is an interrogation;
all objects, query marks,
symbols of wailing and lamentation,
questioning the wisdom of Thy creation.

*

I've been an iconoclast, an expert
at breaking the icons of false gods
that inhabit and inhibit our minds —
the idols of the tribe, the cave, and the market place,
of caste, creed, and class:
the shams of custom and respectability,
of puritanism and piety.
But I find that so long as there is the I,
and the ego invents selfishnesses in self-defence
there can be no emancipation for me;
for the ego builds new idols as soon as
it breaks the old, and enthrones new gods
in place of those dethroned, which lay down the
law and rule my mind with a strict ordinance.
Thus while I break the old idols,
I strew life's path with fresh boulders and rocks
which I find difficult to break or remove.

*

My God! save me this painful reckoning
and call me not to account for sins.

I do not shirk Thy punishment,
I'll not extenuate my guilt;
but the numerous sins I wallowed in
are blurred with the anguished memory
of many uncommitted sins.
And now, when I recount them all
I weep afresh and yearn anew
for the countless sins I could not taste.

Why should man feel ashamed of sin?
What's God's forgiveness for?
When God is great to grant
man pardon for his sins,
when He is indulgent
to allow him transgression,
it bespeaks his lack of faith
to feel ashamed and sad
and stint his transgressions.

*

"Live and let live," my motto reads,
My heart is free and kind.
No enmity to anyone,
I harbour in my mind.

Ill-starred I am, but I thank God
Ill-natured I am not.
I bear no malice in my heart.
O'er fate I grumble not.

MIRZA GHALIB (1797-1869)
translated by J.L. KAUL

Your own Heart is your Candle

All creatures yearn for Self-hood freed:
To bloom is every atom's greed!
Life without self-fruition — death;
Who builds the Self, him the gods speed.
The mustard-seed grows to a hill
With it: without, the hill a seed.
The stars stumble and do not meet —
To all being, severance is decreed;
Pale is the moon of night's last hour
No interclasps of friendship feed.
Your own heart is your candle; you
Yourself are all the light you need;
You are the sole truth of this world,
All else some conjuror's passes breed.
The thorns of the desert bring forth knowledge:
Lament no more, if your feet bleed.

IQBAL (1873-1938)
Poems from Iqbal
translated by V.G. KIERNAN

Slay Thy Self

Paradise is for the weak alone,
Strength is but a means to perdition.
It is wicked to seek greatness and glory,
Penury is sweeter than princedom.
Lightning does not threaten the cornseed:
If the seed become a stack, it is unwise.

If you are sensible, you will be a mote of sand, not a
Sahara,
So that you may enjoy the sunbeams.
O thou that delightest in the slaughter of sheep,
Slay thy self, and thou wilt have honour!
Life is rendered unstable
By violence, oppression, revenge, and exercise of power.
Though trodden underfoot, the grass grows up time after
time
And washes the sleep of death from its eye again and
again.
Forget thy self, if thou art wise!
If thou dost not forget thy self, thou art mad.
Close thine eyes, close thine ears, close thy lips,
That thy thought may reach the lofty sky!
The pasturage of the world is naught, naught:
O fool, do not torment thyself for a phantom!

IQBAL (1873-1938)
The Secrets of the Self

A New Shrine

I'll tell you truth, O Brahmin, if I may make so bold:
These idols in your temples — these idols have grown old.
From them you have learned hatred of those who share
your life,
An Allah to *His* preachers has taught mistrust and strife;
Disgusted, from your temple and our shrine I have run,
Now both our preachers' sermons and your old myths I
shun.

In shapes of stone you fancied God's dwelling-place: I see
In each speck of my country's poor dust, a deity.
Come, let us lift this curtain of alien thoughts again,
And reunite the severed, and wipe division's stain:
Too long has lain deserted the heart's warm habitation;
Let us build in this homeland a new temple's foundation!
And let our shrine be taller than all shrines of this globe,
With lofty pinnacles touching the skirts of heaven's robe;
And there at every sunrise let our sweet chanting move
The hearts of all who worship, and pour the wine of love;
Strength and peace too shall blend in the hymns the votary
    sings —
For in love lies salvation to all earth's living things.

IQBAL (1873-1938)
Poems from Iqbal
translated by V.G. KIERNAN

Sikhism

The founder of Sikhism, Nanak, was a Hindu born in a village in the Punjab. Today Sikhism is the religion of some six and a quarter million Indians.

There is but One God

There is but one God whose name is true, the Creator, devoid of fear and enmity, immortal, unborn, self-existent; by the favour of the Guru.

*

By obeying Him wisdom and understanding enter the
    mind;
By obeying Him man knoweth all worlds;
By obeying Him man suffereth not punishment;
By obeying Him man shall not depart with Jam —
So pure is God's name —
Whoever obeyeth God knowth the pleasure of it in his
    own heart.

*

Make contentment and modesty thine earrings, self-respect
thy wallet, meditation the ashes to smear on thy body;
Make thy body, which is only a morsel for death, thy
beggar's coat, and faith thy rule of life and thy staff.
Make association with men thine Ai Panth, and the conquest
of thy heart the conquest of the world.
To Thee sing, chaste and patient of mankind,
Unyielding heroes of true faith approved.
To Thee sing, pandits and the chiefs of saints;
The ages four and Vedas to them assigned.
To Thee sing maidens who delight the sense,
This world of ours, high heaven, and hell below.
To Thee sing gems from Vishnu's sea that rose,
And eight and sixty spots of pilgrims' haunt.
To Thee sing heroes and the men of might;
The sources four from which all life doth spring.
To Thee sing regions, orbs, and universe,
Created, cherish'd, and upheld by Thee!
To Thee sing those whose deeds delight Thine eye,
The hosts who wear the colours of Thy faith.
All things beside which sing Thy glorious name,
Could ne'er be told by Nanak's lowly song.

Hail! Hail to Him

The primal, the pure, without beginning, the indestructible, the same in every age!

*

Make divine knowledge thy food, compassion thy store-keeper, and a voice is in every heart the pipe to call to repast.

Make Him who hath strung the whole world on His string thy spiritual Lord; let wealth and supernatural power be relishes for others.

Union and separation is the law which regulateth the world. By destiny we receive our portion.

*

False are kings, false their subjects, false the whole world;
False are mansions, false palaces, false those who dwell
     therein;
False is gold; false silver; false he who weareth them;
False the body; false raiment; false peerless beauty;
False husbands; false wives; they waste away and become
     dust.
Man who is false loveth what is false, and forgetteth the
     Creator.
With whom contract friendship? The whole world passeth
     away.
False is sweetness; false honey; in falsehood shiploads are
     drowned.
Nanak humbly asserteth — except Thee, O God, everything
     is thoroughly false.

NANAK (1469-1538)
The Sikh Religion
translated by M.A. MACAULIFFE

The Guru

Under the Guru's instruction *God's* word is heard; under the Guru's instruction its knowledge is acquired; under the Guru's instruction man learns that God is everywhere contained.

The Guru is Shiv; the Guru is Vishnu and Brahma; the Guru is Parbati, Lakhshmi, and Saraswati.

If I knew Him, should I not describe Him? He cannot be described by words.

My Guru explained one thing to me —

That there is but one Bestower on all living beings; may I not forget him!

*

Without the true Guru none hath found God: without the true Guru none hath found God.

God hath put Himself into the true Guru; he hath made manifest and proclaimed this.

Salvation is ever obtained by meeting the true Guru who hath banished worldly love from within him.

Best are the meditations of him who hath fixed his mind on the True One:

He hath found the Giver of life to the world.

NANAK (1469-1538)
translated by M.A. MACAULIFFE

The Ten Stages of Life

In man's first stage he loveth the milk of his mother's
    breasts;
In his second he recogniseth his father and mother;
In his third his brother, his brother's wife, and his own
    sisters;
In the fourth a love of play ariseth in him;
In the fifth he runneth after food and drink;
In the sixth he inquireth not a woman's caste in his lust;
In the seventh he collecteth things for a house to live in;
In the eighth his body is wasted by wrath;
In the ninth he groweth grey and his breathing is difficult;
In the tenth he is burnt and becometh ashes.

NANAK (1469-1538)
translated by M.A. MACAULIFFEE

Futility of Idolatry

Thou in thy house keepest an idol with its attendant gods:
Thou washest it and worshippest it;
Thou offerest it kungu, sandal, and flowers;
Thou fallest at its feet and propitiatest it to the utmost;
Yet it is by continually begging of men thou clothest and
    supported thyself.
For such foolish acts shalt thou receive the punishment
    of the foolish.
The idol giveth thee not when hungry, nor preserveth thee
    from death.
It is like a foolish quarrel among the blind.

NANAK (1469-1538)
translated by M.A. MACAULFFE

Be Not Proud of Thy Caste

Let none be proud of his caste.
He who knoweth God is a Brahman.
O stupid fool, be not proud of thy caste;
From such pride many sins result.
Everybody saith there are four castes,
But they all proceeded from God's seed.
The world is all made out of one clay,
But the Potter fashioned it into vessels of many sorts.
The body is formed from the union of five elements;
Let any one consider if he hath less or more in his
    composition.
Saith Nanak, the soul is fettered by its acts.
Without meeting the true Guru Salvation is not obtained.

AMAR DAS (1552-74)
translated by M.A. MACAULIFFE

Adi Granth

The First Book (Adi Granth) of the Sikhs was compiled by their fifth Guru (spiritual teacher) Arjun, 1581-1606. It was an official collection of the hymns and sayings of Nanak and his three successors, together with a large selection from Kabir and other saints whose message was consonant with the Sikh teachers.

Three things have been put into the vessel — truth, patience, and meditation.

The ambrosial name of God the support of all hath also been put therein.

He who eateth and enjoyeth it shall be saved.

This provision should never be abandoned; ever clasp it to your hearts.

By embracing God's feet we cross the ocean of darkness; Nanak, everything is an extension of God.

GURU ARJUN (1581-1606)
translated by M.A. MACAULIFFE

Neither a Hindu nor a Musalman

I practise no fasting, nor observe the Ramzan:
I serve Him who will preserve me at the last hour.
The one Lord of the earth is my God,
Who judgeth both Hindus and Musalmans.
I go not on a pilgrimage to Makka, nor worship at Hindu
    places of Pilgrimages.
I serve the one God and none other.
I neither worship as the Hindus, nor pray as the Musalmans.
I take the Formless God into my heart, and there make
    obeisance unto Him.
I am neither a Hindu nor a Musalman.
The soul and body belong to God whether He be called
    Allah or Ram.
Kabir hath delivered this lecture.
When I meet a true guru or pir, I recognise my own
    Master.

GURU ARJUN (1581-1606)
translated by M.A. MACAULIFFE

The Inauguration of the Khalsa
1699

The final transformation of the Sikhs into a militant brotherhood took place in the time of their tenth teacher, Guru Gobind Singh, 1675-1708.

By the order of the immortal God the great Guru obtained inspiration.

Then he gradually established the Khalsa, whole-bodied and manly.

Then arose the roaring of the Singhs (lions) which terrified the whole world.

They levelled with the earth the shrines of Hindus and Muhammadans.

They cancelled the Veds, the Purans, the six Hindu systems and Quran.

They abolished the call to prayer and the prayer-carpet of the Muhammadans and killed the Turkish monarchs.

Temporal and spiritual leaders all hid themselves or became converted to Sikhism.

The Mullas and the Qazis grew weary of reading, but found not God's secret.

Hundreds of thousands of Pandits, Brahmans, and Astrologers had become entangled in worldly affairs.

Worshipping stones and temples they had become exceedingly superstitious.

Both the Hindus and the Muhammadans were altogether engaged in deception.

Consequently a third religion, the Khalsa, arose and became renowned.

The Singhs by the order of Guru Gobind Singh seized the sword and wielded it.

They killed all their enemies and caused the name of the Immortal God to be repeated.

Then God's order was promulgated in the world.

The drum of victory resounded and drowned the cry of sorrow.

The great sagacious guru established a third sect.

Well done! Well done Gobind Singh! thou wert at once Guru and disciple!

GURDAS, a Sikh writer
translated by M.A. MACAULIFFE

Religion Consisteth Not

O man with the garb, religion consisteth not in wearing a garb.

It consisteth not in wearing matted hair and long nails, or in smearing ashes on the body, or dyeing thy raiment.

If man obtain Jog by dwelling in the forest, the bird ever dwelleth there.

The elephant ever throweth dust on his head; consider this in thy heart.

Frogs and fishes ever bathe at places of pilgrimage.

The cat, the wolf, and the crane meditate; what know they of religion?

As thou endurest pain to deceive men, do also for God's sake,

Thus shalt thou know great divine knowledge and quaff the supreme nectar.

GOBIND SINGH (1675-1708)
translated by M.A. MACAULIFFE

All Men are the Same

The temple and the mosque are the same; the Hindu worship and the Musalman prayer are the same; all men are the same; it is through error they appear different.

Deities, demons, Yakshas, heavenly singers, Musalmans, and Hindus adopt the customary dress of their different countries.

All men have the same eyes, the same ears, the same body, the same build, a compound of earth, air, fire, and water.

Allah and Abhekh are the same; the Purans and the Quran are the same; they are all alike; it is the one God who created all.

GOBIND SINGH (1675-1708)
translated by M.A. MACAULIFFE

Hail to Thee, O Sword

Thou art the Subduer of countries, the Destroyer of the armies of the wicked, in the battlefield Thou greatly adornest the brave.

Thine arm is infrangible, They brightness refulgent, Thy radiance and splendour dazzle like the sun.

Thou bestowest happiness on the good, Thou terrifiest the evil, Thou scatterest sinners, I seek Thy protection.

Hail! hail to the Creator of the world, the Saviour of creation, my Cherisher, hail to Thee, O Sword!

GOBIND SINGH (1675-1708)
translated by M.A. MACAULIFFE

Epilogue

Let my Country Awake

Where the mind is without fear and the head is held high;
Where knowledge is free;
Where the world has not been broken up into fragments
   by narrow domestic walls;
Where words come out from the depth of truth;
Where tireless striving stretches its arms towards perfection;
Where the clear stream of reason has not lost its way into
   the dreary desert sand of dead habit;
Where the mind is led forward by Thee into ever-widening
   thought and action –
Into that heaven of freedom, my Father, let my country
   awake.

RABINDRANATH TAGORE (1861-1941)
Gitanjali

Dates in Indian History

B.C.

3250-2750	The period of the Indus valley civilisation.
1500-1200	Aryan invasion of the Indian subcontinent; composition of the earliest hymns of the *Rigveda*.
1200-900	Composition of the *Rigveda* and the great war depicted in the *Mahabharata* epic.
800	Aryans reach Bengal.
900-600	The period of the composition of later Vedas, Brahmanas, and early Upanishads.
563-483	Gautam Buddha.
480	First Buddhist council at Rajagriha.
468	Death of Mahavira, the Jain prophet.
327-325	Invasion of Alexander of Macedon.
322-298	Chandragupta Maurya.
321-300	Composition of Kautilya's *Arthasâstra*.
300	Megasthenes, Greek ambassador of Seleucus Nicator, visits court of Chandragupta.
269-232	Asoka.
200-200 A. D.	The period of greatest Jain and Buddhist influence in India.
185	End of Mauryan dynasty.

A. D.

1st century	Kushans invade India.
320-540	The Gupta period – the golden age.
319-335	Chandragupta I.
335-376	Samudragupta.

400-500	The composition of Vatsyayana's *Kama Sutra*.
405	Fa-hsien, Chinese pilgrim, arrives in India.
606-47	Reign of King Harsha of Kanuj in North India.
629-45	Chinese pilgrim Hsuan-tsang visits India.
711-15	Conquest of Sind by the Arab Muslims under Muhammad ibn Qasim.
907-1310	Hindu Chola Empire at Tanjore.
999-1026	Mahmud of Ghazni raids India.
1192	Muhammad Ghori defeats Prithvi Raj. Delhi becomes Ghori's headquarters in India.
1306-1310	Ala al din Khalji of Delhi conquers South India.
1336-1565	Vijayanagar, last great Hindu kingdom in India.
1398-99	Timur's invasion of India and sack of Delhi. Rise of independent "Provincial" Muslim principalities.
1440-1518	Kabir, poet and saint.
1469	Birth of Guru Nanak, founder of Sikhism.
1498	Vasco da Gama lands on the Malabar coast.
1526	First battle of Panipat. Babur defeats Ibrahim Lodi and establishes Mogul rule in Delhi and Agra.
1532-1623	Tulsi Das.
1556	Accession of Akbar.
1582	Promulgation of Din-i-Ilahi, Akbar's Divine Faith.
1600	Foundation of the East India Company.
1605-27	Reign of Jahangir.
1627-58	Reign of Shahjahan.
1651	Foundation of East India Company's factory at Hugli in Bengal.
1658-1707	Reign of Aurangzeb.
1668	Bombay acquired by the East India Company.
1690	Calcutta founded by Job Charnock.
1739	Sack of Delhi by Nadir Shah.
1757	Battle of Plassey: Robert Clive defeats Siraj-ud Daula, the Nawab of Bengal.
1765	The East India Company virtually acquires the control of Bengal, Bihar and Orissa under the Diwani settlements.
1773	Warren Hastings appointed first Governor-General of Bengal.

1799	Lord Wellesley defeats Tipu Sultan and ends Muslim rule in Mysore.
1818	Defeat of Maratha Peshwa ends effective Indian resistance to British rule.
1828	Rammohan Roy (1772-1833) founds Brahma Samaj.
1829	Lord Bentinck abolishes *suttee* in India.
1833	East India Company deprived by Parliament of all commercial functions.
1835	English system of education introduced.
1848	Lord Dalhousie conquers the Punjab.
1857-58	Mutiny of Sepoy troops and widespread rebellion in Northern India.
1858	East India Company's rule replaced by that of a Viceroy appointed by the British Crown.
1875	Swami Dayanand (1824-83) founds the Arya Samaj at Bombay. Syed Ahmad Khan (1817-98) founds Muhammadan Anglo Oriental College at Aligarh.
1877	Queen Victoria proclaimed Empress of India.
1885	Indian National Congress inaugurated in Bombay.
1886	Death of Sri Ramakrishna (born 1834).
1893	M. K. Gandhi (1869-1948) begins twenty years' work as lawyer in South Africa.
1894	Death of Bankim Chandra Chatterjee (born 1838).
1897	Swami Vivekananda (1863-1902) founds Ramakrishna Mission.
1905	Partition of Bengal by Lord Curzon arouses nationalist agitation.
1906	Muslim League founded.
1911	Transfer of the Indian capital from Calcutta to Delhi announced.
1913	Rabindranath Tagore awarded Nobel Prize for his *Gitanjali.*
1920	Mahatma Gandhi starts first nation-wide civil disobedience movement.
1930	Muhammad Iqbal (1873-1938) proposes separate state for India's Muslims. C. V. Raman awarded Nobel Prize for Physics.
1930-34	Second civil disobedience movement.

1935	Government of India Act grants provincial self-government.
1940	Muslim League, under President Jinnah (1876-1948), demands creation of Pakistan.
1941	Subhas Chandra Bose (1897-1945) escapes from India to organise Indian National Army.
1942	Indian National Congress rejects Cripps' offer and demands British quit India.
1945-47	The Labour Government prepares to grant India complete self-government.
1947	India divided: India, under Prime Minister Jawaharlal Nehru (1889-1964), and Pakistan, under Prime Minister Liaquat Ali Khan (1895-1951), become independent nations.
1948	Gandhi assassinated in New Delhi. Death of Jinnah.
1950	India becomes a republic within the Commonwealth.
1951-52	Congress party wins first national elections. First Five-year Plan begins.
1964	Death of Jawaharlal Nehru.

First Lines of Poems

List of Authors

463

List of Translators

Place Names

The following places are not found on most atlases. Some have a modern name; others are ruined towns, no longer centres of population. A few still exist under the same name but are obscure.

AMBER. Ruined capital of Jaipur district, 5 miles from Jaipur.

ARH. Arrah.

BADAKSHAN. Province of Afghanistan.

BAJOUR. Bajaur in W. Pakistan.

BALUCHISTAN. Part of W. Pakistan.

BEHREH. Bhera in W. Pakistan.

BENARES. Varanasi.

BENGAL. Now W. Bengal and E. Pakistan.

BOMBAY PROVINCE. Now Maharashtra.

CHANDAHAR. Kandahar.

CHITORE. Now Chittur (Chittoor) in Rajputana.

CORAZON. Khorazon, a province of Persia. Corresponds nowadays with the modern Turkmen SSR and adjoining areas of Persia and Afghanistan.

GOLKONDA. Now Golconda.

KANCHI. Now part of Orissa.

KHORSAN. Khurasan, an area to the east of Iran.

KHWARIZM. Province of Iraq.

KOROMANDEL. Eastern sea-coast of India from Nagapattinam to Masulipatnam.

KOT. Now Kota.

KUNDUZ. Town in Afghanistan.

MANDOR. Ruined town in Rajputana.

MAWERALNAHER. Name given at time of Arab expansion in the 7th century A. D. to country beyond the Oxus. Now the Uzbek SSR.

MIDDLE KINGDOM. Now Uttar Pradesh.

MOKA. Mokha in the Yemen.

MUTTRA. Now Mathura.

N. W. FRONTIER PROVINCE. Now north-western part of Pakistan.

OGOULI. Part of Calcutta.

PAUNJAB. Punjab.

PATELEPUTRA. Now Patna.

SALARPUR. Name of several villages in Uttar Pradesh and Bihar.

Savatthi or Sravasti. Once thought to be the ruins of Set Mehet in the Gonda district of Uttar Pradesh. Now thought to be on the upper Rapti river in Nepal.

TAMRAPARNI. Tamraparni, a river in the Tinnevelly district.

TUGHLIKPUR. Tughlakpur, two villages near Delhi.